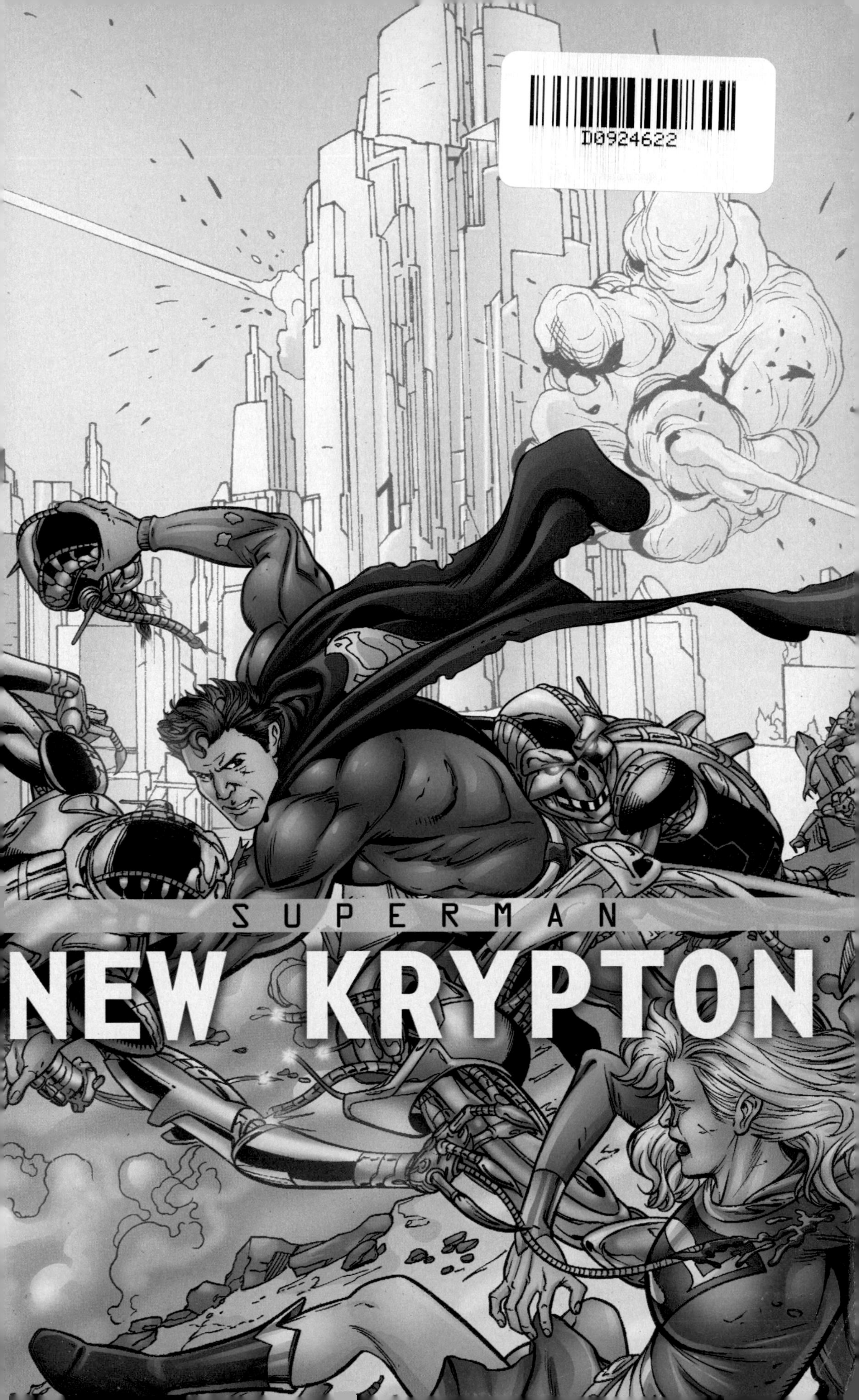
SUPERMAN
NEW KRYPTON

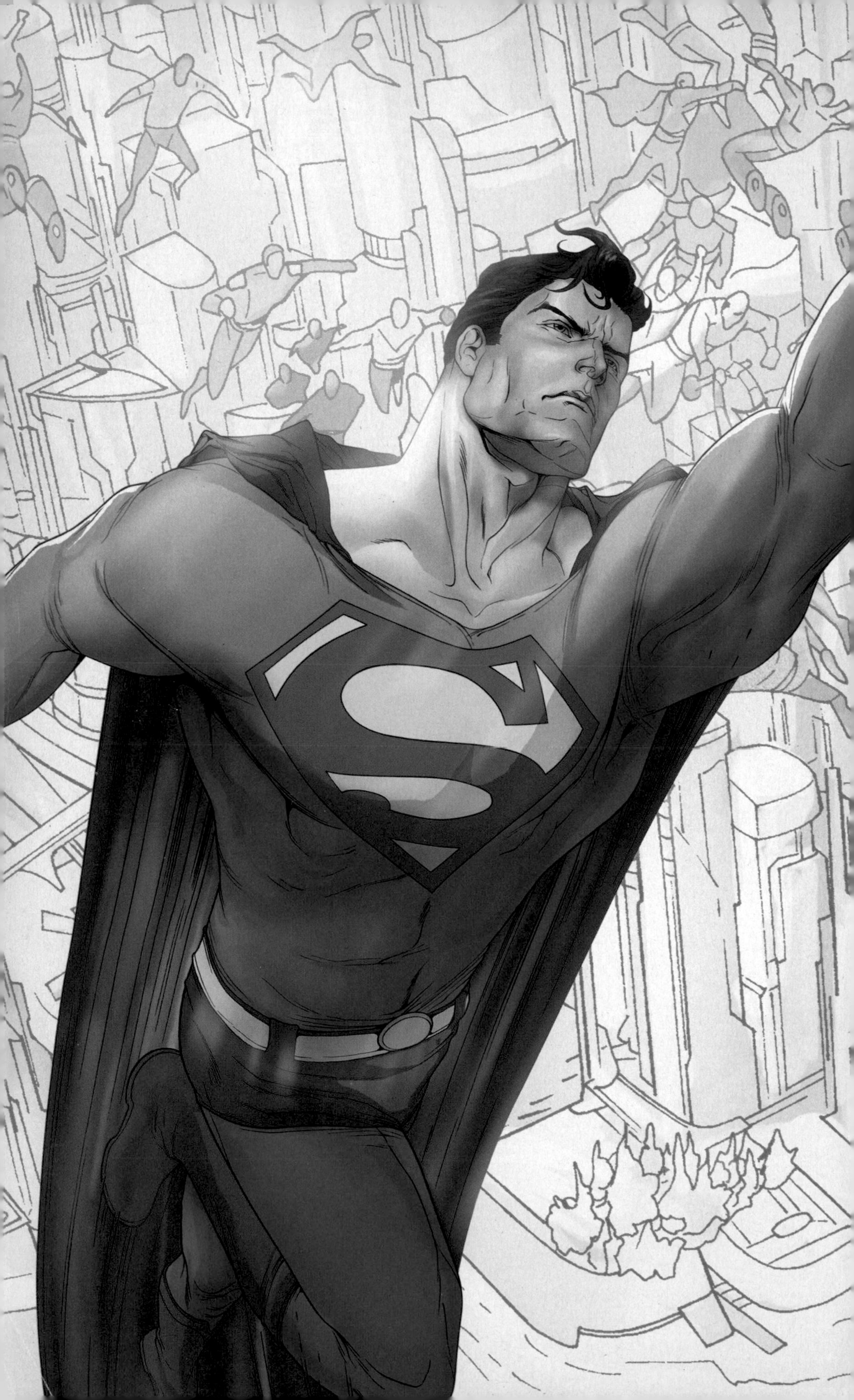

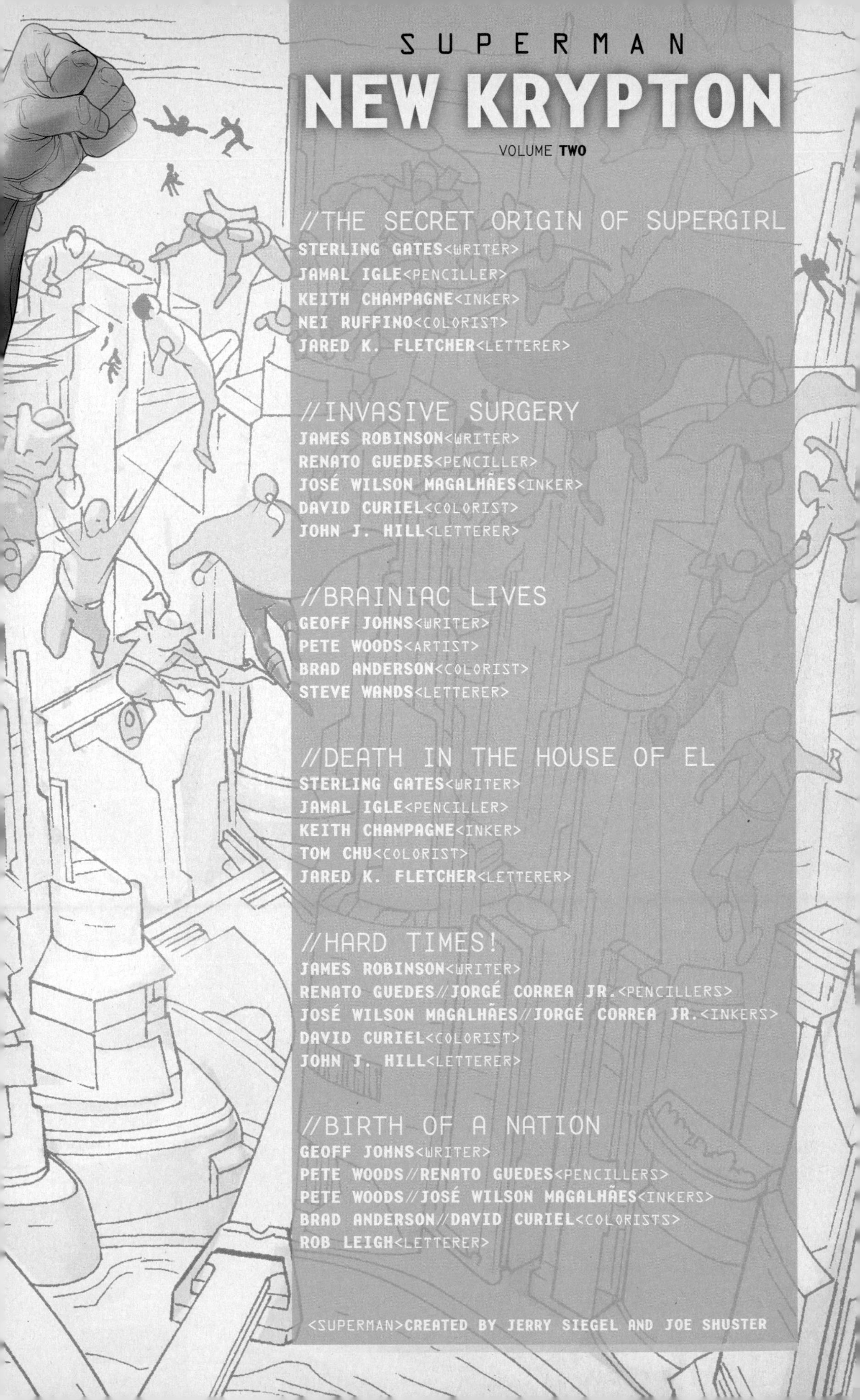

SUPERMAN

NEW KRYPTON

VOLUME **TWO**

//THE SECRET ORIGIN OF SUPERGIRL

STERLING GATES<WRITER>
JAMAL IGLE<PENCILLER>
KEITH CHAMPAGNE<INKER>
NEI RUFFINO<COLORIST>
JARED K. FLETCHER<LETTERER>

//INVASIVE SURGERY

JAMES ROBINSON<WRITER>
RENATO GUEDES<PENCILLER>
JOSÉ WILSON MAGALHÃES<INKER>
DAVID CURIEL<COLORIST>
JOHN J. HILL<LETTERER>

//BRAINIAC LIVES

GEOFF JOHNS<WRITER>
PETE WOODS<ARTIST>
BRAD ANDERSON<COLORIST>
STEVE WANDS<LETTERER>

//DEATH IN THE HOUSE OF EL

STERLING GATES<WRITER>
JAMAL IGLE<PENCILLER>
KEITH CHAMPAGNE<INKER>
TOM CHU<COLORIST>
JARED K. FLETCHER<LETTERER>

//HARD TIMES!

JAMES ROBINSON<WRITER>
RENATO GUEDES//JORGÉ CORREA JR.<PENCILLERS>
JOSÉ WILSON MAGALHÃES//JORGÉ CORREA JR.<INKERS>
DAVID CURIEL<COLORIST>
JOHN J. HILL<LETTERER>

//BIRTH OF A NATION

GEOFF JOHNS<WRITER>
PETE WOODS//RENATO GUEDES<PENCILLERS>
PETE WOODS//JOSÉ WILSON MAGALHÃES<INKERS>
BRAD ANDERSON//DAVID CURIEL<COLORISTS>
ROB LEIGH<LETTERER>

<SUPERMAN>**CREATED BY JERRY SIEGEL AND JOE SHUSTER**

//
DAN DIDIO <SENIOR VP-EXECUTIVE EDITOR>
MATT IDELSON <EDITOR-ORIGINAL SERIES>
WIL MOSS <ASSISTANT EDITOR-ORIGINAL SERIES>
BOB HARRAS <EDITOR-COLLECTED EDITION>
ROBBIN BROSTERMAN <SENIOR ART DIRECTOR>
PAUL LEVITZ <PRESIDENT & PUBLISHER>
GEORG BREWER <VP-DESIGN & DC DIRECT CREATIVE>
RICHARD BRUNING <SENIOR VP-CREATIVE DIRECTOR>
PATRICK CALDON <EXECUTIVE VP-FINANCE & OPERATIONS>
CHRIS CARAMALIS <VP-FINANCE>
JOHN CUNNINGHAM <VP-MARKETING>
TERRI CUNNINGHAM <VP-MANAGING EDITOR>
AMY GENKINS <SENIOR VP-BUSINESS & LEGAL AFFAIRS>
ALISON GILL <VP-MANUFACTURING>
DAVID HYDE <VP-PUBLICITY>
HANK KANALZ <VP-GENERAL MANAGER, WILDSTORM>
JIM LEE <EDITORIAL DIRECTOR-WILDSTORM>
GREGORY NOVECK <SENIOR VP-CREATIVE AFFAIRS>
SUE POHJA <VP-BOOK TRADE SALES>
STEVE ROTTERDAM <SENIOR VP-SALES & MARKETING>
CHERYL RUBIN <SENIOR VP-BRAND MANAGEMENT>
ALYSSE SOLL <VP-ADVERTISING & CUSTOM PUBLISHING>
JEFF TROJAN <VP-BUSINESS DEVELOPMENT, DC DIRECT>
BOB WAYNE <VP-SALES>

//
Cover by Alex Ross
Publication design by ROBBIE BIEDERMAN

SUPERMAN: NEW KRYPTON Volume 2
Published by DC Comics. Cover and compilation Copyright © 2009
DC Comics. All Rights Reserved.

Originally published in single magazine form in SUPERGIRL 35, 36,
SUPERMAN 682, 683, ACTION COMICS 872, 873 Copyright © 2008, 2009
DC Comics. All Rights Reserved. All characters, their distinctive
likenesses and related elements featured in this publication are
trademarks of DC Comics. The stories, characters and incidents
featured in this publication are entirely fictional. DC Comics
does not read or accept unsolicited submissions of ideas,
stories or artwork.

DC Comics, 1700 Broadway, New York, NY 10019
A Warner Bros. Entertainment Company
Printed by RR Donnelley, Salem, VA, USA. 8/11/10
ISBN: 978-1-4012-2320-5

<THE SECRET ORIGIN OF SUPERGIRL> SUPERGIRL 35 COVER ART BY **ALEX ROSS**

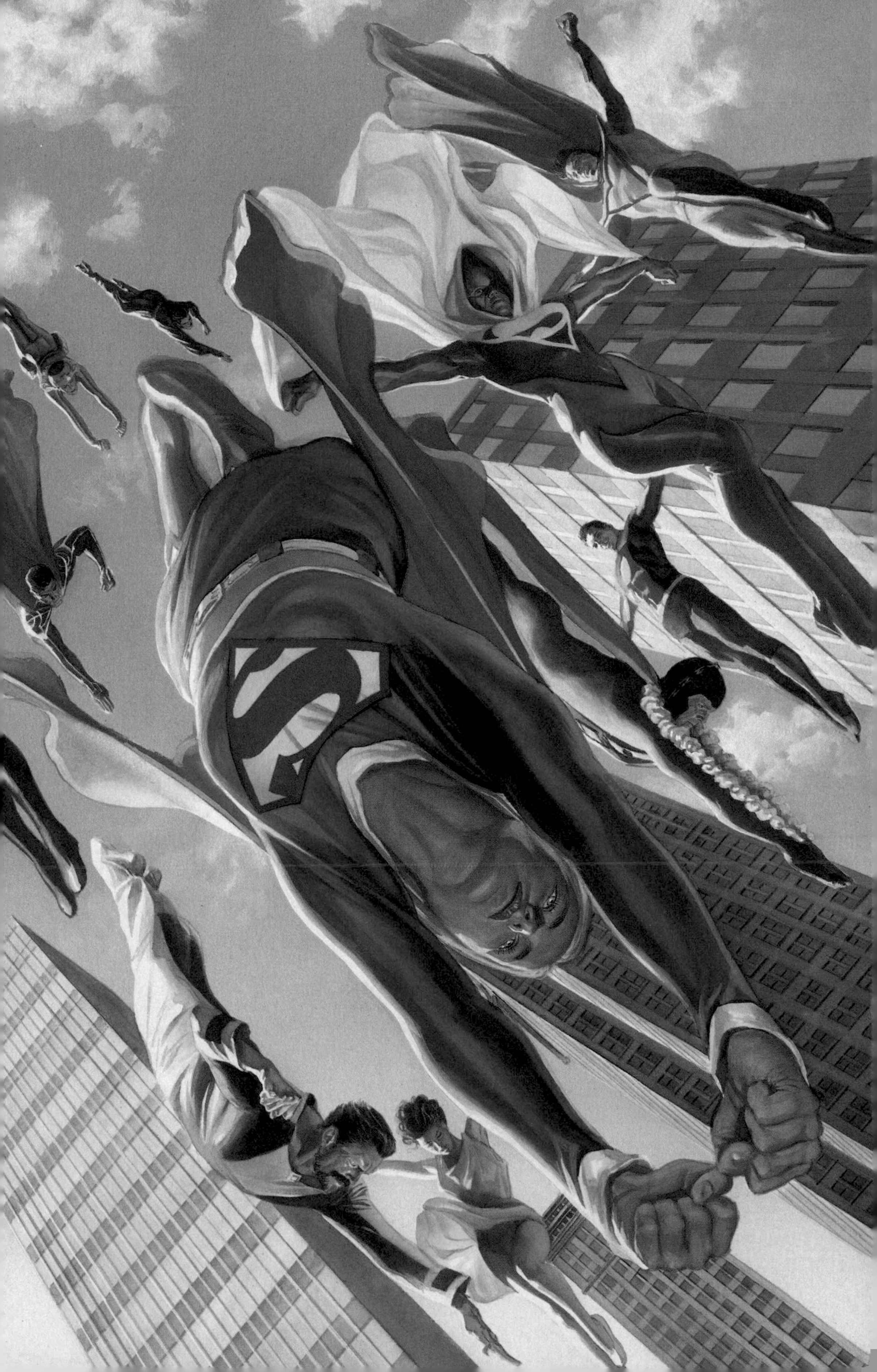

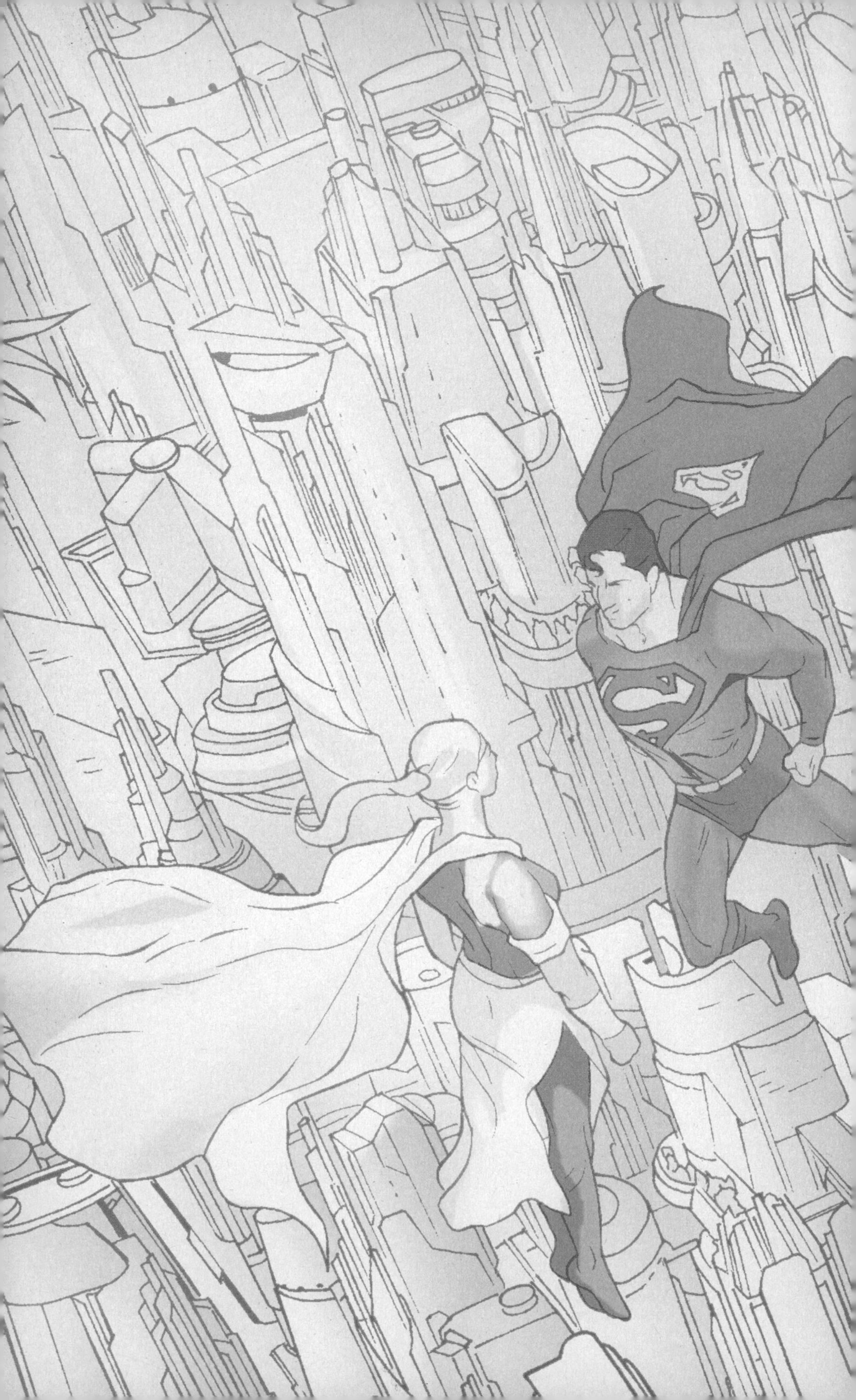

DC COMICS *proudly presents*

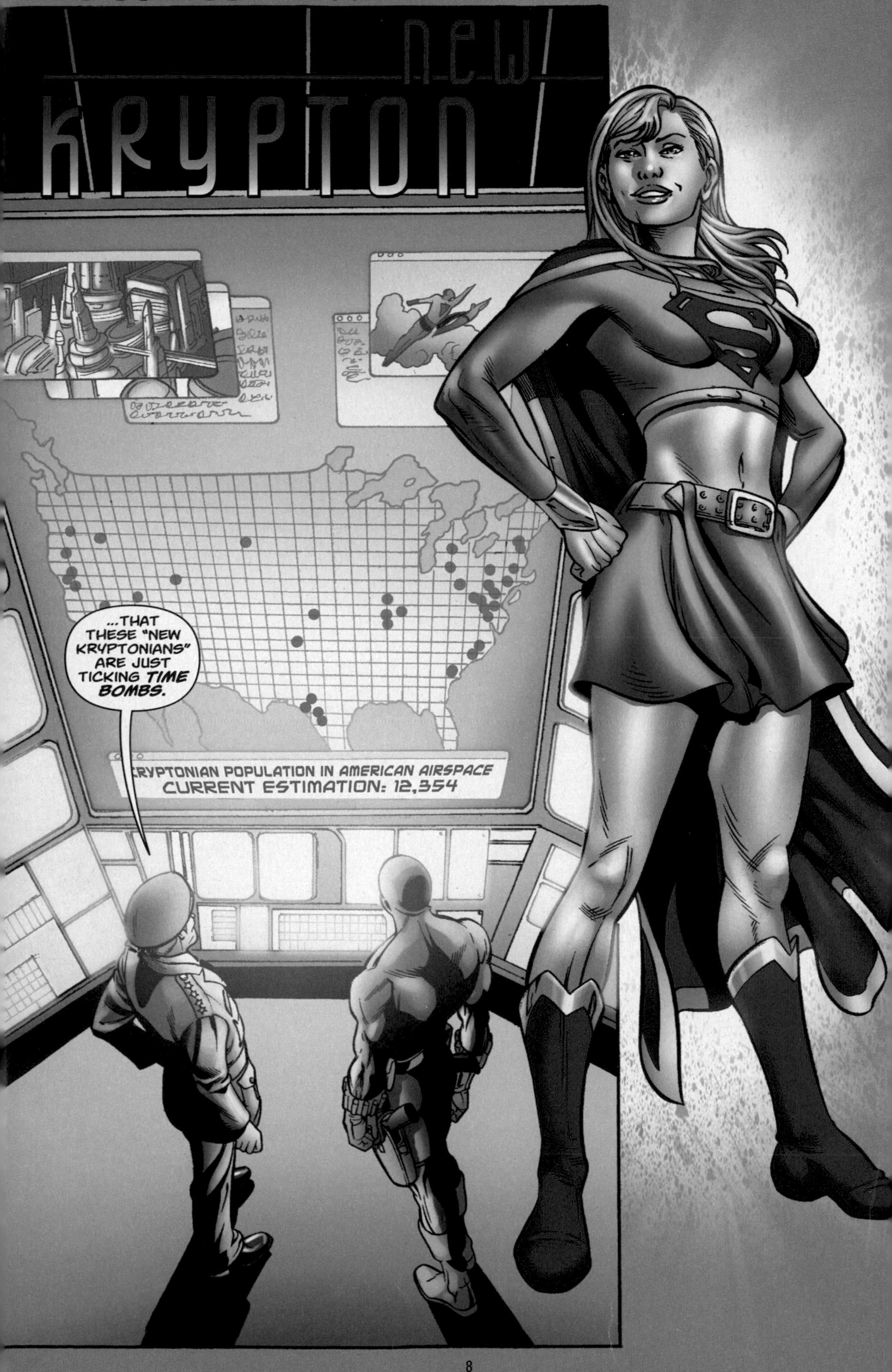
NEW KRYPTON
...THAT THESE "NEW KRYPTONIANS" ARE JUST TICKING TIME BOMBS.
KRYPTONIAN POPULATION IN AMERICAN AIRSPACE
CURRENT ESTIMATION: 12,354

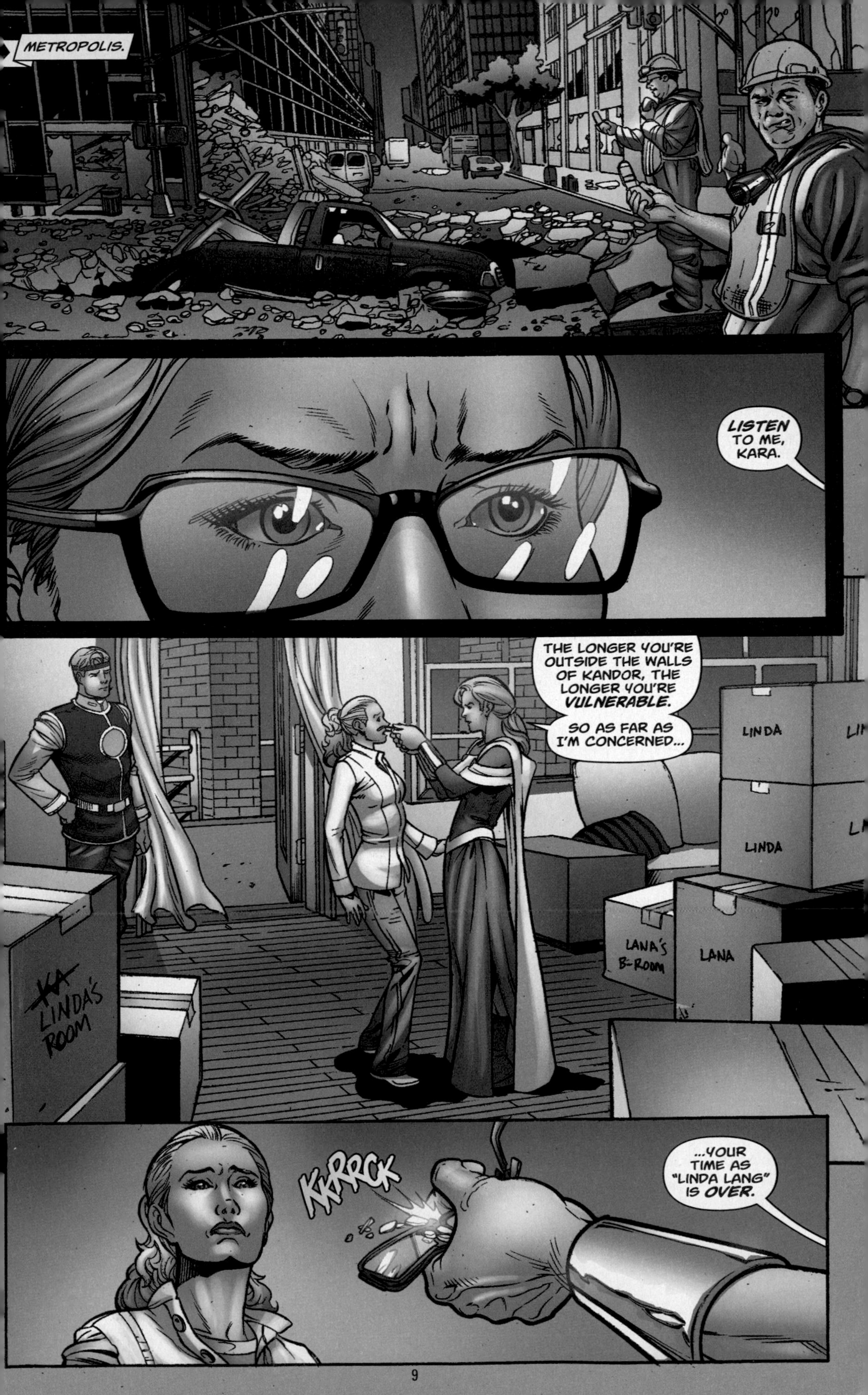
METROPOLIS.
LISTEN TO ME, KARA.
THE LONGER YOU'RE OUTSIDE THE WALLS OF KANDOR, THE LONGER YOU'RE VULNERABLE.
SO AS FAR AS I'M CONCERNED...
LINDA
LINDA
LANA'S B-ROOM
LANA
KA LINDA'S ROOM
KKRRCK
...YOUR TIME AS "LINDA LANG" IS OVER.

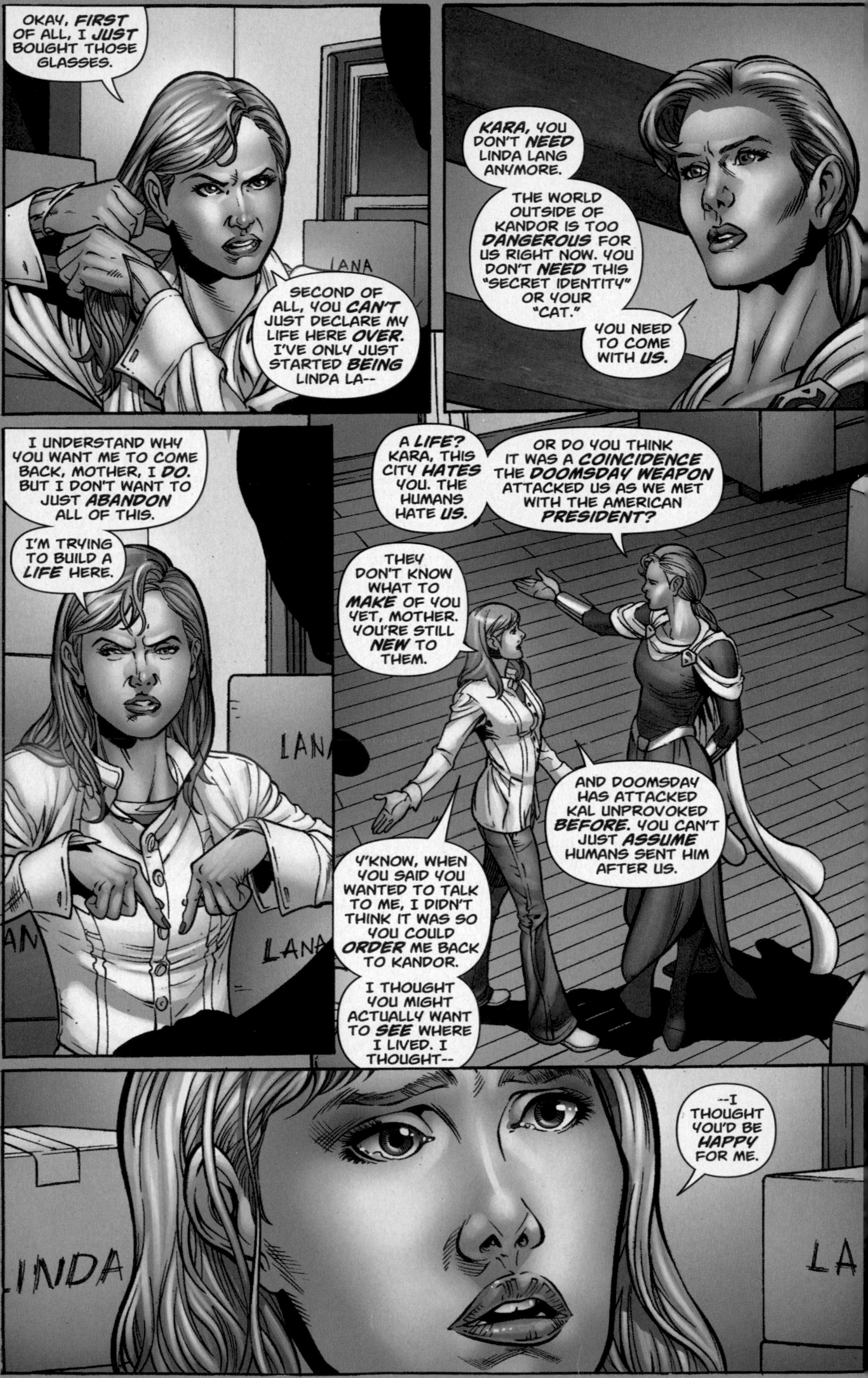
OKAY, FIRST OF ALL, I JUST BOUGHT THOSE GLASSES.
LANA
SECOND OF ALL, YOU CAN'T JUST DECLARE MY LIFE HERE OVER. I'VE ONLY JUST STARTED BEING LINDA LA--
KARA, YOU DON'T NEED LINDA LANG ANYMORE.
THE WORLD OUTSIDE OF KANDOR IS TOO DANGEROUS FOR US RIGHT NOW. YOU DON'T NEED THIS "SECRET IDENTITY" OR YOUR "CAT."
YOU NEED TO COME WITH US.
I UNDERSTAND WHY YOU WANT ME TO COME BACK, MOTHER, I DO. BUT I DON'T WANT TO JUST ABANDON ALL OF THIS.
I'M TRYING TO BUILD A LIFE HERE.
LANA
LANA
A LIFE? KARA, THIS CITY HATES YOU. THE HUMANS HATE US.
OR DO YOU THINK IT WAS A COINCIDENCE THE DOOMSDAY WEAPON ATTACKED US AS WE MET WITH THE AMERICAN PRESIDENT?
THEY DON'T KNOW WHAT TO MAKE OF YOU YET, MOTHER. YOU'RE STILL NEW TO THEM.
AND DOOMSDAY HAS ATTACKED KAL UNPROVOKED BEFORE. YOU CAN'T JUST ASSUME HUMANS SENT HIM AFTER US.
Y'KNOW, WHEN YOU SAID YOU WANTED TO TALK TO ME, I DIDN'T THINK IT WAS SO YOU COULD ORDER ME BACK TO KANDOR.
I THOUGHT YOU MIGHT ACTUALLY WANT TO SEE WHERE I LIVED. I THOUGHT--
--I THOUGHT YOU'D BE HAPPY FOR ME.
LINDA
LA

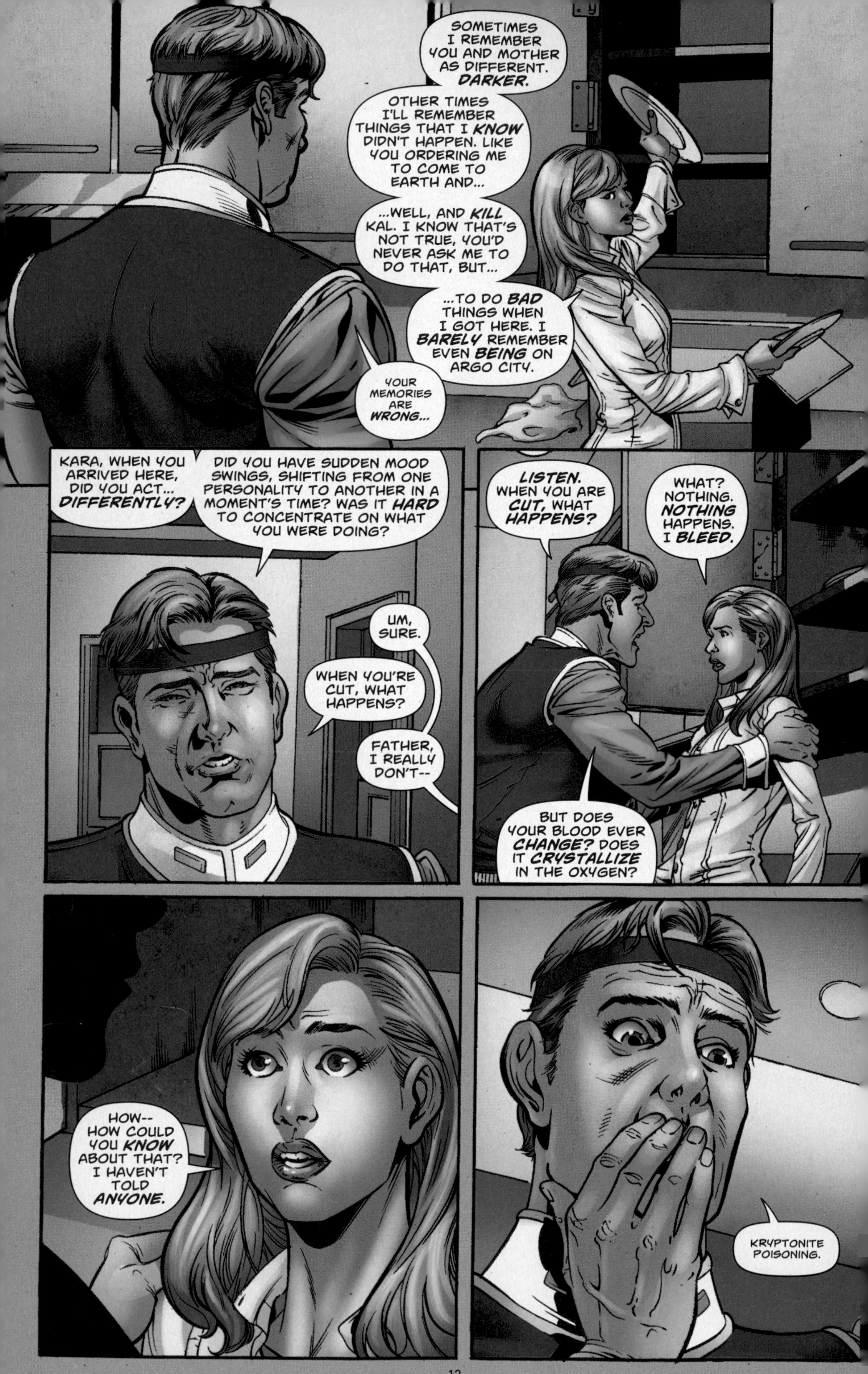
SOMETIMES I REMEMBER YOU AND MOTHER AS DIFFERENT. DARKER.
OTHER TIMES I'LL REMEMBER THINGS THAT I KNOW DIDN'T HAPPEN. LIKE YOU ORDERING ME TO COME TO EARTH AND...
...WELL, AND KILL KAL. I KNOW THAT'S NOT TRUE, YOU'D NEVER ASK ME TO DO THAT, BUT...
...TO DO BAD THINGS WHEN I GOT HERE. I BARELY REMEMBER EVEN BEING ON ARGO CITY.
YOUR MEMORIES ARE WRONG...
KARA, WHEN YOU ARRIVED HERE, DID YOU ACT... DIFFERENTLY?
DID YOU HAVE SUDDEN MOOD SWINGS, SHIFTING FROM ONE PERSONALITY TO ANOTHER IN A MOMENT'S TIME? WAS IT HARD TO CONCENTRATE ON WHAT YOU WERE DOING?
UM, SURE.
WHEN YOU'RE CUT, WHAT HAPPENS?
FATHER, I REALLY DON'T--
LISTEN. WHEN YOU ARE CUT, WHAT HAPPENS?
WHAT? NOTHING. NOTHING HAPPENS. I BLEED.
BUT DOES YOUR BLOOD EVER CHANGE? DOES IT CRYSTALLIZE IN THE OXYGEN?
HOW-- HOW COULD YOU KNOW ABOUT THAT? I HAVEN'T TOLD ANYONE.
KRYPTONITE POISONING.

FRONT PAGE?!

THEY'RE GIVING YOU A FRONT-PAGE *FEATURE* FOR YOUR HATEFUL *GARBAGE?*

IT'S NOT GARBAGE, LANA. IT'S A *STORY.*

THE PUBLISHERS ARE *SHREWD* PEOPLE, AND THEY'RE LOOKING TO *ME* TO ASK THE *TOUGH* QUESTIONS.

PERRY TOLD ME THEY *SO* LIKED THE SALES SPIKE THEY GOT FROM MY FIRST SUPERGIRL ARTICLE, THEY WANT *ALL* MAJOR SUPERGIRL NEWS TO COME FROM ME.

SUPERMAN CLAIMS DOOMSDAY'S DEATH WAS SELF-DEFENSE, BUT SINCE HE RETURNED THE REMAINS TO THE US GOVERNMENT, SUPERGIRL AND HER PARENTS HAVEN'T SHOWN THEM-SELVES.

SEEMS LIKE WHAT *GUILTY* PEOPLE DO, DOESN'T IT? NOT THAT I THINK THEY *MURDERED* THAT BEAST.

AND LANA, ARTICLES LIKE *MINE* GENERATE SALES. AND SALES ARE *GOOD BUSINESS.*

AS THE PLANET'S BUSINESS EDITOR, THAT'S SOMETHING *YOU* SHOULD KNOW ABOUT.

SUPERGIRL SHOULD BE DELIRIOUS WITH *JOY.* ALL THESE *ALIENS* RUNNING AROUND--

DAILY PLANET
KRYPTONIANS!

--AND I'M GOING TO MAKE SURE SHE'S THE MOST *FAMOUS* OF THEM *ALL.*

IS SUPERGIRL LEA... KRYPTONIAN INVASION...

AN ARTICLE BY CAT GRANT

This is the start of the Kryptonian invasion.

Following an attack at a peace summit by the monster known only as "Doomsday," this Daily Planet reporter was shocked to learn that Supergirl's ... were in part responsible for the ... eath. Was Supergirl sent as a ... parents to find out our ... And what nation ... the death

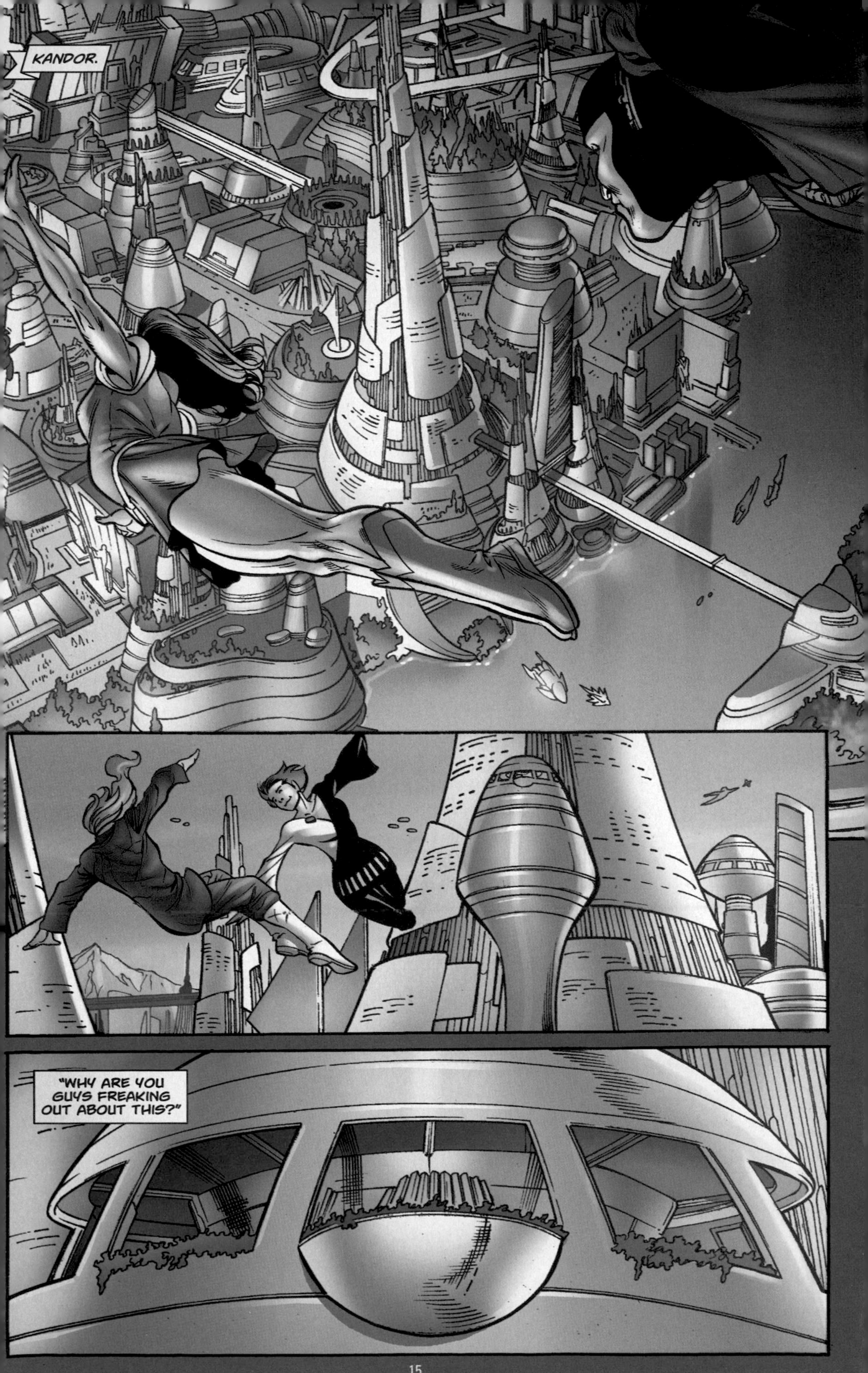
KANDOR.
"WHY ARE YOU GUYS FREAKING OUT ABOUT THIS?"

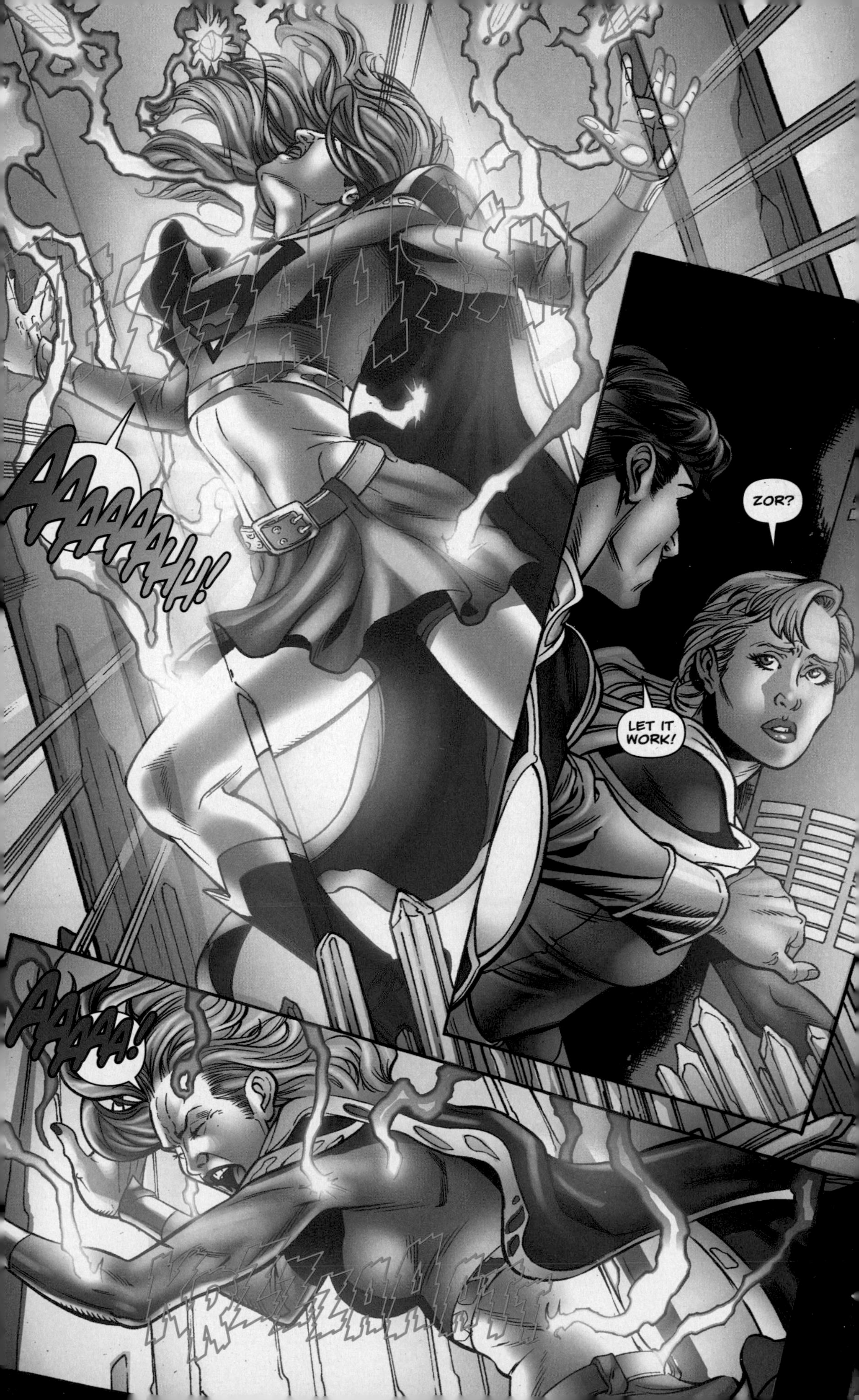
AAAAAAHH!
ZOR?
LET IT WORK!
AAAAA!

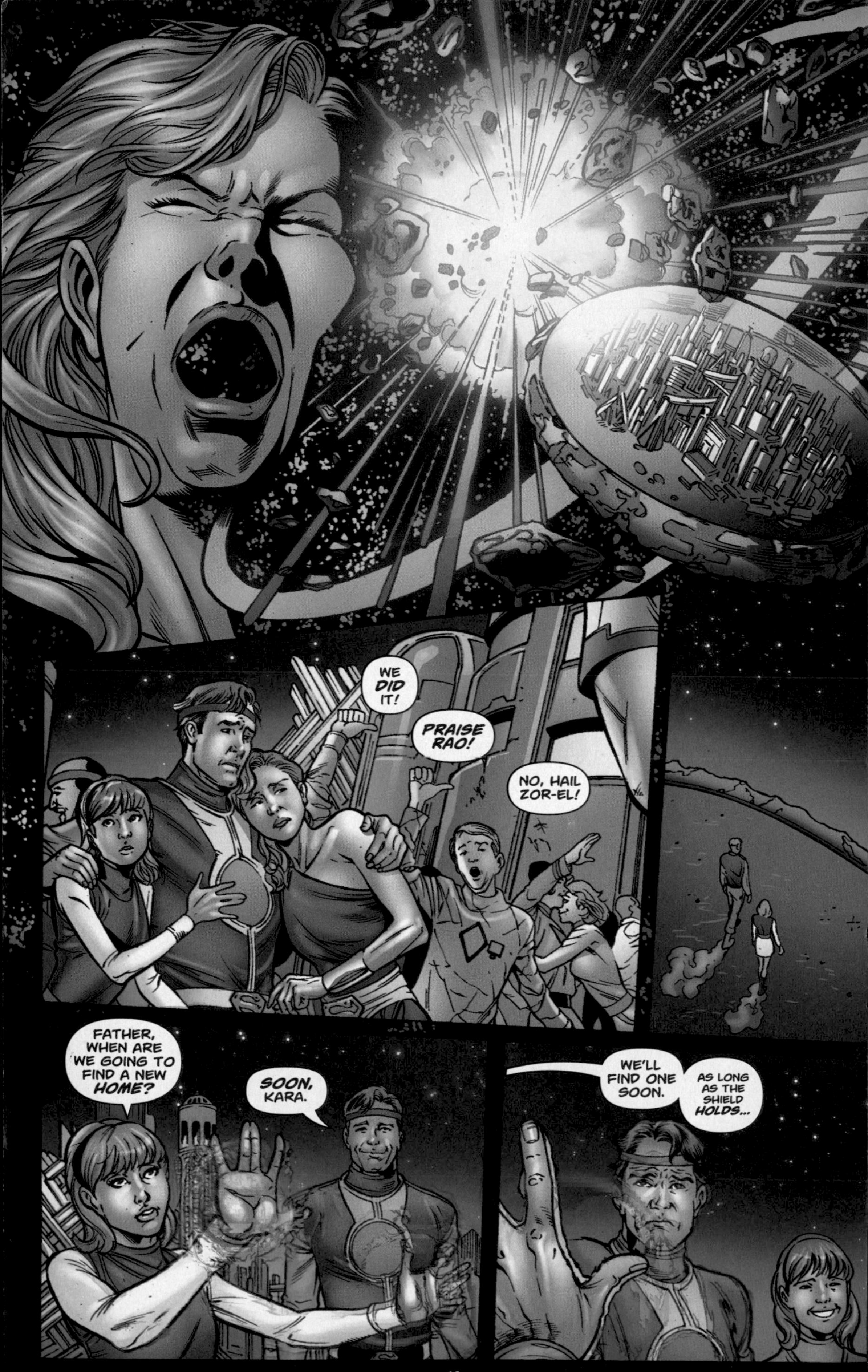
WE DID IT!
PRAISE RAO!
NO, HAIL ZOR-EL!
FATHER, WHEN ARE WE GOING TO FIND A NEW HOME?
SOON, KARA.
WE'LL FIND ONE SOON.
AS LONG AS THE SHIELD HOLDS...

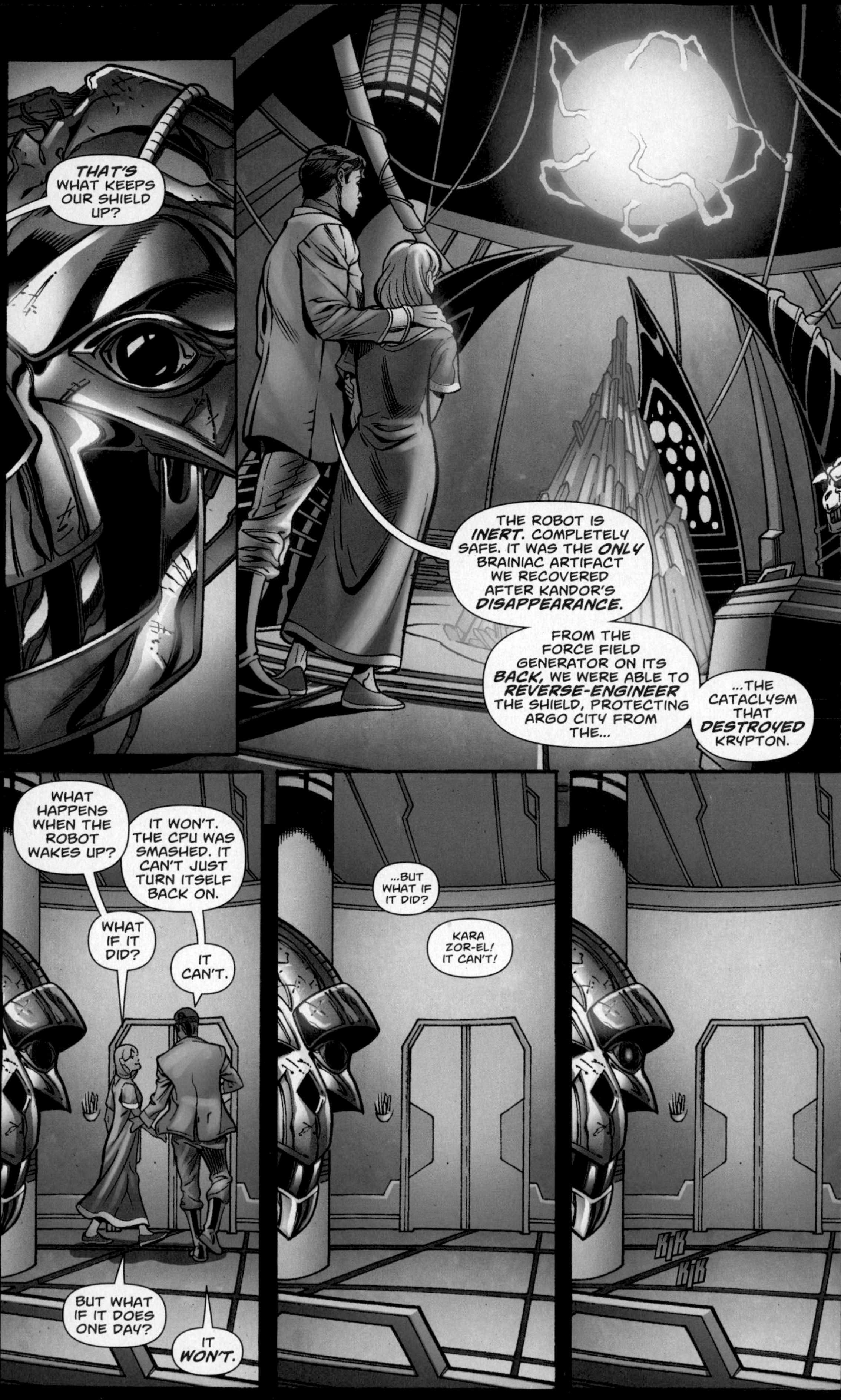
THAT'S WHAT KEEPS OUR SHIELD UP?
THE ROBOT IS INERT. COMPLETELY SAFE. IT WAS THE ONLY BRAINIAC ARTIFACT WE RECOVERED AFTER KANDOR'S DISAPPEARANCE.
FROM THE FORCE FIELD GENERATOR ON ITS BACK, WE WERE ABLE TO REVERSE-ENGINEER THE SHIELD, PROTECTING ARGO CITY FROM THE...
...THE CATACLYSM THAT DESTROYED KRYPTON.
WHAT HAPPENS WHEN THE ROBOT WAKES UP?
IT WON'T. THE CPU WAS SMASHED. IT CAN'T JUST TURN ITSELF BACK ON.
WHAT IF IT DID?
IT CAN'T.
BUT WHAT IF IT DOES ONE DAY?
IT WON'T.
...BUT WHAT IF IT DID?
KARA ZOR-EL! IT CAN'T!
KIK KIK

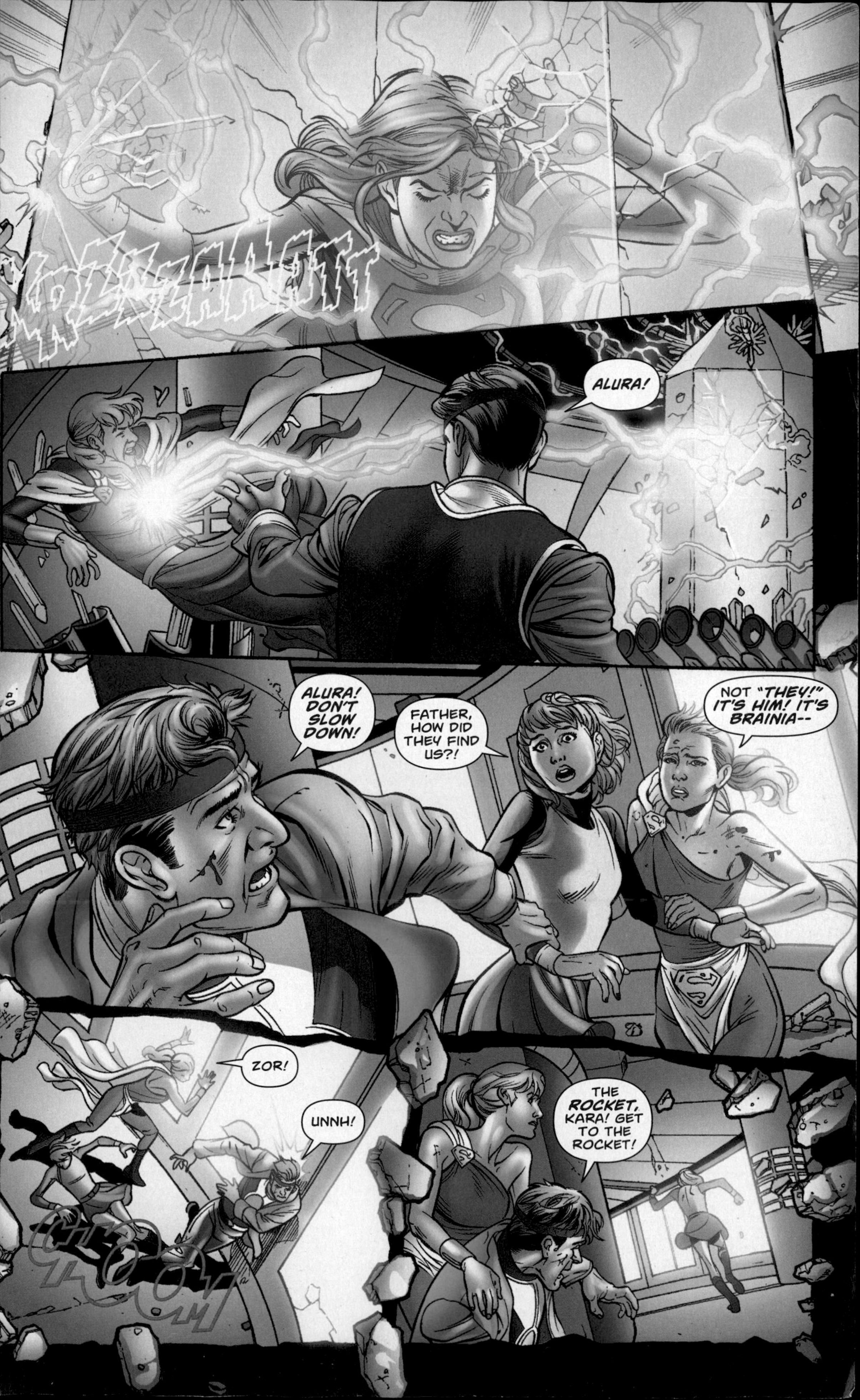
ALURA!
ALURA! DON'T SLOW DOWN!
FATHER, HOW DID THEY FIND US?!
NOT "THEY!" IT'S HIM! IT'S BRAINIA--
ZOR!
UNNH!
THE ROCKET, KARA! GET TO THE ROCKET!

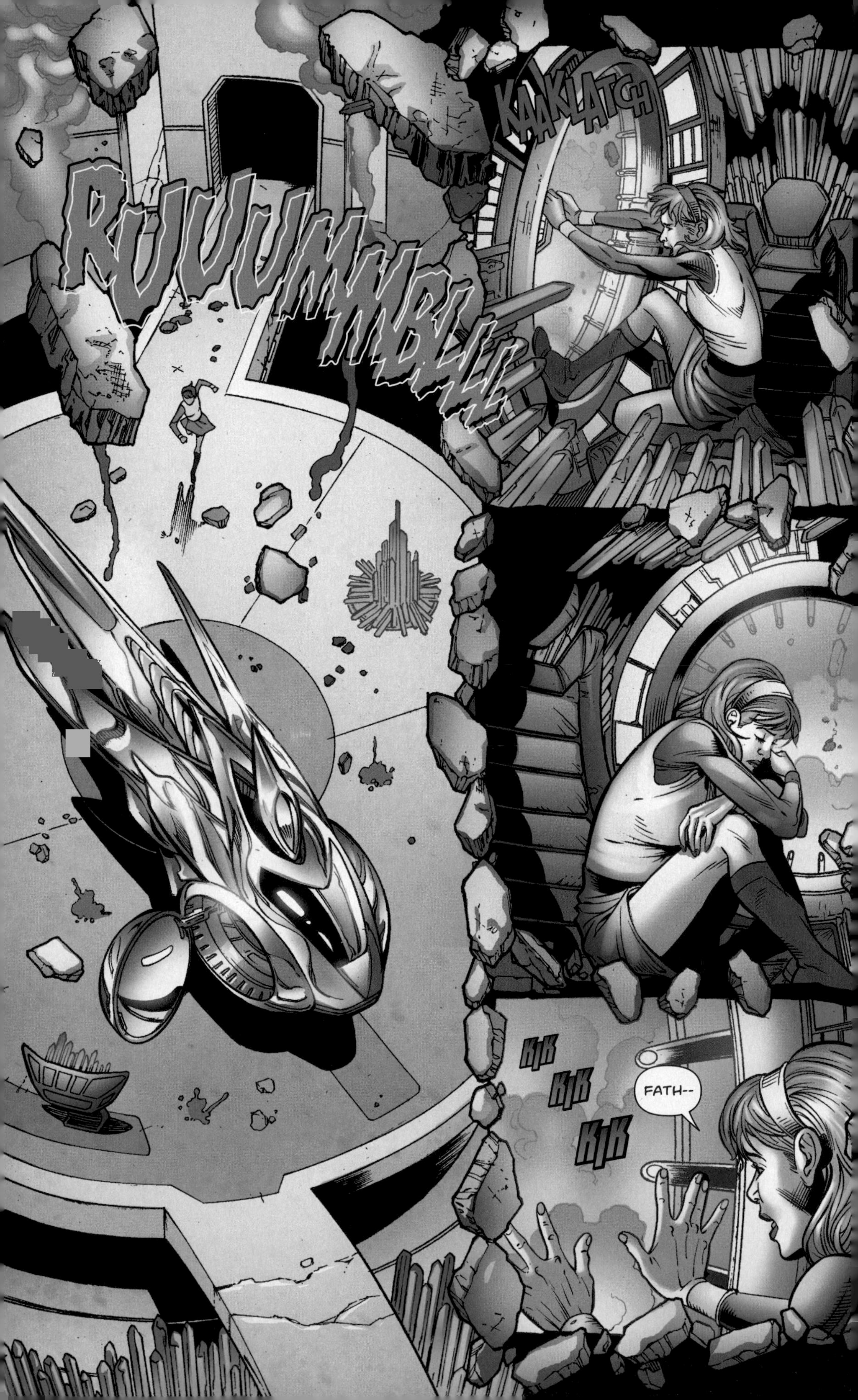
RUUUMMBLLL
KAAKLATCH
KIK
KIK
KIK
FATH--

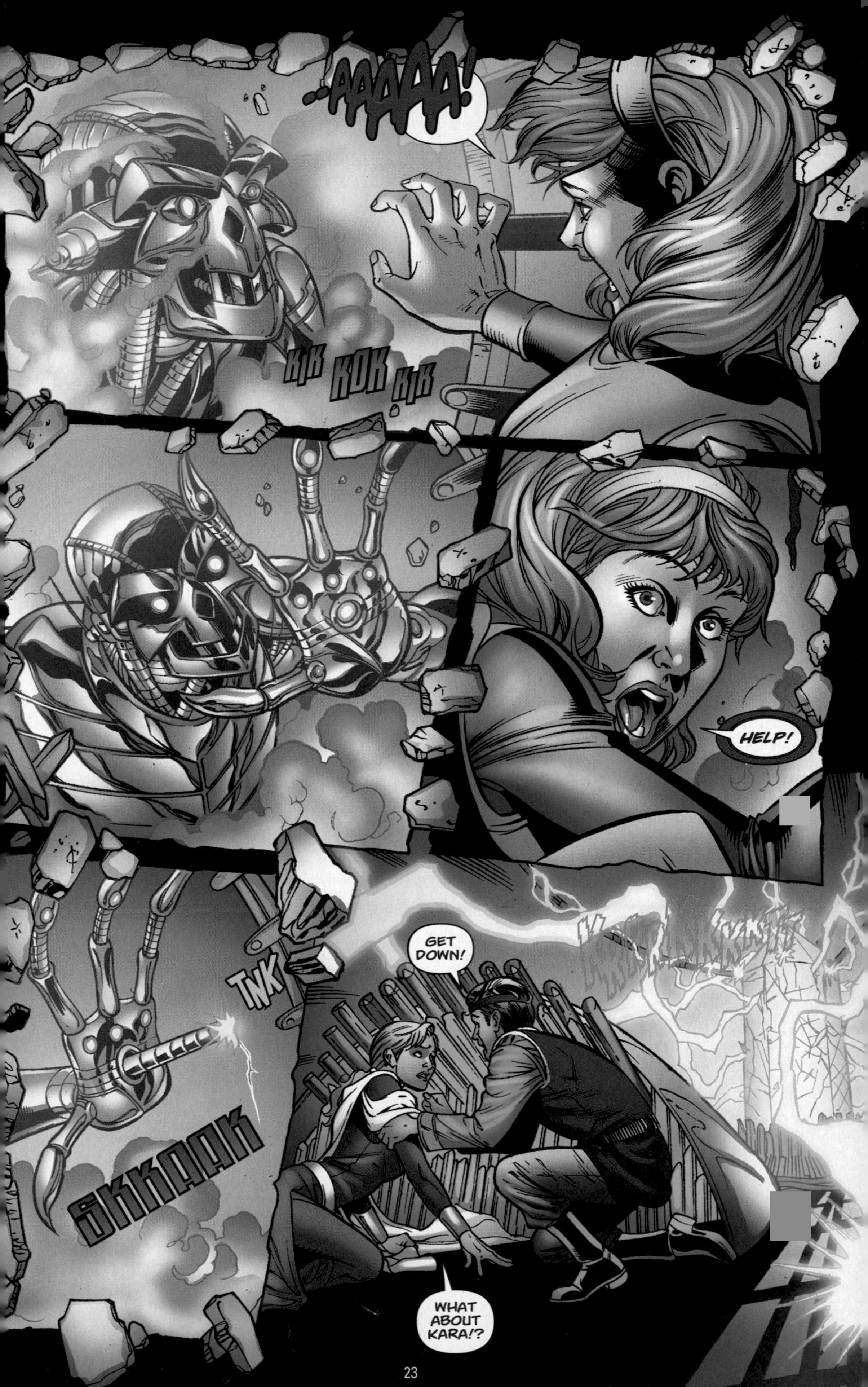
--AAAAA!
KIK KOK KIK
HELP!
TNK
SKKAAK
GET DOWN!
WHAT ABOUT KARA!?

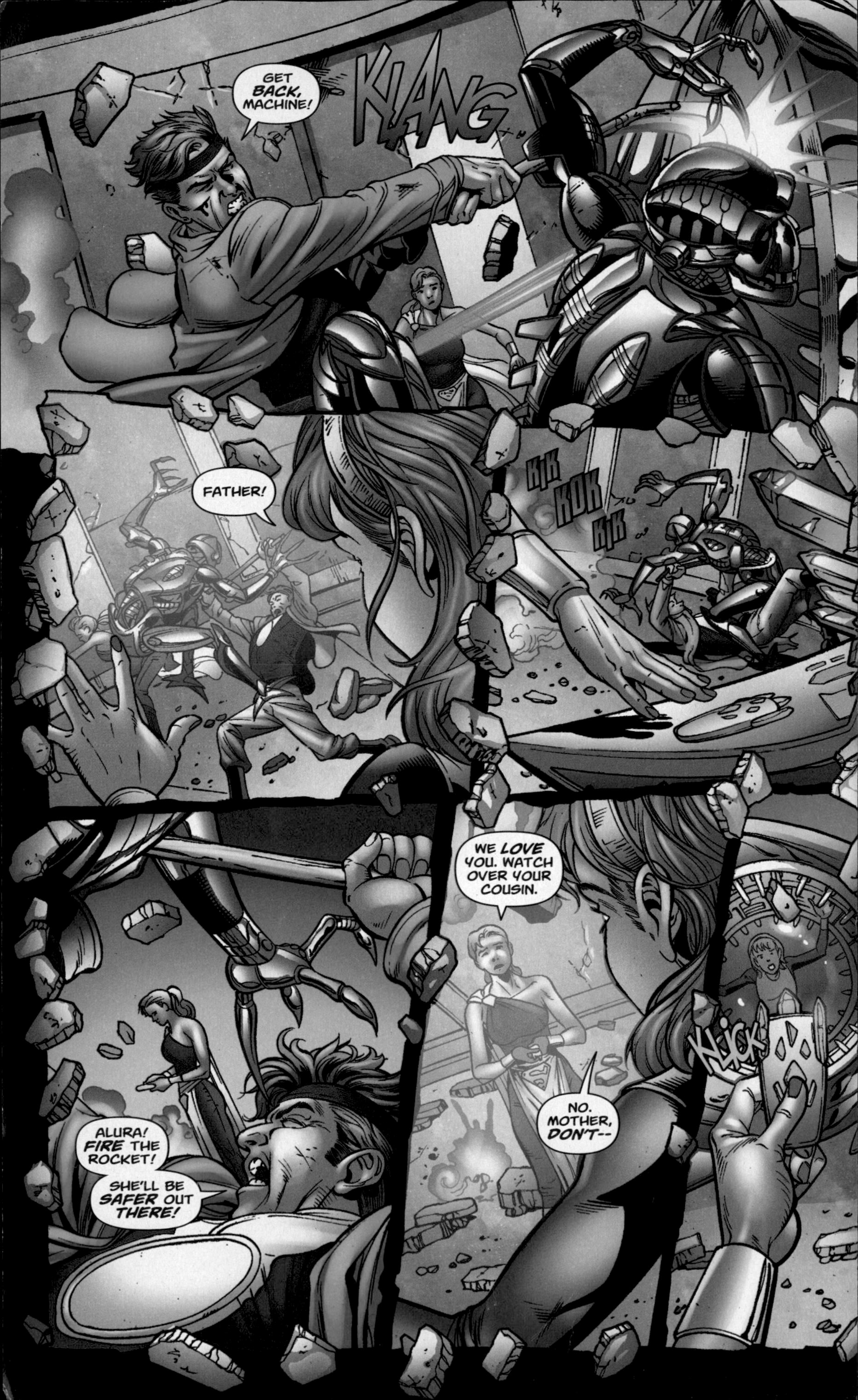
GET BACK, MACHINE!
KLANG
FATHER!
KIK KOK KIK
ALURA! FIRE THE ROCKET!
SHE'LL BE SAFER OUT THERE!
WE LOVE YOU. WATCH OVER YOUR COUSIN.
NO. MOTHER, DON'T--
KLICK

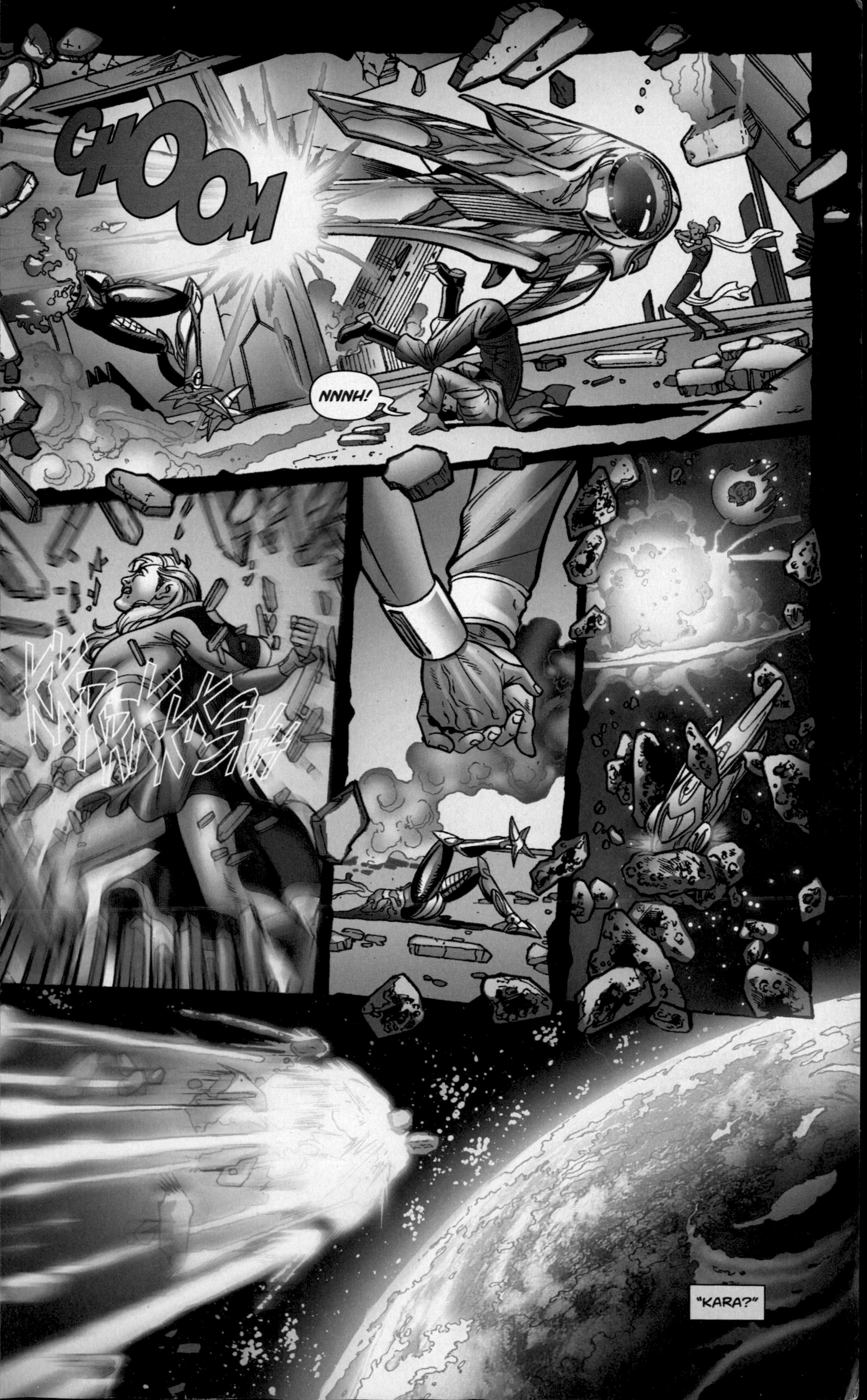
CHOOM
NNNH!
KRAKKSH
"KARA?"

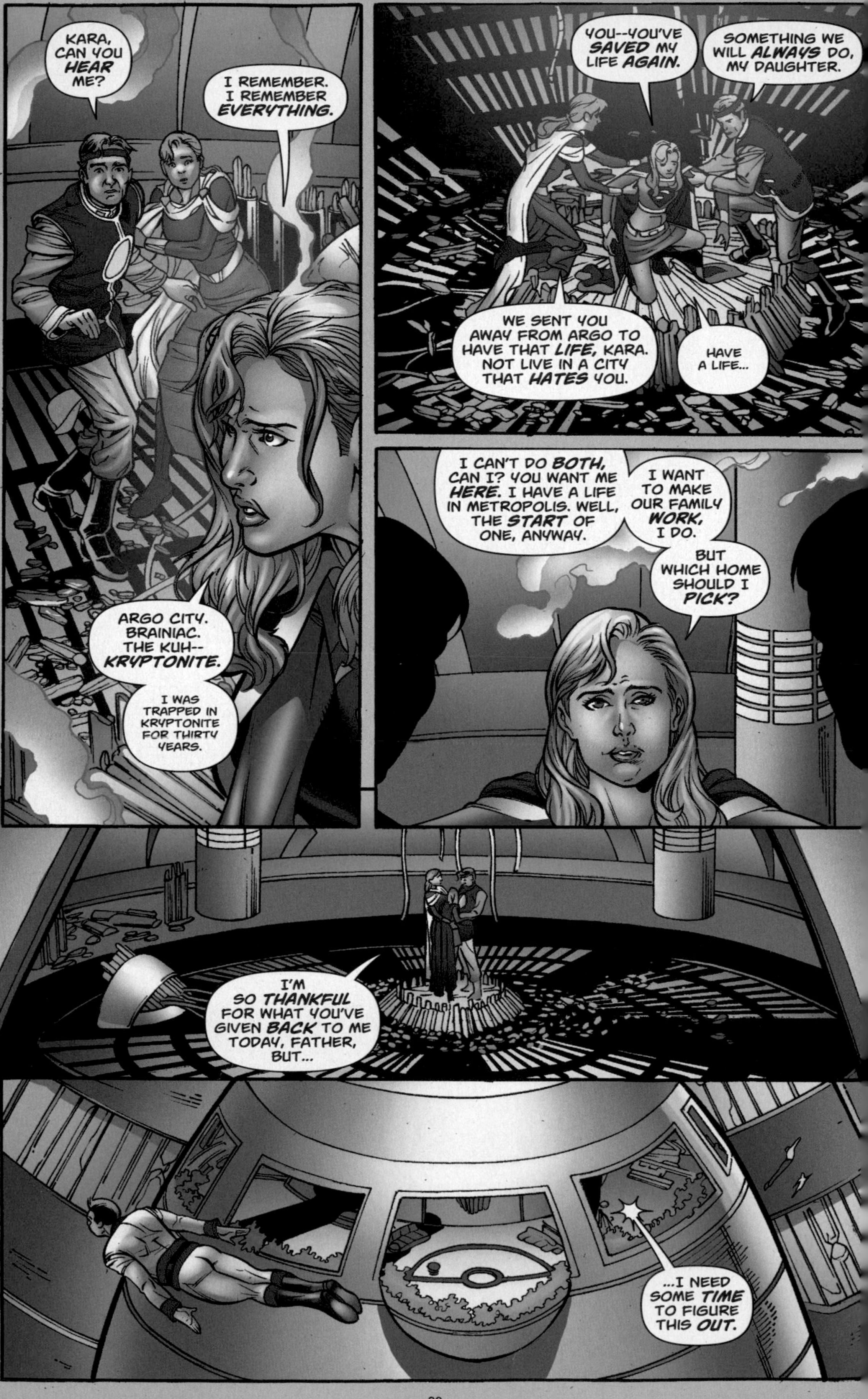
KARA, CAN YOU HEAR ME?
I REMEMBER. I REMEMBER EVERYTHING.
ARGO CITY. BRAINIAC. THE KUH-- KRYPTONITE.
I WAS TRAPPED IN KRYPTONITE FOR THIRTY YEARS.
YOU--YOU'VE SAVED MY LIFE AGAIN.
SOMETHING WE WILL ALWAYS DO, MY DAUGHTER.
WE SENT YOU AWAY FROM ARGO TO HAVE THAT LIFE, KARA. NOT LIVE IN A CITY THAT HATES YOU.
HAVE A LIFE...
I CAN'T DO BOTH, CAN I? YOU WANT ME HERE. I HAVE A LIFE IN METROPOLIS. WELL, THE START OF ONE, ANYWAY.
I WANT TO MAKE OUR FAMILY WORK, I DO.
BUT WHICH HOME SHOULD I PICK?
I'M SO THANKFUL FOR WHAT YOU'VE GIVEN BACK TO ME TODAY, FATHER, BUT...
...I NEED SOME TIME TO FIGURE THIS OUT.

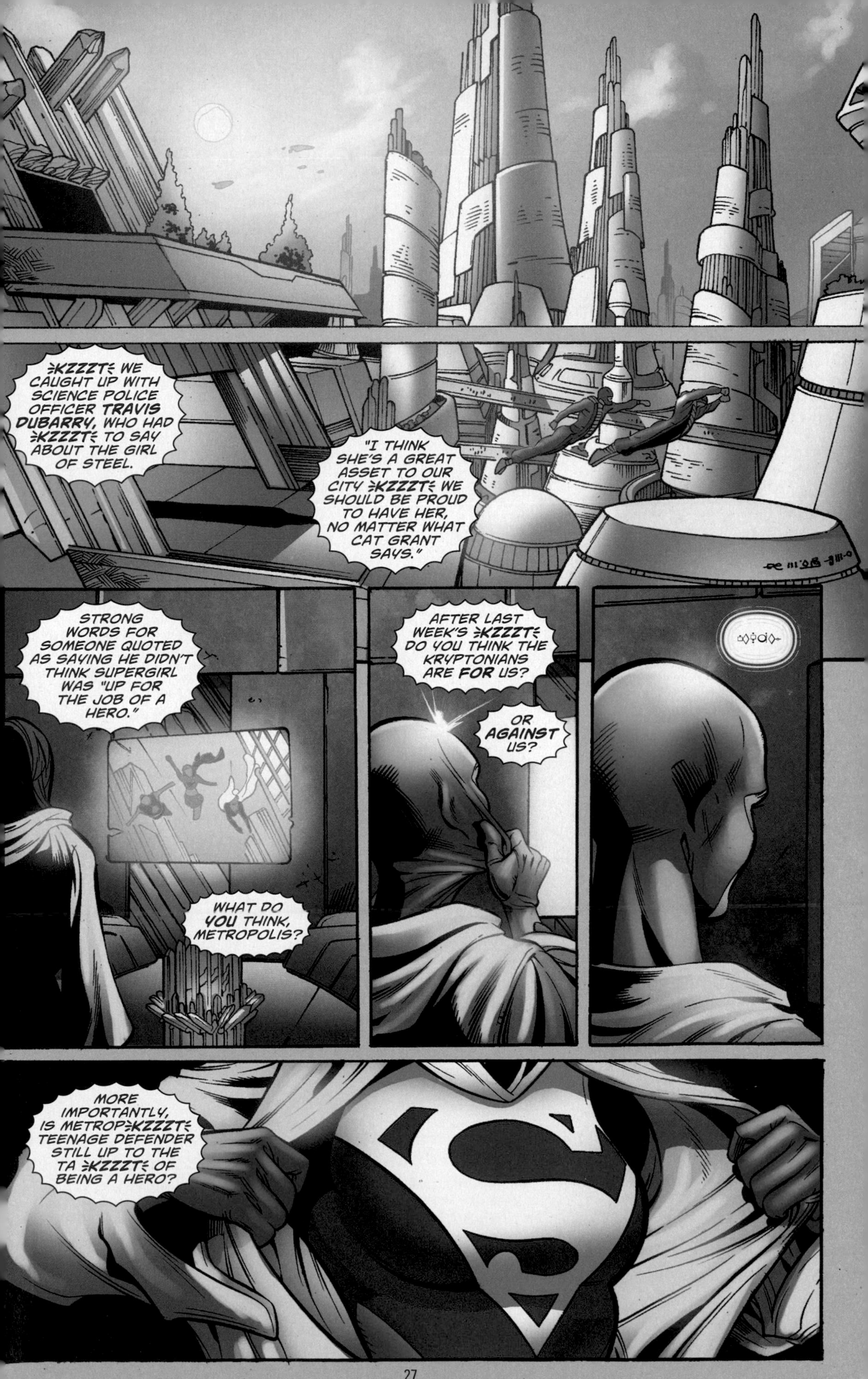

≡KZZZT≡ WE CAUGHT UP WITH SCIENCE POLICE OFFICER TRAVIS DUBARRY, WHO HAD ≡KZZZT≡ TO SAY ABOUT THE GIRL OF STEEL.
"I THINK SHE'S A GREAT ASSET TO OUR CITY ≡KZZZT≡ WE SHOULD BE PROUD TO HAVE HER, NO MATTER WHAT CAT GRANT SAYS."
STRONG WORDS FOR SOMEONE QUOTED AS SAYING HE DIDN'T THINK SUPERGIRL WAS "UP FOR THE JOB OF A HERO."
WHAT DO YOU THINK, METROPOLIS?
AFTER LAST WEEK'S ≡KZZZT≡ DO YOU THINK THE KRYPTONIANS ARE FOR US?
OR AGAINST US?
MORE IMPORTANTLY, IS METROP≡KZZZT≡ TEENAGE DEFENDER STILL UP TO THE TA ≡KZZZT≡ OF BEING A HERO?

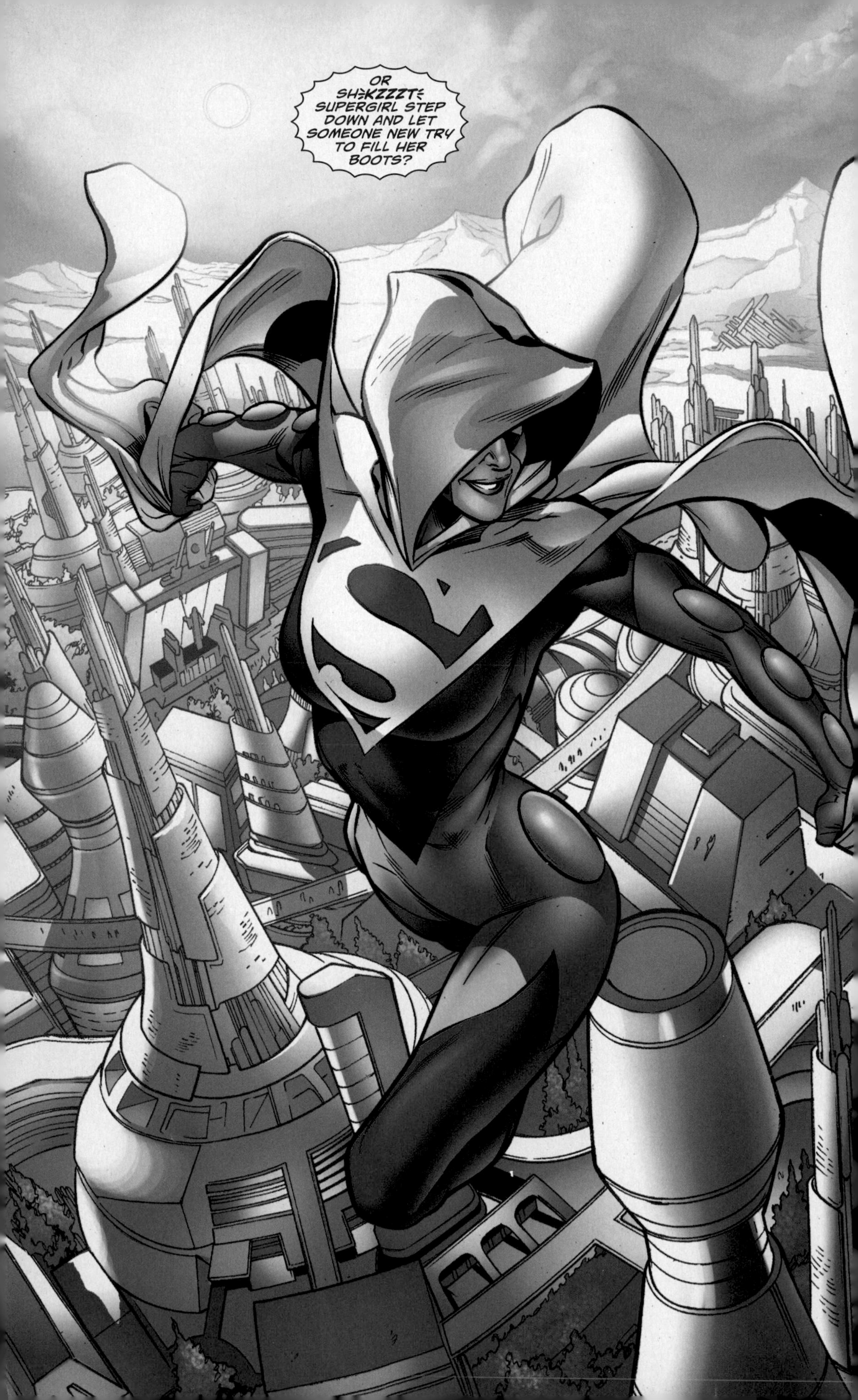
OR SH=KZZZT= SUPERGIRL STEP DOWN AND LET SOMEONE NEW TRY TO FILL HER BOOTS?

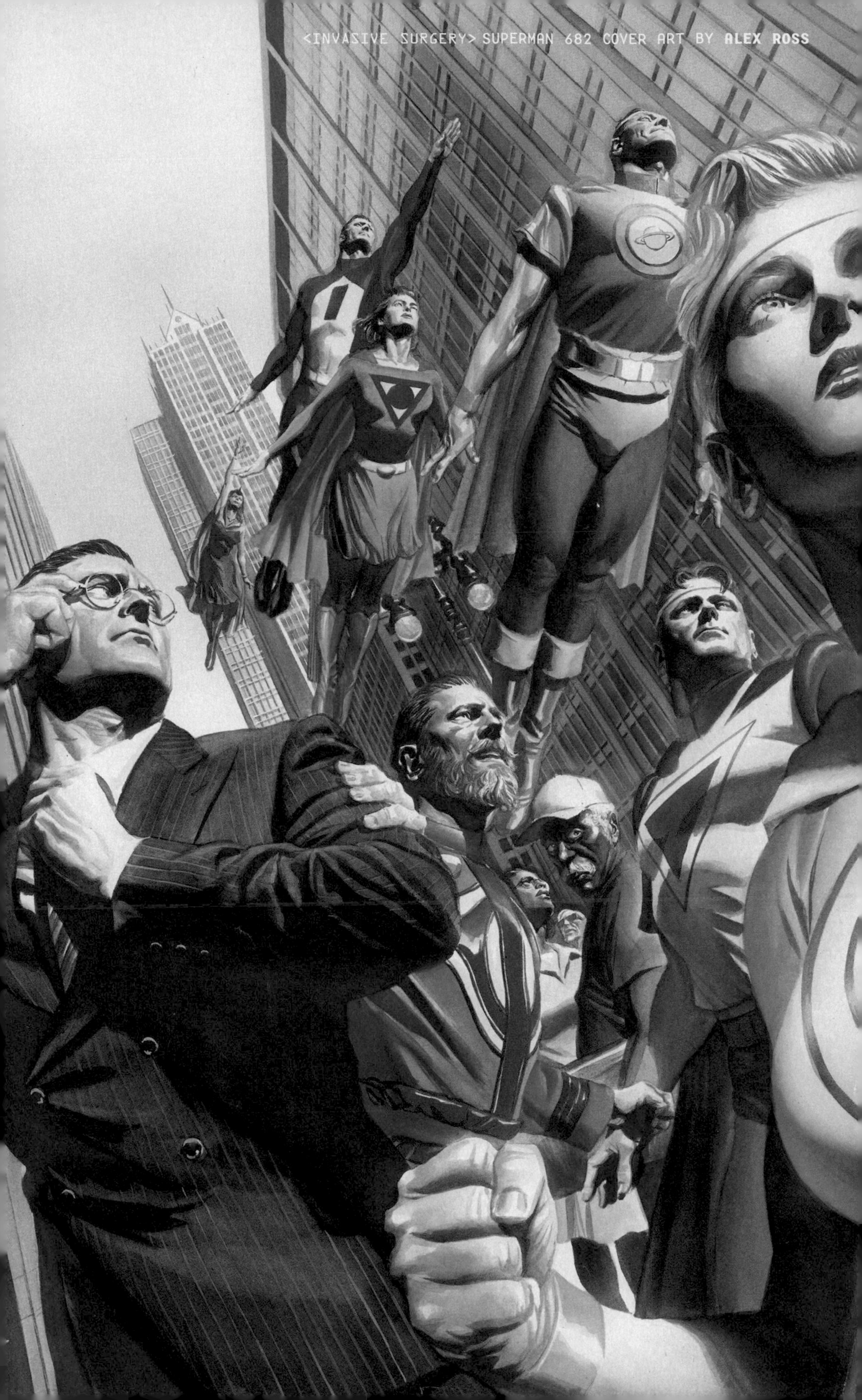

<INVASIVE SURGERY> SUPERMAN 682 COVER ART BY **ALEX ROSS**

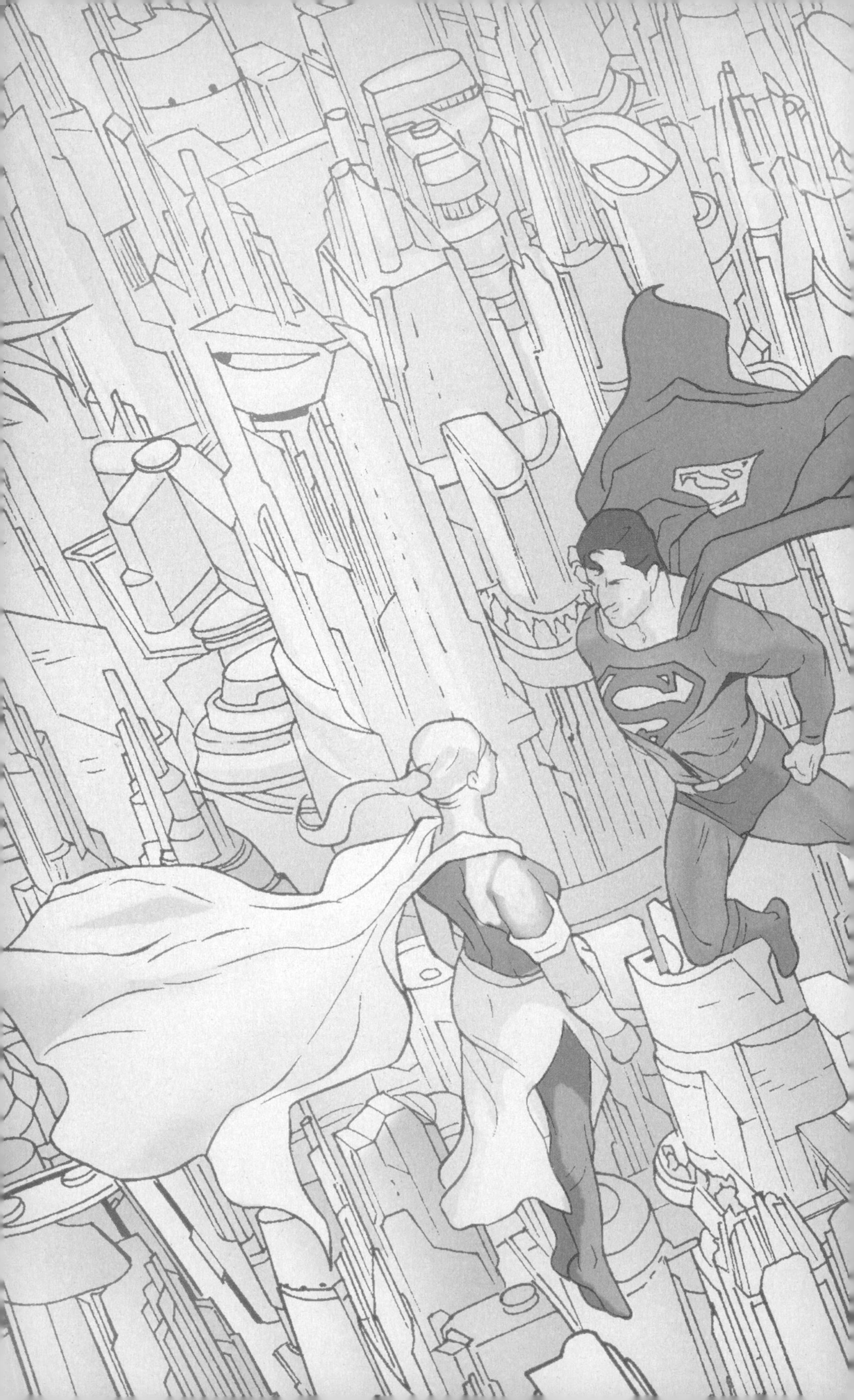

31

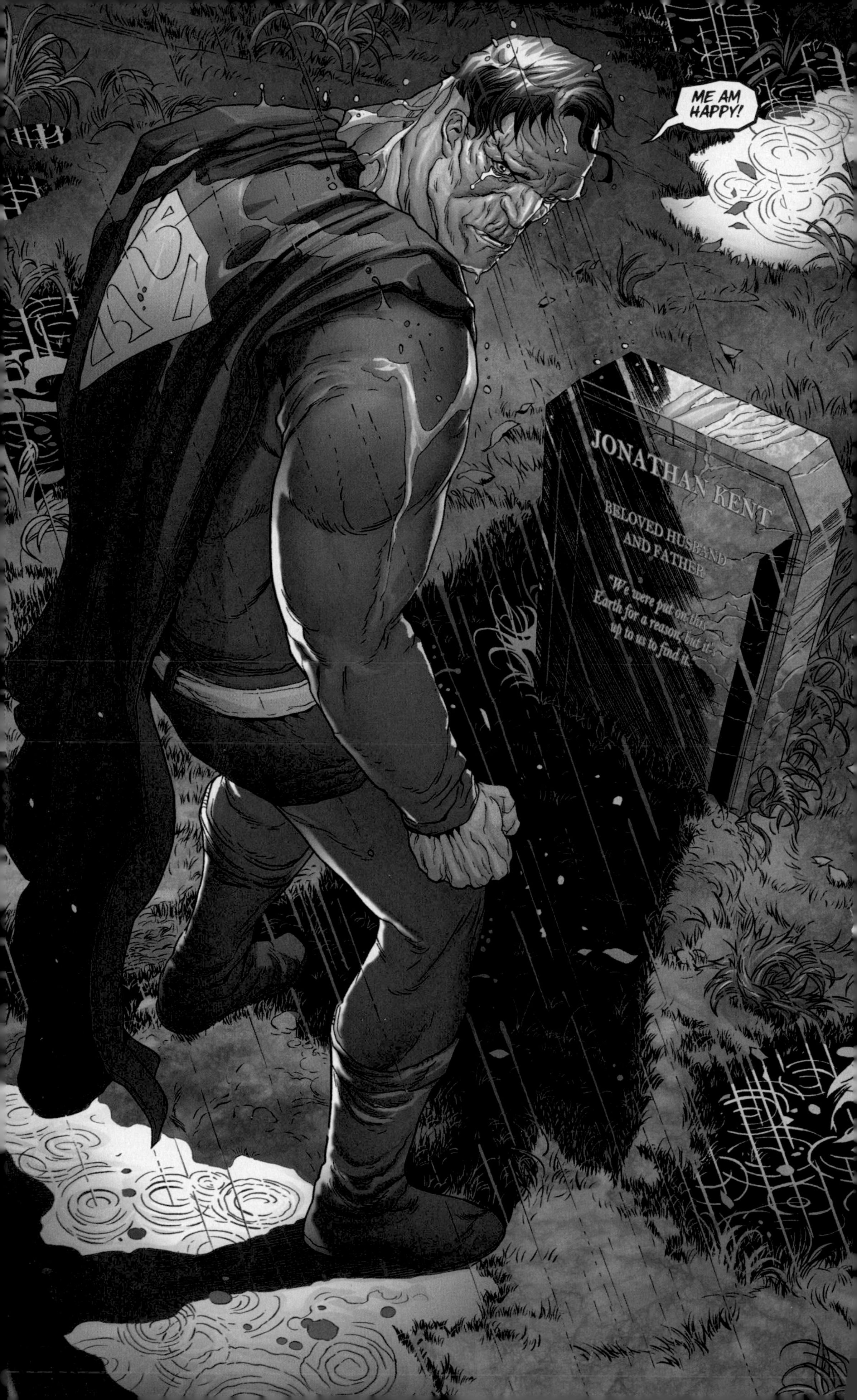
ME AM HAPPY!
JONATHAN KENT
BELOVED HUSBAND AND FATHER
"We were put on this Earth for a reason, but it's up to us to find it."

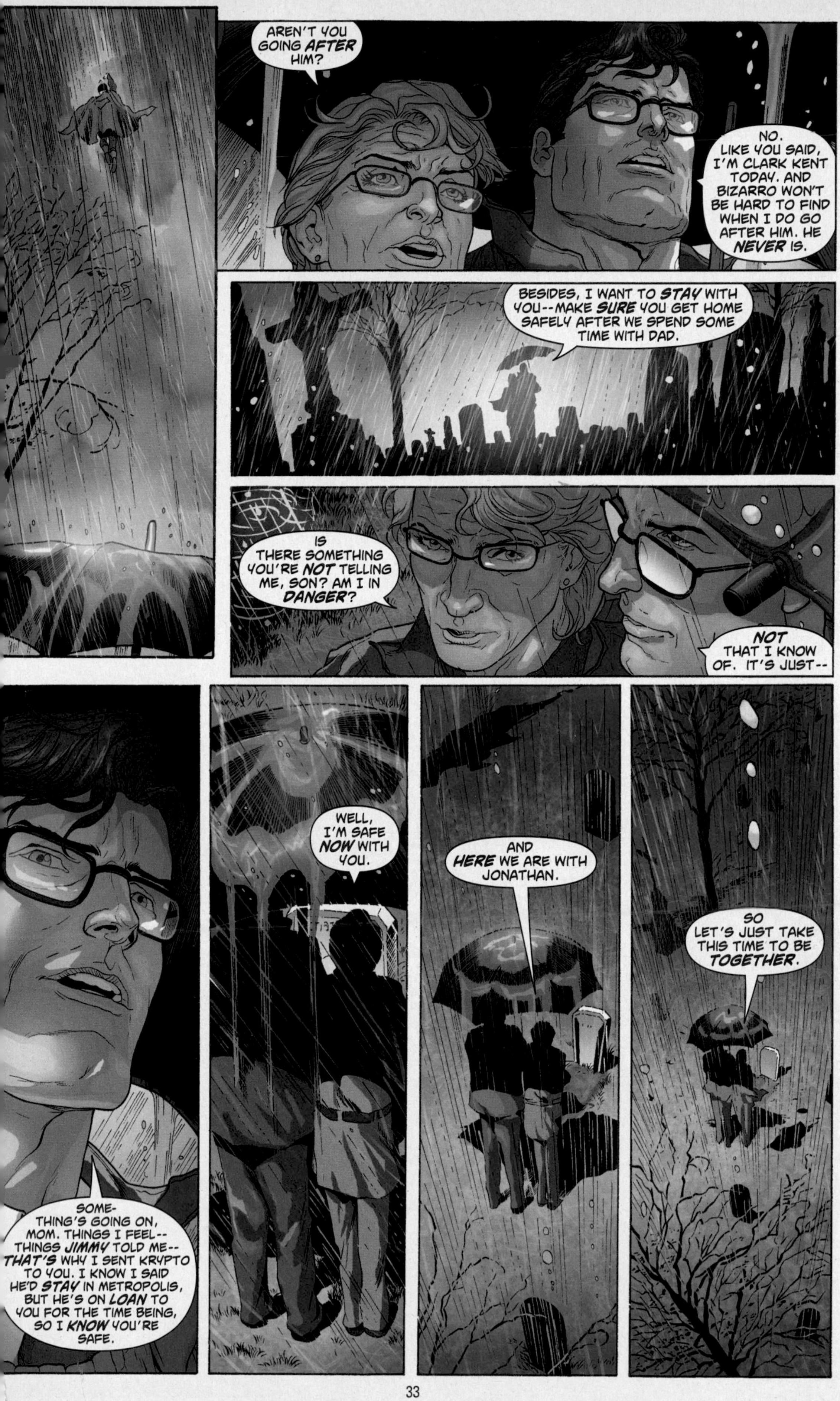

AREN'T YOU GOING AFTER HIM?
NO. LIKE YOU SAID, I'M CLARK KENT TODAY. AND BIZARRO WON'T BE HARD TO FIND WHEN I DO GO AFTER HIM. HE NEVER IS.
BESIDES, I WANT TO STAY WITH YOU--MAKE SURE YOU GET HOME SAFELY AFTER WE SPEND SOME TIME WITH DAD.
IS THERE SOMETHING YOU'RE NOT TELLING ME, SON? AM I IN DANGER?
NOT THAT I KNOW OF. IT'S JUST--
SOME-THING'S GOING ON, MOM. THINGS I FEEL--THINGS JIMMY TOLD ME--THAT'S WHY I SENT KRYPTO TO YOU. I KNOW I SAID HE'D STAY IN METROPOLIS, BUT HE'S ON LOAN TO YOU FOR THE TIME BEING, SO I KNOW YOU'RE SAFE.
WELL, I'M SAFE NOW WITH YOU.
AND HERE WE ARE WITH JONATHAN.
SO LET'S JUST TAKE THIS TIME TO BE TOGETHER.

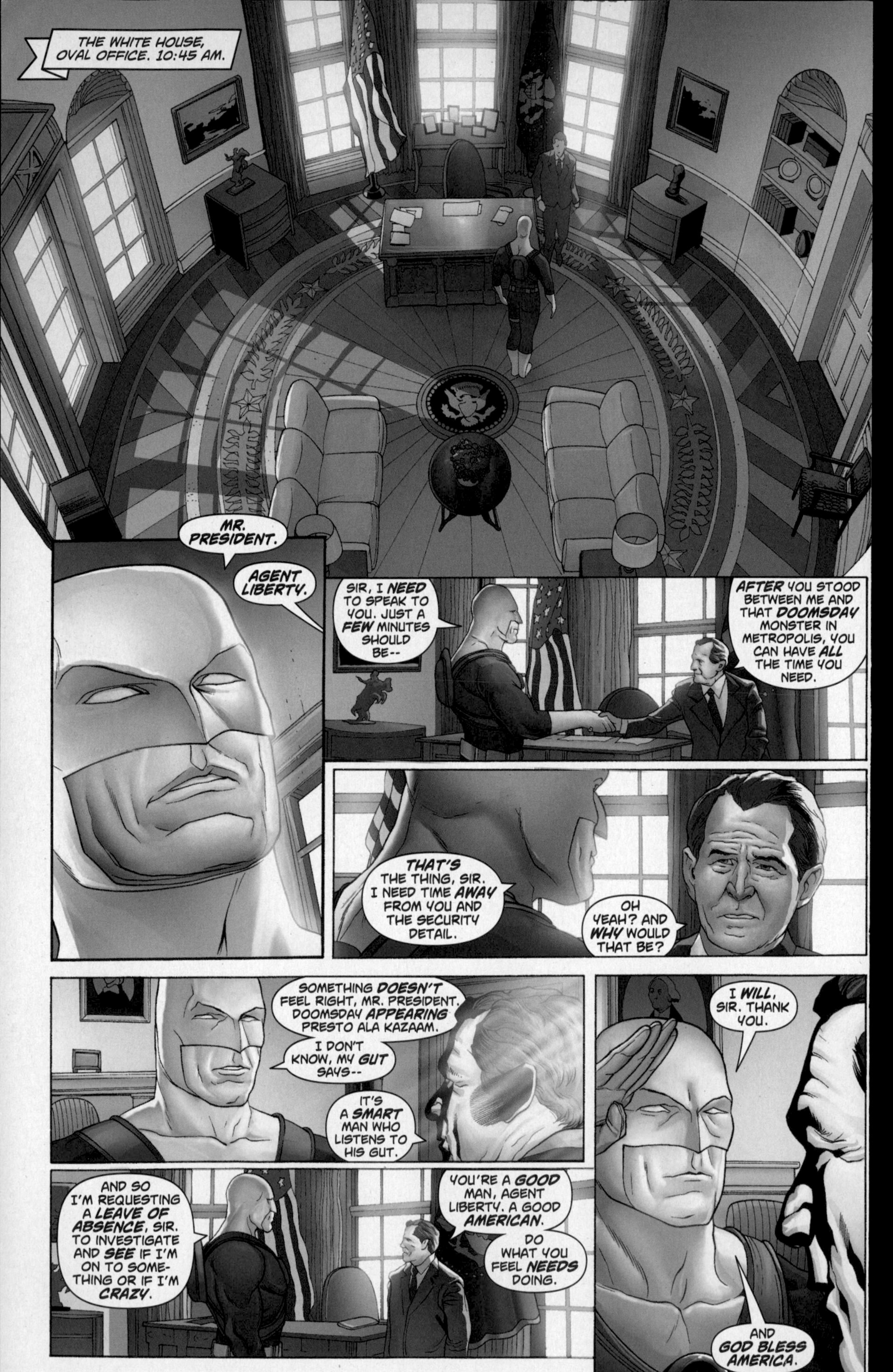
THE WHITE HOUSE, OVAL OFFICE. 10:45 AM.
MR. PRESIDENT.
AGENT LIBERTY.
SIR, I NEED TO SPEAK TO YOU. JUST A FEW MINUTES SHOULD BE--
AFTER YOU STOOD BETWEEN ME AND THAT DOOMSDAY MONSTER IN METROPOLIS, YOU CAN HAVE ALL THE TIME YOU NEED.
THAT'S THE THING, SIR. I NEED TIME AWAY FROM YOU AND THE SECURITY DETAIL.
OH YEAH? AND WHY WOULD THAT BE?
SOMETHING DOESN'T FEEL RIGHT, MR. PRESIDENT. DOOMSDAY APPEARING PRESTO ALA KAZAAM.
I DON'T KNOW, MY GUT SAYS--
IT'S A SMART MAN WHO LISTENS TO HIS GUT.
AND SO I'M REQUESTING A LEAVE OF ABSENCE, SIR. TO INVESTIGATE AND SEE IF I'M ON TO SOME-THING OR IF I'M CRAZY.
YOU'RE A GOOD MAN, AGENT LIBERTY. A GOOD AMERICAN.
DO WHAT YOU FEEL NEEDS DOING.
I WILL, SIR. THANK YOU.
AND GOD BLESS AMERICA.

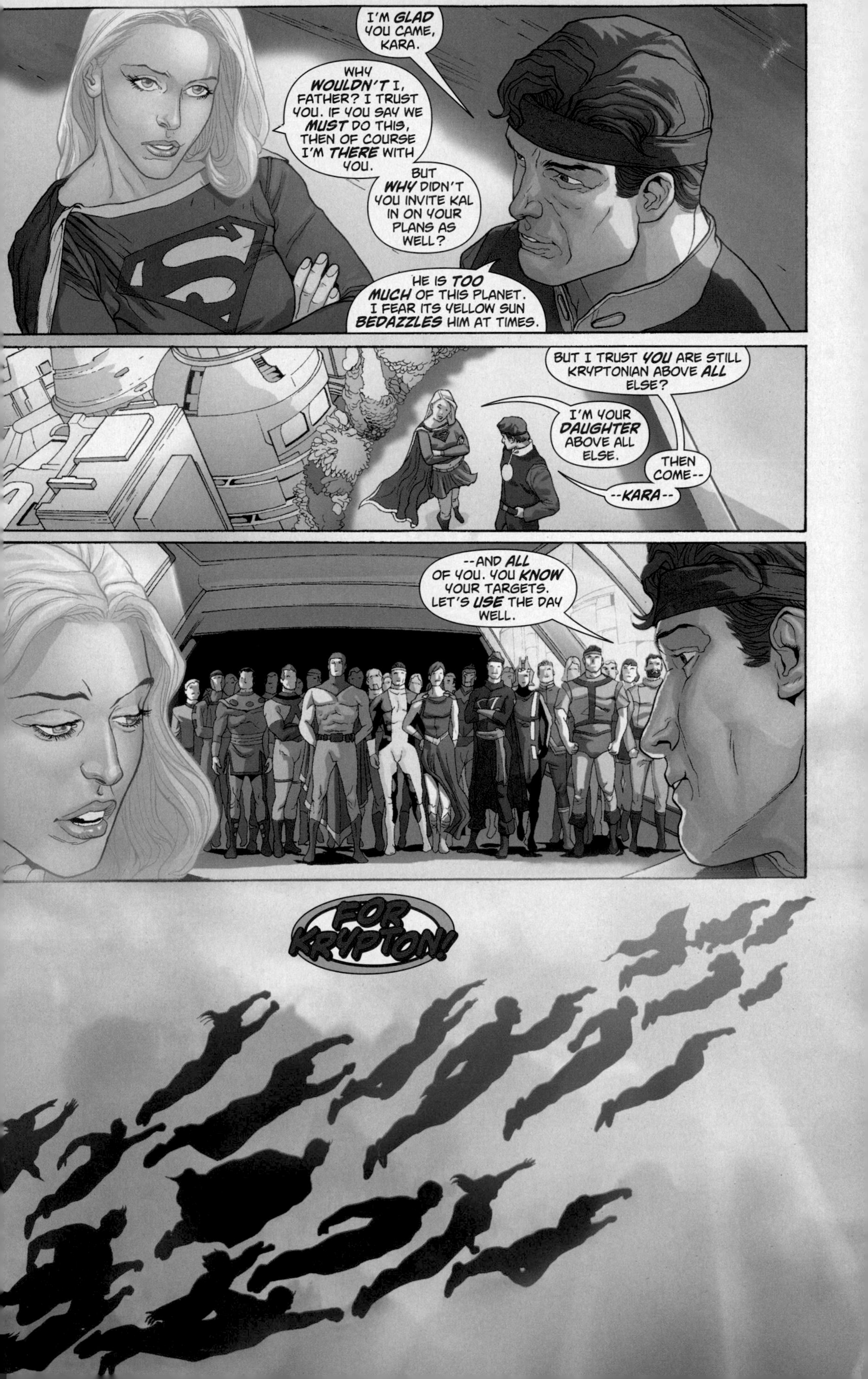
I'M GLAD YOU CAME, KARA.
WHY WOULDN'T I, FATHER? I TRUST YOU. IF YOU SAY WE MUST DO THIS, THEN OF COURSE I'M THERE WITH YOU.
BUT WHY DIDN'T YOU INVITE KAL IN ON YOUR PLANS AS WELL?
HE IS TOO MUCH OF THIS PLANET. I FEAR ITS YELLOW SUN BEDAZZLES HIM AT TIMES.
BUT I TRUST YOU ARE STILL KRYPTONIAN ABOVE ALL ELSE?
I'M YOUR DAUGHTER ABOVE ALL ELSE.
THEN COME--
--KARA--
--AND ALL OF YOU. YOU KNOW YOUR TARGETS. LET'S USE THE DAY WELL.
FOR KRYPTON!

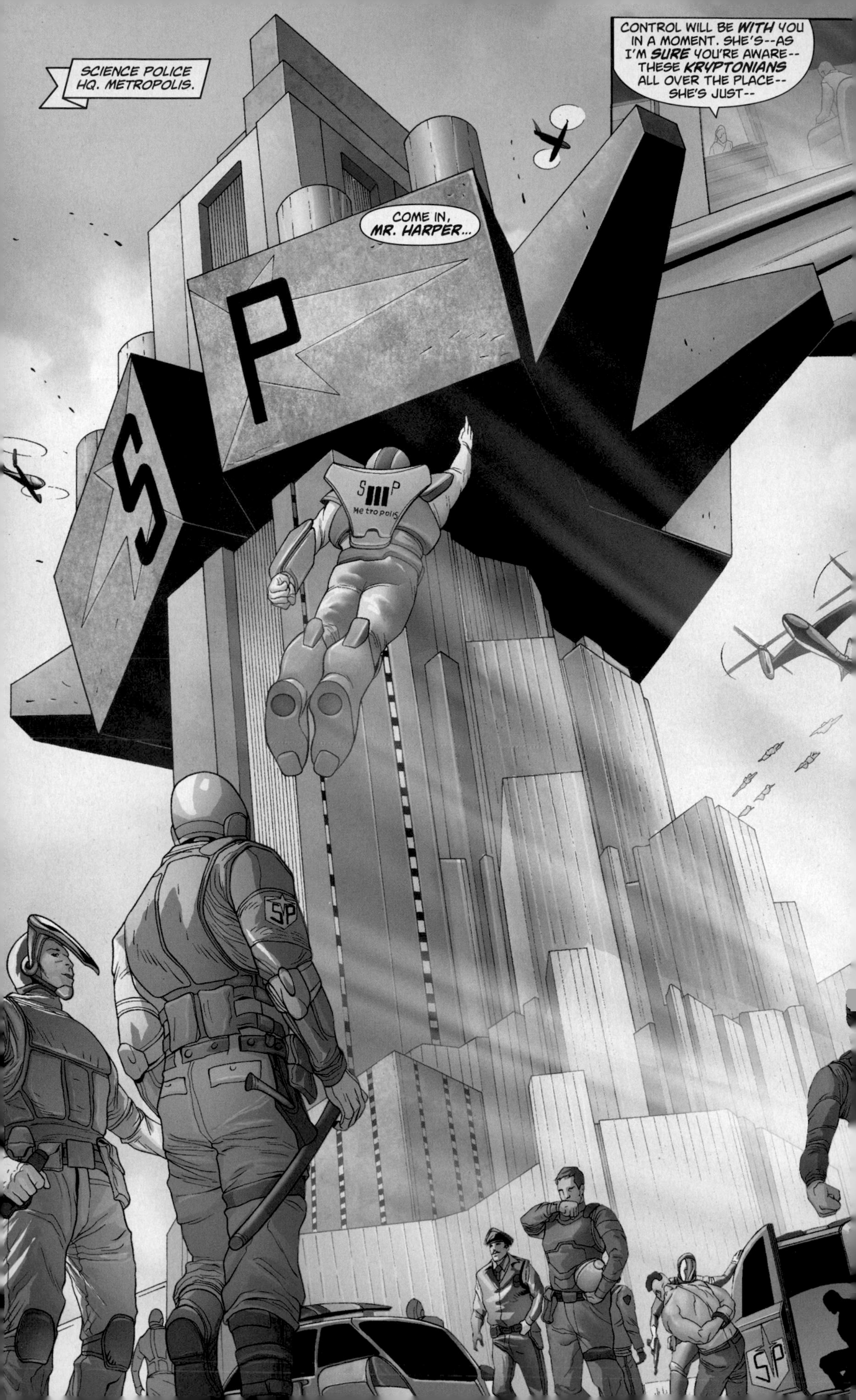
SCIENCE POLICE HQ. METROPOLIS.
CONTROL WILL BE WITH YOU IN A MOMENT. SHE'S--AS I'M SURE YOU'RE AWARE--THESE KRYPTONIANS ALL OVER THE PLACE--SHE'S JUST--
COME IN, MR. HARPER...
S P
Metropolis

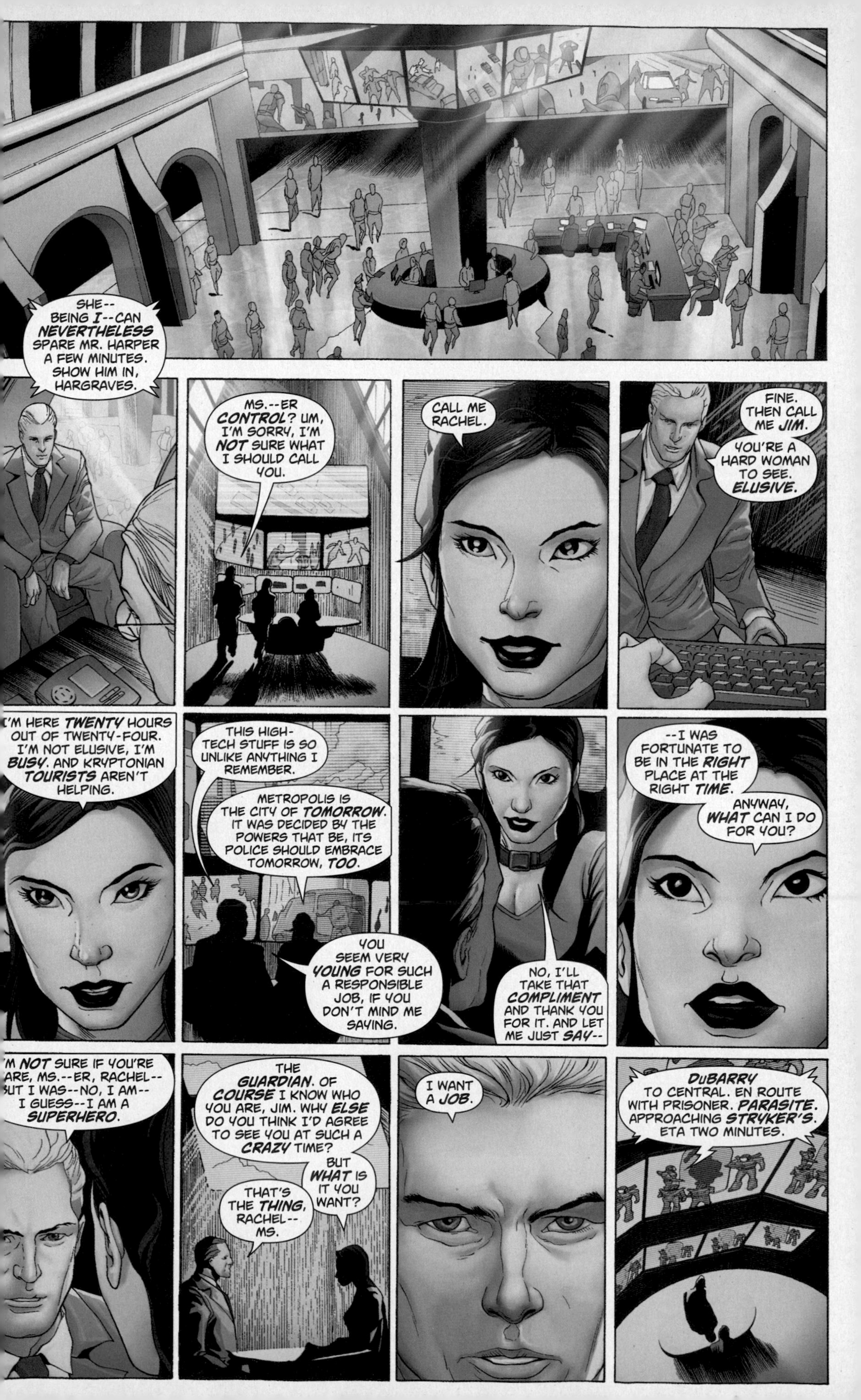
SHE--
BEING I--CAN NEVERTHELESS SPARE MR. HARPER A FEW MINUTES. SHOW HIM IN, HARGRAVES.
MS.--ER CONTROL? UM, I'M SORRY, I'M NOT SURE WHAT I SHOULD CALL YOU.
CALL ME RACHEL.
FINE. THEN CALL ME JIM.
YOU'RE A HARD WOMAN TO SEE. ELUSIVE.
I'M HERE TWENTY HOURS OUT OF TWENTY-FOUR. I'M NOT ELUSIVE, I'M BUSY. AND KRYPTONIAN TOURISTS AREN'T HELPING.
THIS HIGH-TECH STUFF IS SO UNLIKE ANYTHING I REMEMBER.
METROPOLIS IS THE CITY OF TOMORROW. IT WAS DECIDED BY THE POWERS THAT BE, ITS POLICE SHOULD EMBRACE TOMORROW, TOO.
YOU SEEM VERY YOUNG FOR SUCH A RESPONSIBLE JOB, IF YOU DON'T MIND ME SAYING.
NO, I'LL TAKE THAT COMPLIMENT AND THANK YOU FOR IT. AND LET ME JUST SAY--
--I WAS FORTUNATE TO BE IN THE RIGHT PLACE AT THE RIGHT TIME.
ANYWAY, WHAT CAN I DO FOR YOU?
I'M NOT SURE IF YOU'RE AWARE, MS.--ER, RACHEL--BUT I WAS--NO, I AM--I GUESS--I AM A SUPERHERO.
THE GUARDIAN. OF COURSE I KNOW WHO YOU ARE, JIM. WHY ELSE DO YOU THINK I'D AGREE TO SEE YOU AT SUCH A CRAZY TIME?
BUT WHAT IS IT YOU WANT?
THAT'S THE THING, RACHEL--MS.
I WANT A JOB.
DUBARRY TO CENTRAL. EN ROUTE WITH PRISONER. PARASITE. APPROACHING STRYKER'S. ETA TWO MINUTES.

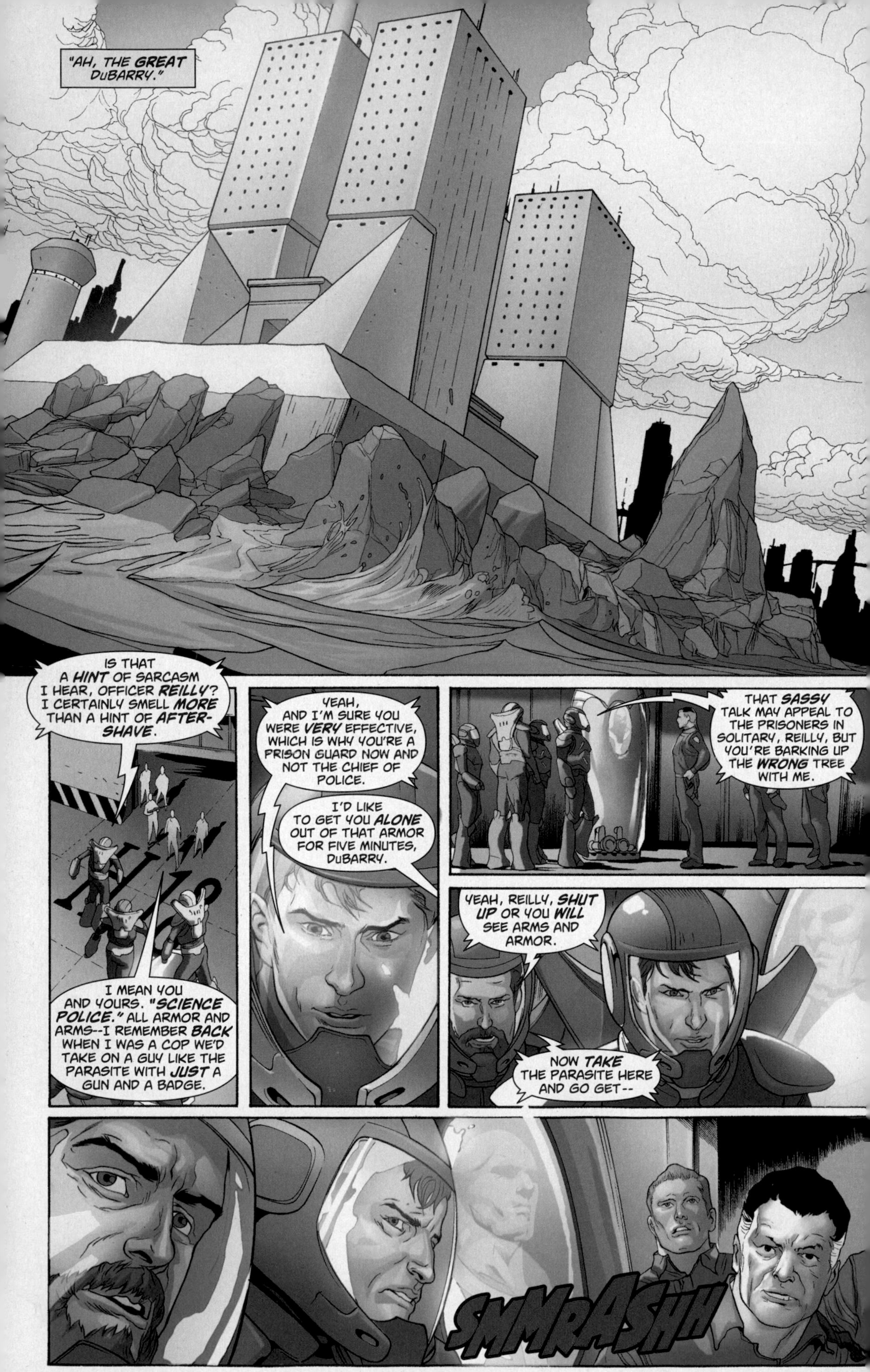
"AH, THE GREAT DuBARRY."
IS THAT A HINT OF SARCASM I HEAR, OFFICER REILLY? I CERTAINLY SMELL MORE THAN A HINT OF AFTER-SHAVE.
I MEAN YOU AND YOURS. "SCIENCE POLICE." ALL ARMOR AND ARMS--I REMEMBER BACK WHEN I WAS A COP WE'D TAKE ON A GUY LIKE THE PARASITE WITH JUST A GUN AND A BADGE.
YEAH, AND I'M SURE YOU WERE VERY EFFECTIVE, WHICH IS WHY YOU'RE A PRISON GUARD NOW AND NOT THE CHIEF OF POLICE.
I'D LIKE TO GET YOU ALONE OUT OF THAT ARMOR FOR FIVE MINUTES, DuBARRY.
THAT SASSY TALK MAY APPEAL TO THE PRISONERS IN SOLITARY, REILLY, BUT YOU'RE BARKING UP THE WRONG TREE WITH ME.
YEAH, REILLY, SHUT UP OR YOU WILL SEE ARMS AND ARMOR.
NOW TAKE THE PARASITE HERE AND GO GET--
SMMRASHH

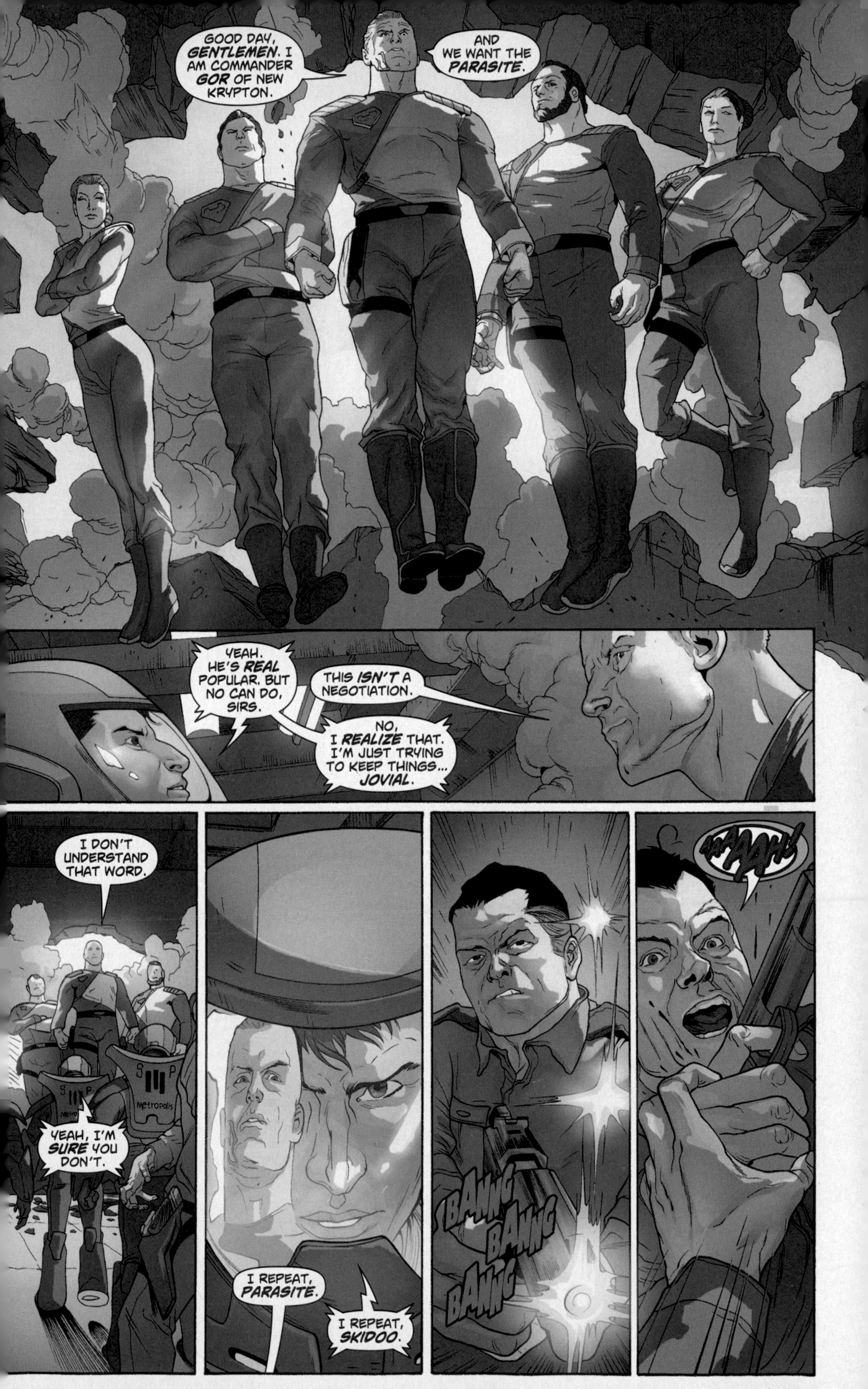
GOOD DAY, GENTLEMEN. I AM COMMANDER GOR OF NEW KRYPTON.
AND WE WANT THE PARASITE.
YEAH. HE'S REAL POPULAR. BUT NO CAN DO, SIRS.
THIS ISN'T A NEGOTIATION.
NO, I REALIZE THAT. I'M JUST TRYING TO KEEP THINGS... JOVIAL.
I DON'T UNDERSTAND THAT WORD.
YEAH, I'M SURE YOU DON'T.
I REPEAT, PARASITE.
I REPEAT, SKIDOO.
BANNG BANNG BANNG
AAAAAH!

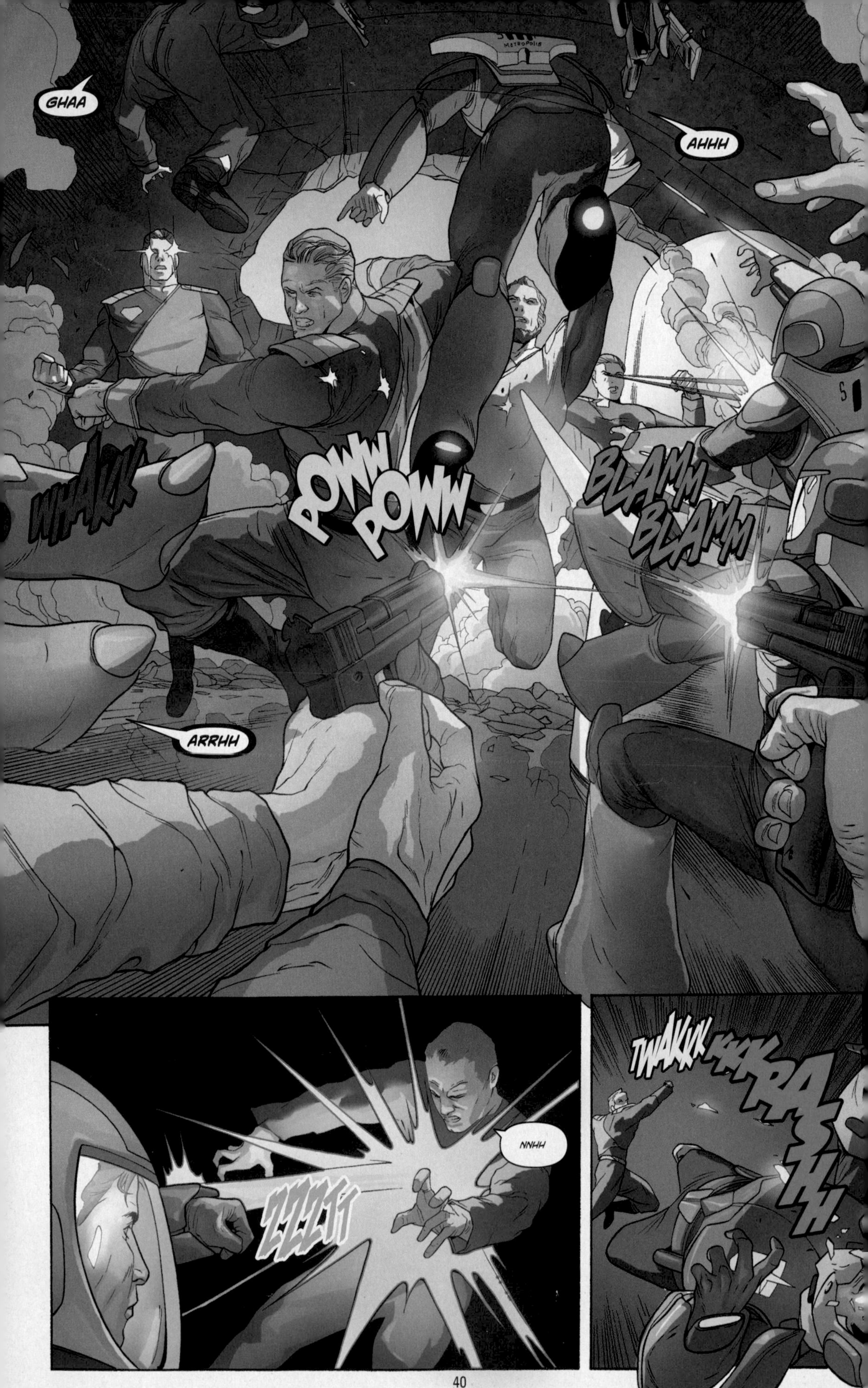
GHAA
METROPOLIS
AHHH
WHAKK
POWW POWW
BLAMM BLAMM
ARRHH
NNHH
ZZZTT
TWAKKK KKKRAAHH

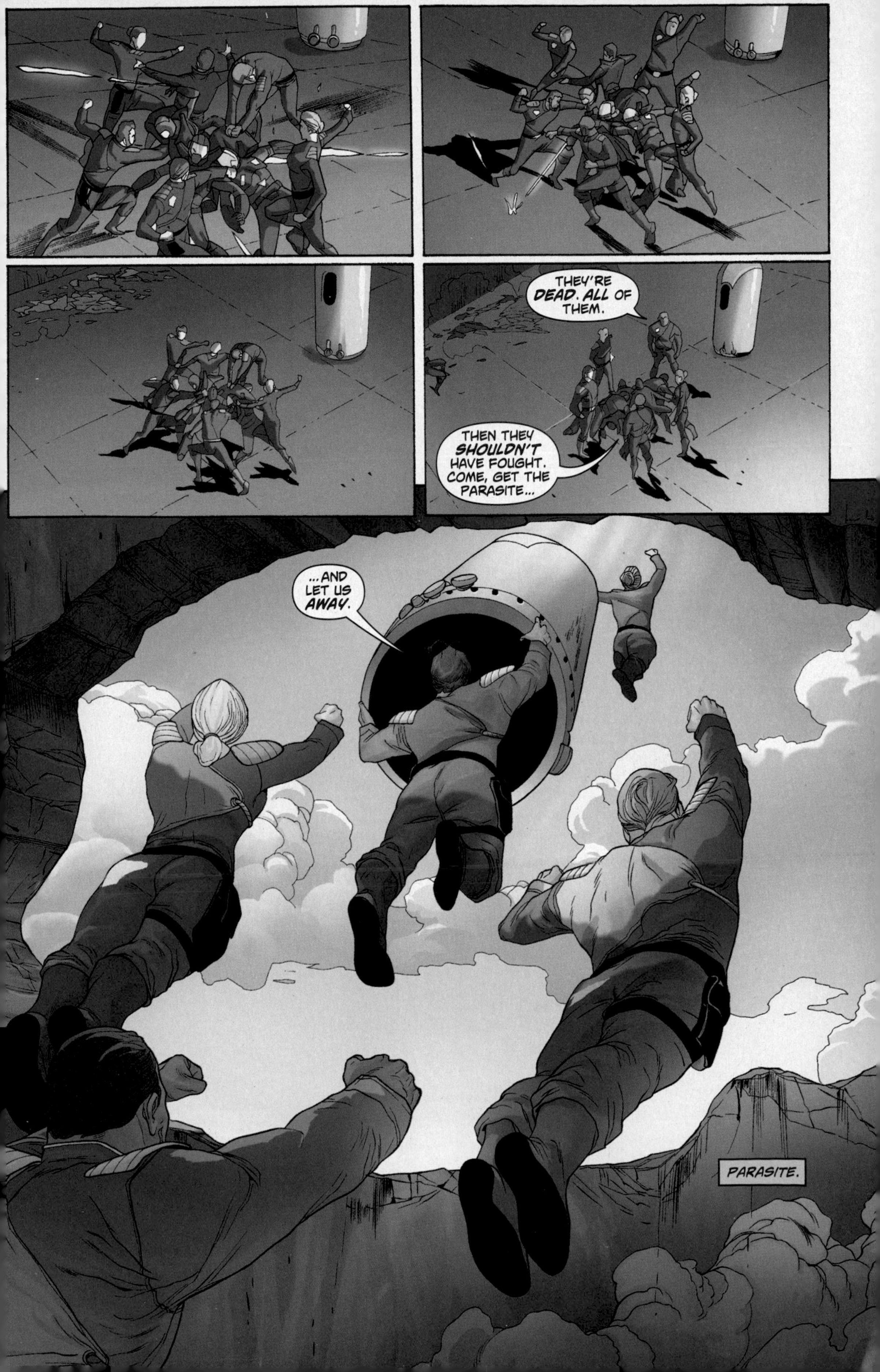
THEY'RE DEAD. ALL OF THEM.
THEN THEY SHOULDN'T HAVE FOUGHT. COME, GET THE PARASITE...
...AND LET US AWAY.
PARASITE.

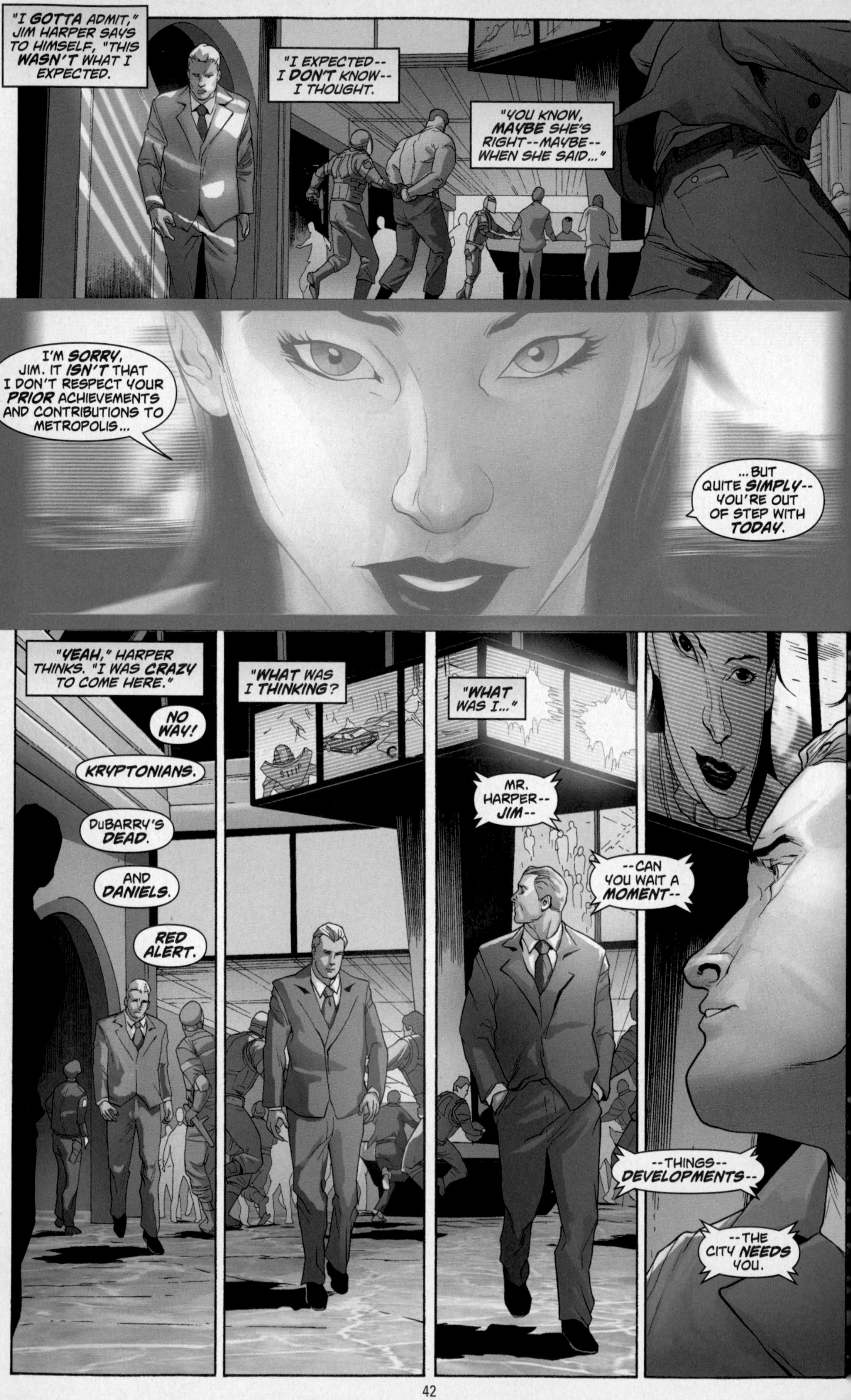
"I GOTTA ADMIT," JIM HARPER SAYS TO HIMSELF, "THIS WASN'T WHAT I EXPECTED.
"I EXPECTED-- I DON'T KNOW-- I THOUGHT.
"YOU KNOW, MAYBE SHE'S RIGHT--MAYBE-- WHEN SHE SAID..."
I'M SORRY, JIM. IT ISN'T THAT I DON'T RESPECT YOUR PRIOR ACHIEVEMENTS AND CONTRIBUTIONS TO METROPOLIS...
...BUT QUITE SIMPLY-- YOU'RE OUT OF STEP WITH TODAY.
"YEAH," HARPER THINKS. "I WAS CRAZY TO COME HERE."
NO WAY!
KRYPTONIANS.
DuBARRY'S DEAD.
AND DANIELS.
RED ALERT.
"WHAT WAS I THINKING?
"WHAT WAS I..."
MR. HARPER-- JIM--
--CAN YOU WAIT A MOMENT--
--THINGS-- DEVELOPMENTS--
--THE CITY NEEDS YOU.

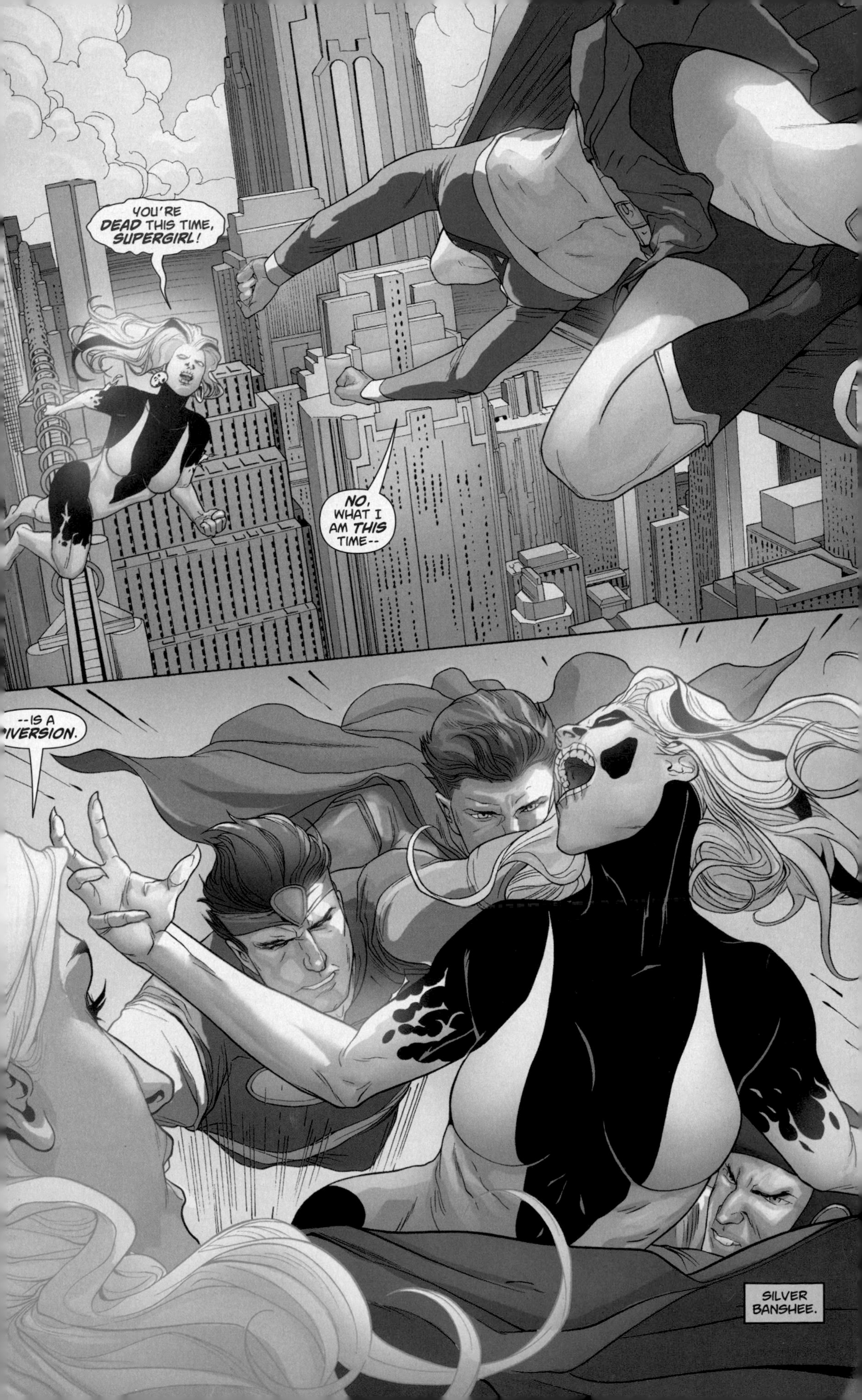
YOU'RE DEAD THIS TIME, SUPERGIRL!
NO, WHAT I AM THIS TIME--
--IS A DIVERSION.
SILVER BANSHEE.

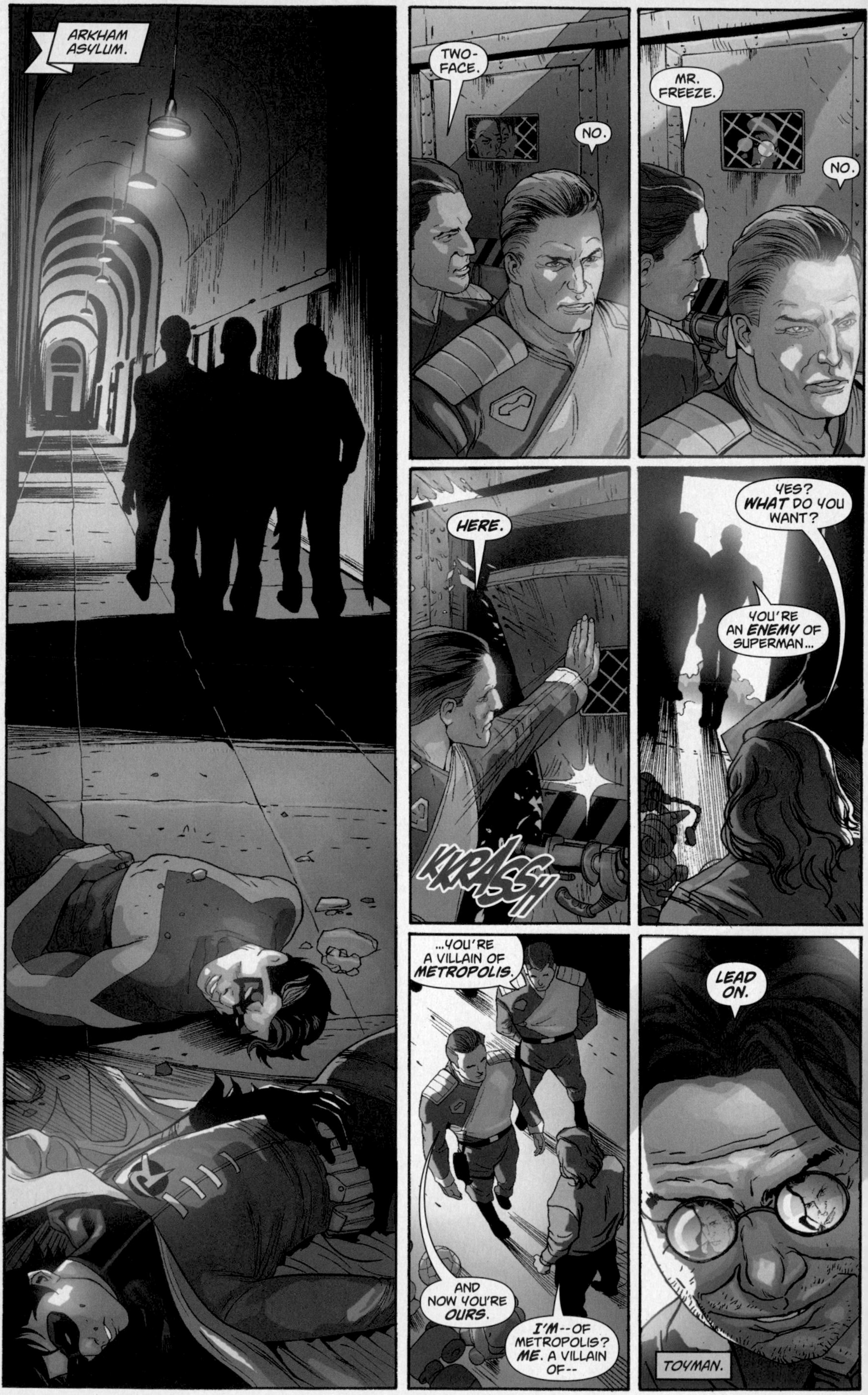
ARKHAM ASYLUM.
TWO-FACE.
NO.
MR. FREEZE.
NO.
HERE.
KKRASSH
YES? WHAT DO YOU WANT?
YOU'RE AN ENEMY OF SUPERMAN...
...YOU'RE A VILLAIN OF METROPOLIS.
AND NOW YOU'RE OURS.
I'M--OF METROPOLIS? ME. A VILLAIN OF--
LEAD ON.
TOYMAN.

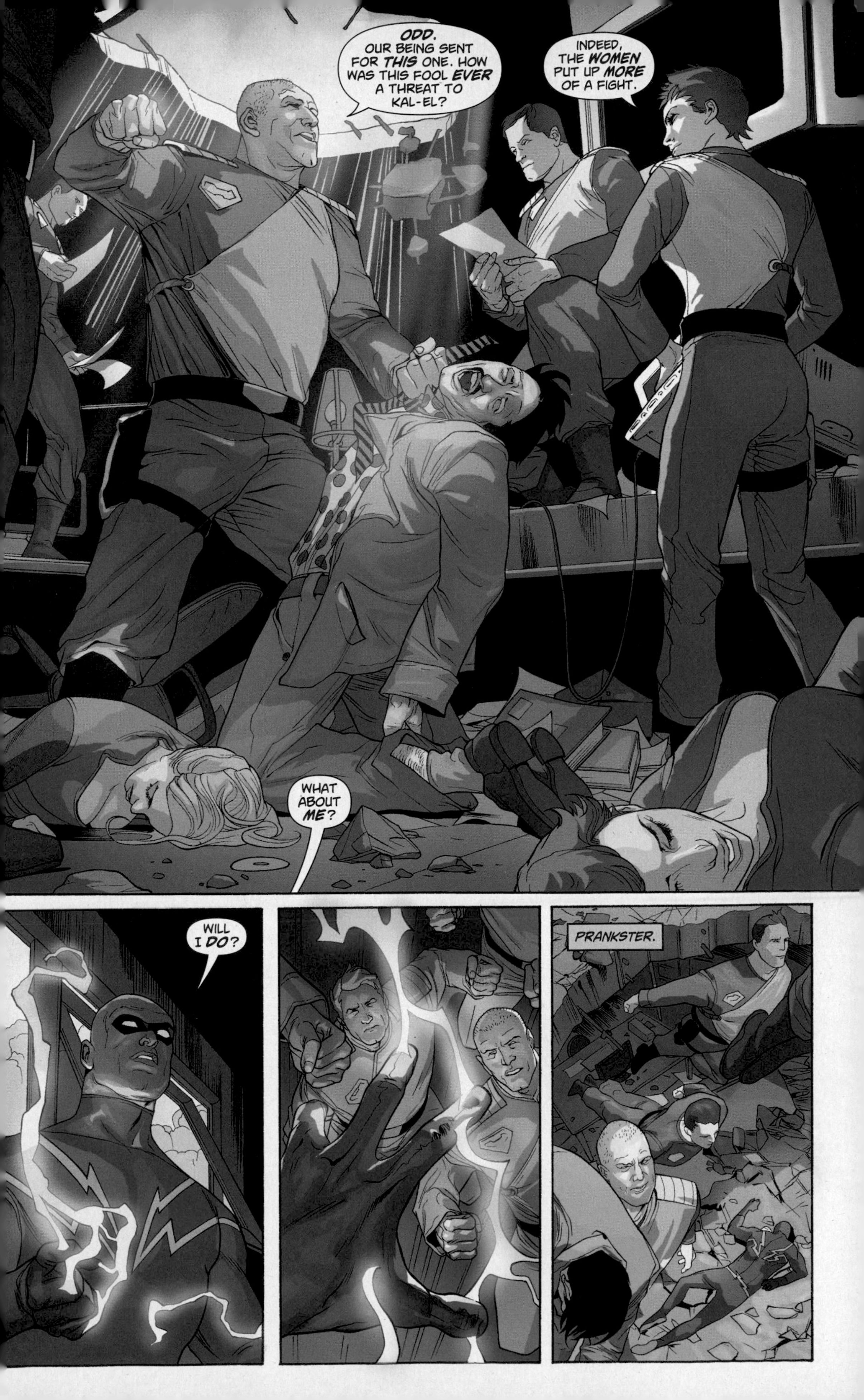
ODD. OUR BEING SENT FOR THIS ONE. HOW WAS THIS FOOL EVER A THREAT TO KAL-EL?
INDEED, THE WOMEN PUT UP MORE OF A FIGHT.
WHAT ABOUT ME?
WILL I DO?
PRANKSTER.

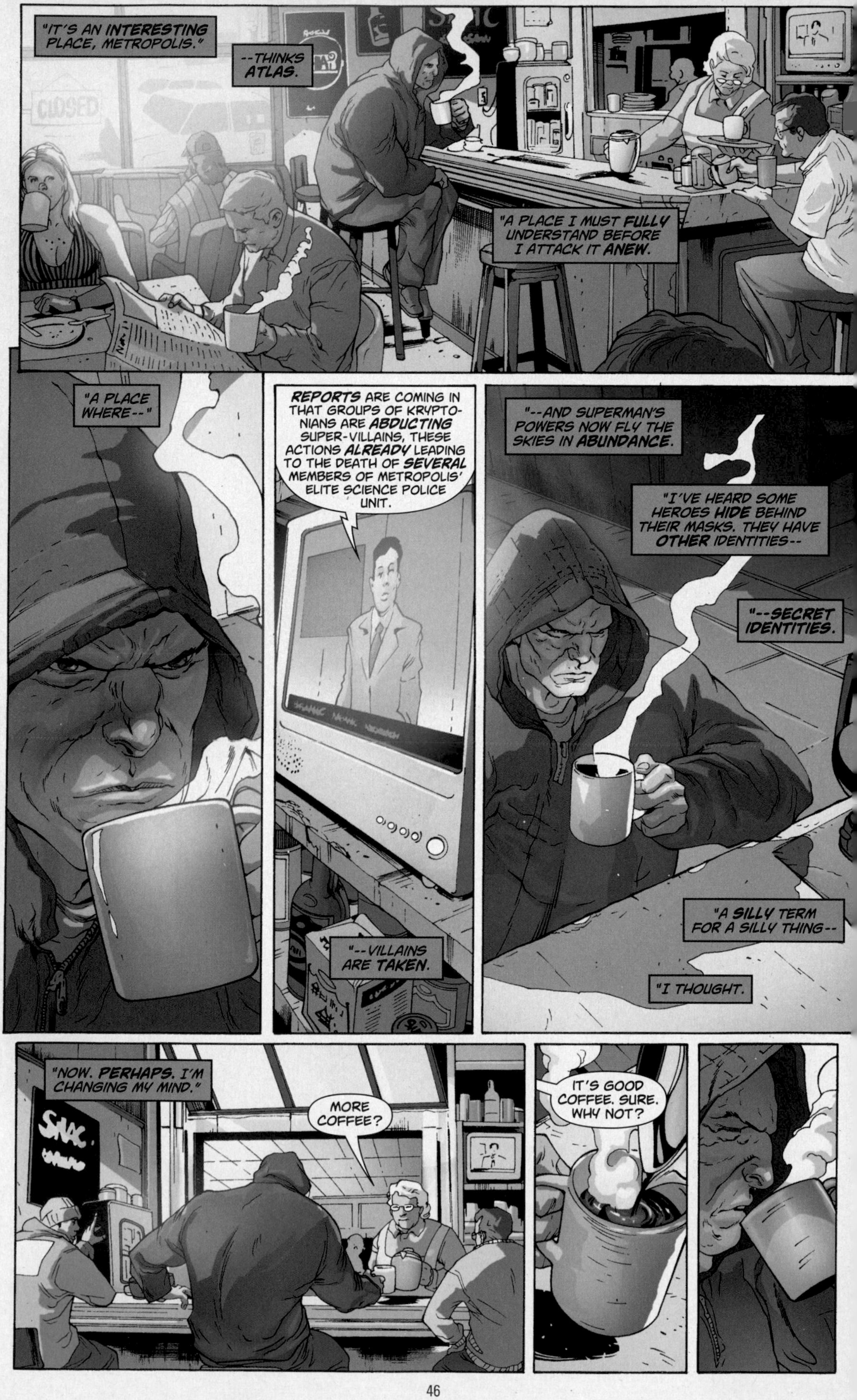
"IT'S AN INTERESTING PLACE, METROPOLIS."
--THINKS ATLAS.
CLOSED
"A PLACE I MUST FULLY UNDERSTAND BEFORE I ATTACK IT ANEW.
"A PLACE WHERE--"
REPORTS ARE COMING IN THAT GROUPS OF KRYPTONIANS ARE ABDUCTING SUPER-VILLAINS, THESE ACTIONS ALREADY LEADING TO THE DEATH OF SEVERAL MEMBERS OF METROPOLIS' ELITE SCIENCE POLICE UNIT.
"--VILLAINS ARE TAKEN.
"--AND SUPERMAN'S POWERS NOW FLY THE SKIES IN ABUNDANCE.
"I'VE HEARD SOME HEROES HIDE BEHIND THEIR MASKS. THEY HAVE OTHER IDENTITIES--
"--SECRET IDENTITIES.
"A SILLY TERM FOR A SILLY THING--
"I THOUGHT.
"NOW. PERHAPS. I'M CHANGING MY MIND."
MORE COFFEE?
IT'S GOOD COFFEE. SURE. WHY NOT?

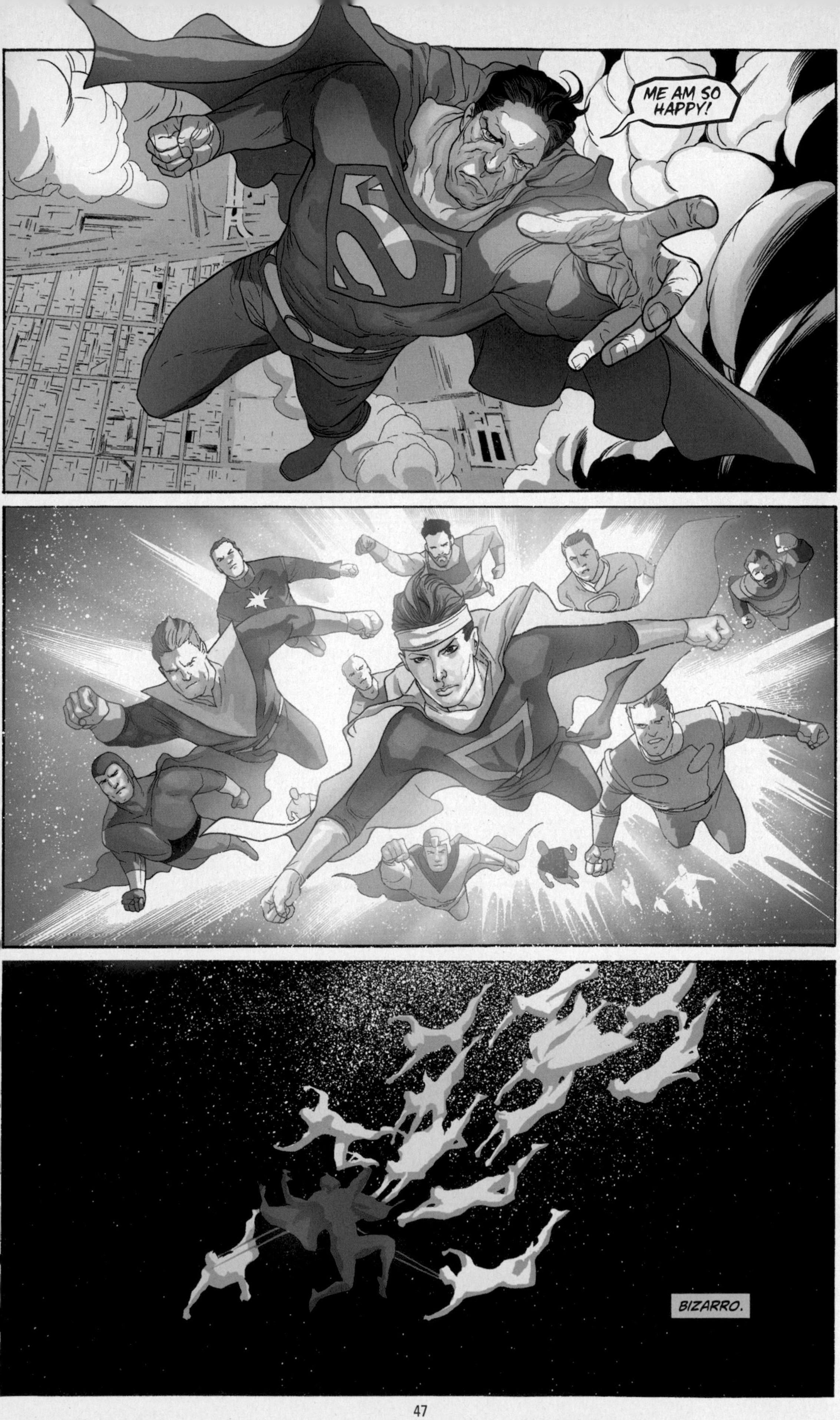
ME AM SO HAPPY!
BIZARRO.

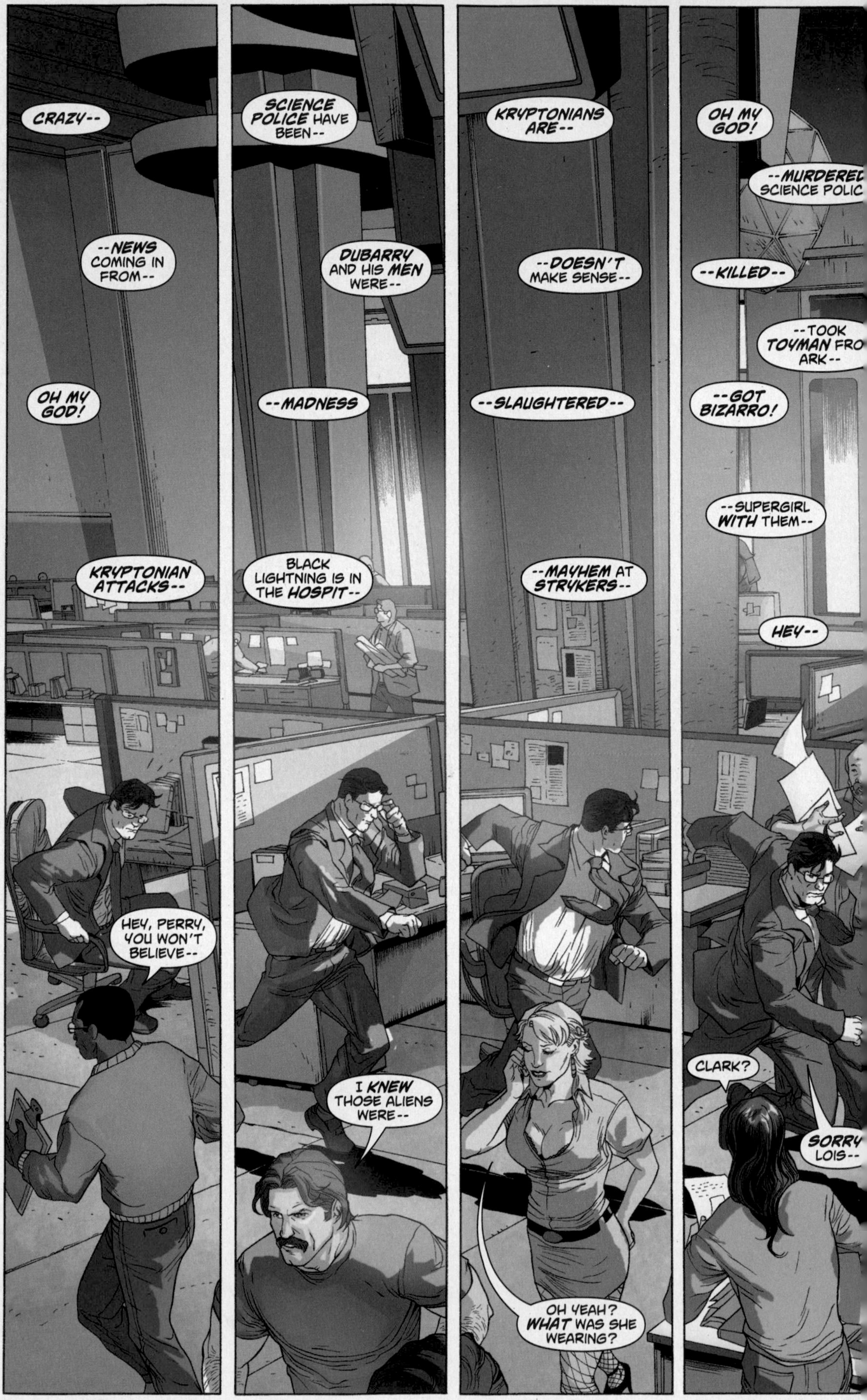
CRAZY--
--NEWS COMING IN FROM--
OH MY GOD!
KRYPTONIAN ATTACKS--
HEY, PERRY, YOU WON'T BELIEVE--
SCIENCE POLICE HAVE BEEN--
DUBARRY AND HIS MEN WERE--
--MADNESS
BLACK LIGHTNING IS IN THE HOSPIT--
I KNEW THOSE ALIENS WERE--
KRYPTONIANS ARE--
--DOESN'T MAKE SENSE--
--SLAUGHTERED--
--MAYHEM AT STRYKERS--
OH YEAH? WHAT WAS SHE WEARING?
OH MY GOD!
--MURDERED SCIENCE POLIC
--KILLED--
--TOOK TOYMAN FRO ARK--
--GOT BIZARRO!
--SUPERGIRL WITH THEM--
HEY--
CLARK?
SORRY LOIS--

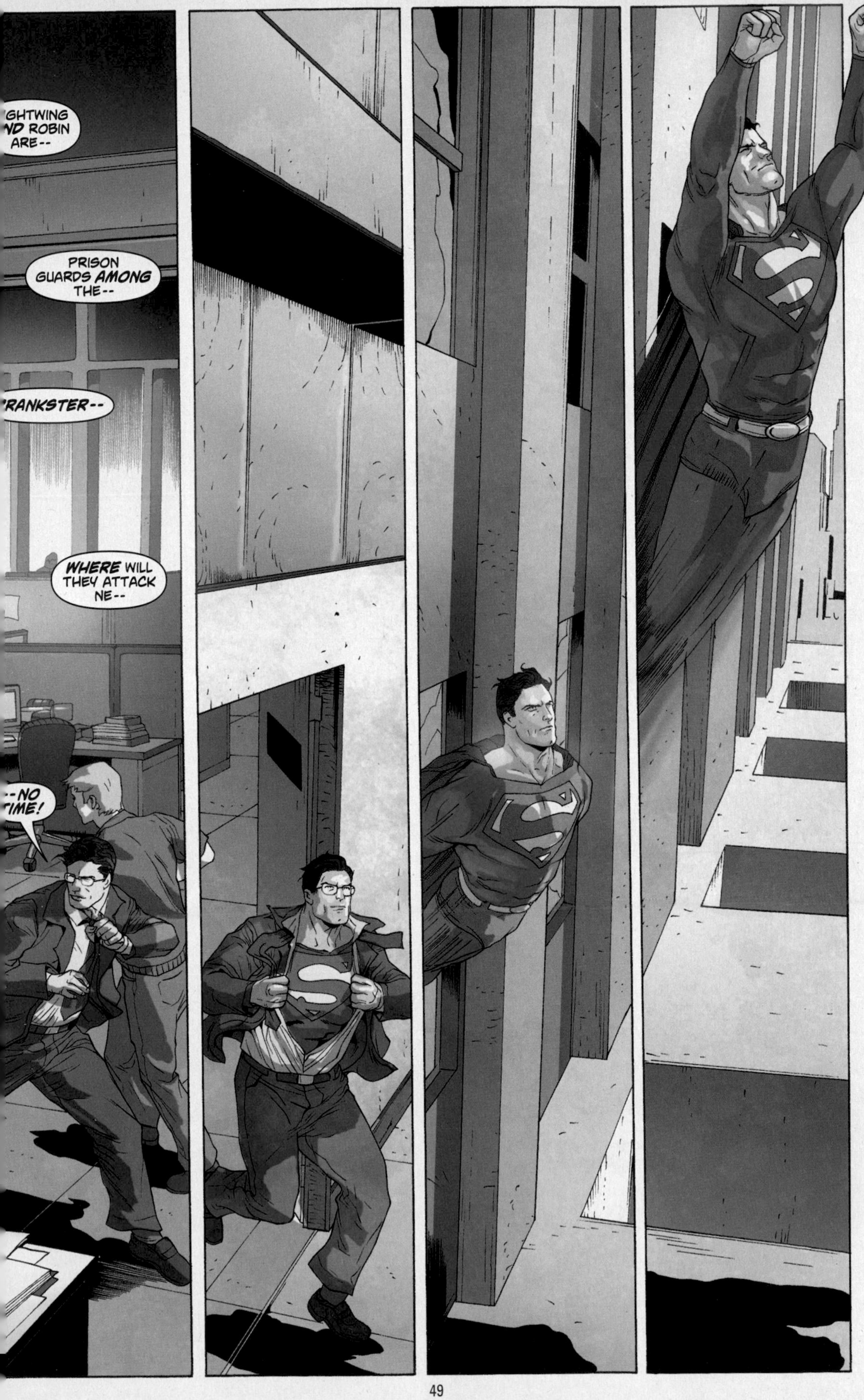
GHTWING ND ROBIN ARE--
PRISON GUARDS AMONG THE--
RANKSTER--
WHERE WILL THEY ATTACK NE--
--NO TIME!

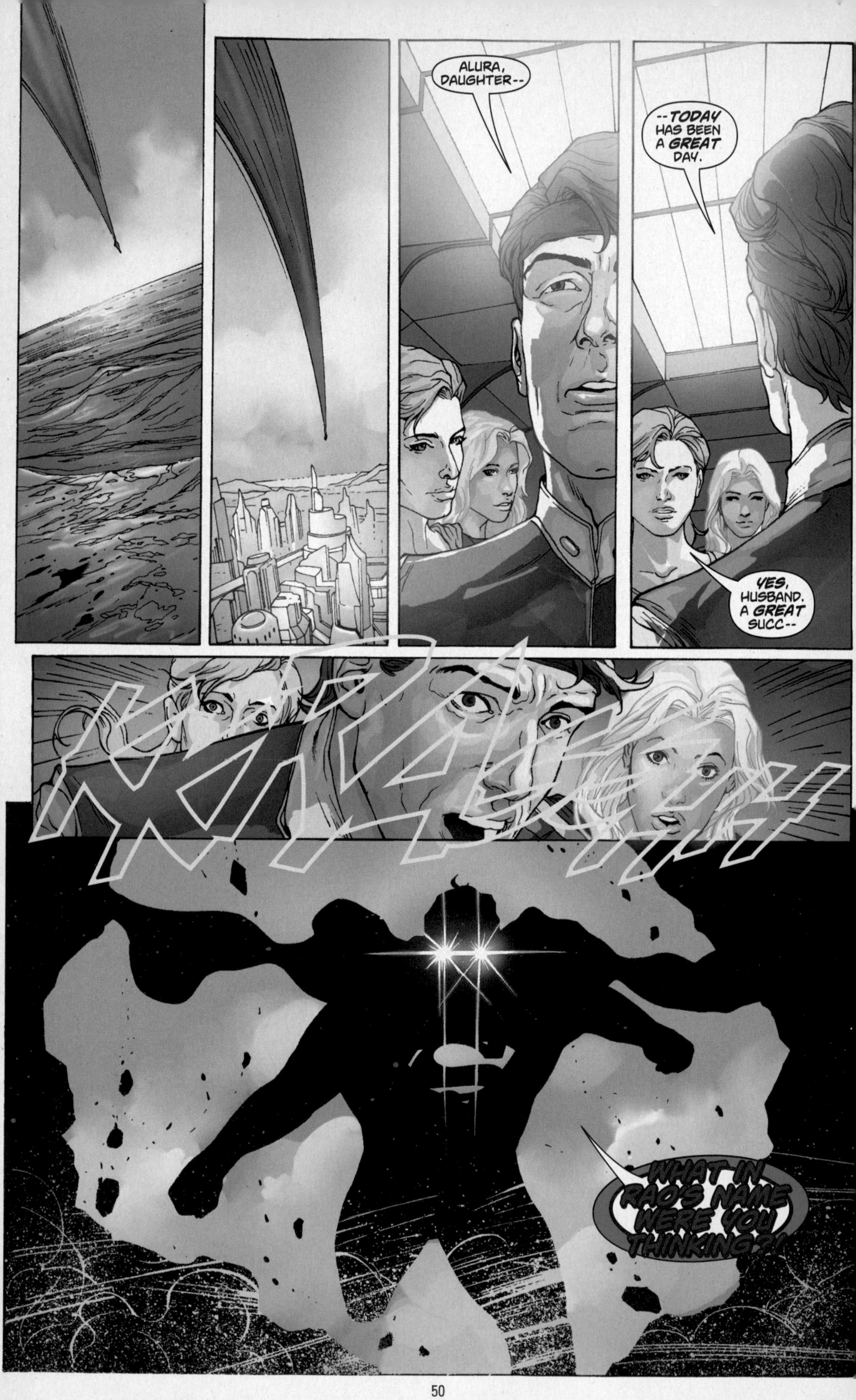
ALURA, DAUGHTER--
--TODAY HAS BEEN A GREAT DAY.
YES, HUSBAND. A GREAT SUCC--
WHAT IN RAO'S NAME WERE YOU THINKING?!

KAL, ARE YOU *INSANE?*

I MUST SAY, KAL, THIS IS A *SURPRISE.* WE WERE EXPECTING SOMETHING *MORE* IN THE WAY OF THANKS.

ME? AFTER *EVERYTHING* YOU'VE--

KAL, CALM DOWN, YOU *DON'T* UNDERSTAND.

YOU'RE *RIGHT,* KARA, I'M *BEWILDERED.*

AFTER OUR BRUSH WITH *DOOMSDAY,* WE WANTED TO KNOW WE WERE *SAFE* FROM *OTHERS* WHO MIGHT ATTACK US TO GET TO YOU. YOUR FOES ARE NO LONGER SOMETHING *YOU* HAVE TO DEAL WITH.

NO. NO! DO NOT TELL ME YOU'VE *MURDERED* THEM LIKE YOU DID THOSE POOR COPS.

COPS?

NO. *NO! FATHER,* THIS IS *TERRIBLE.* I NEVER WANTED--

NEITHER DID I.

ALURA? YOU SPEAK AS IF YOU *ALREADY*--

KNEW? I *DID.* I LEARNED OF EVENTS UPON *RETURNING* HERE.

AND YOU CHOSE TO *KEEP* THIS FROM ME?

I DIDN'T SEE IT AS IMPORTANT ENOUGH TO BOTHER YOU WITH.

POLICEMEN. GOOD MEN OF MY CITY, *KILLED* BY SOME OF YOU IN THE COURSE OF THIS *INSANITY.*

OH, *KAL.* NO.

THEY *FOUGHT BACK.* THESE "COPS". THAT WAS *THEIR* MISTAKE.

MOTHER!

ALURA-- THE WAY YOU ACT IS *ALARMING.* I DON'T UNDER- STAND--

THEN *DON'T* TRY, KAL. THERE'S AN EARTH TERM I'VE *LEARNED* OF LATE--*COLLATERAL DAMAGE.* THESE POLICEMEN WERE *UNLUCKY.*

HAVEN'T YOU LISTENED TO *ANYTHING* I'VE TOLD YOU? THERE ARE *LAWS* ON EARTH--INTERNATIONAL LAWS. YOU *CAN'T* JUST DO AS YOU PLEASE.

I'LL NEED THE NAMES OF THOSE INVOLVED IN THE KILLINGS. THEY'LL HAVE TO *ANSWER* FOR THIS.

DO YOU *HONESTLY* THINK WE'LL HAND OVER OUR PEOPLE?

MOTHER, KAL'S *RIGHT*-- YOU'VE GOT TO LISTEN.

NO, KARA, YOU'VE GOT TO *HOLD YOUR TONGUE.*

AND *AS FOR* THE VILLAINS, KAL, *DON'T WORRY.* THEY'RE ALIVE--

"--AND SOMEWHERE VERY *SAFE.*"

THE PHANTOM ZONE.

AND *MON-EL,* THE ONE GOOD MAN WHO ABIDES THERE.

WHAT IN *SARD'S NAME* IS GOING ON?

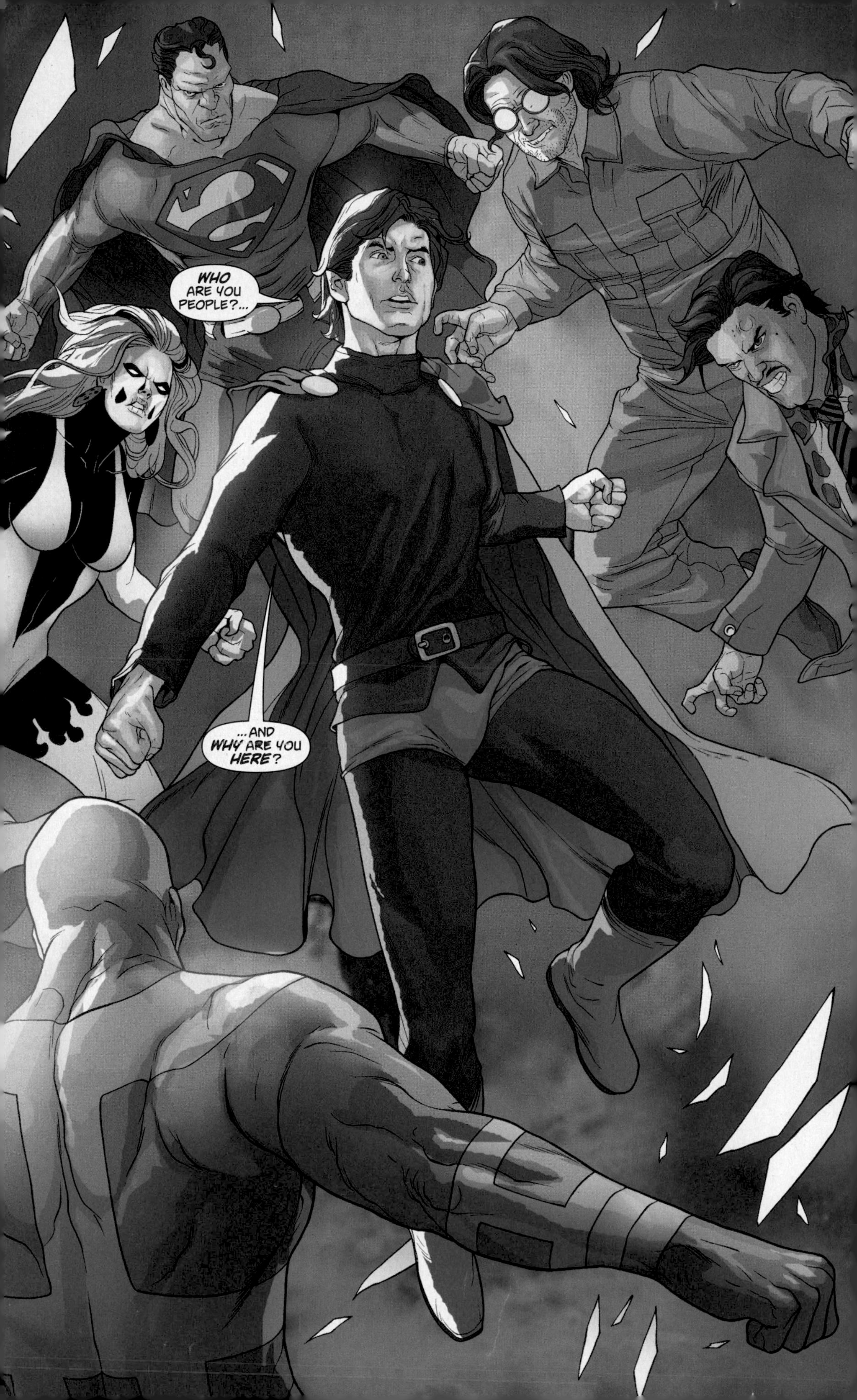
WHO ARE YOU PEOPLE?...
...AND WHY ARE YOU HERE?

<BRAINIAC LIVES> ACTION COMICS 872 COVER ART BY **GARY FRANK** WITH **BRAD ANDERSON**

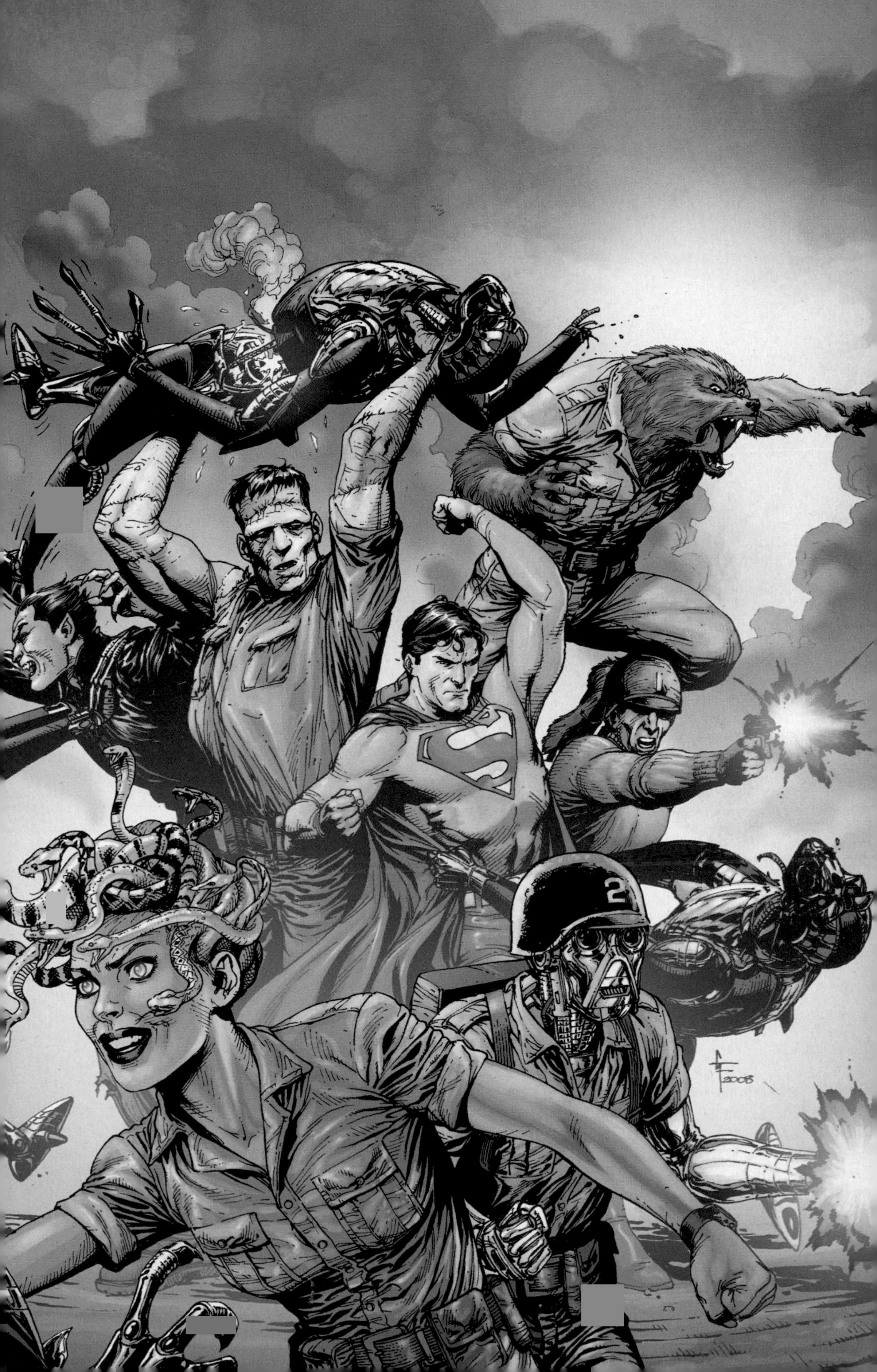

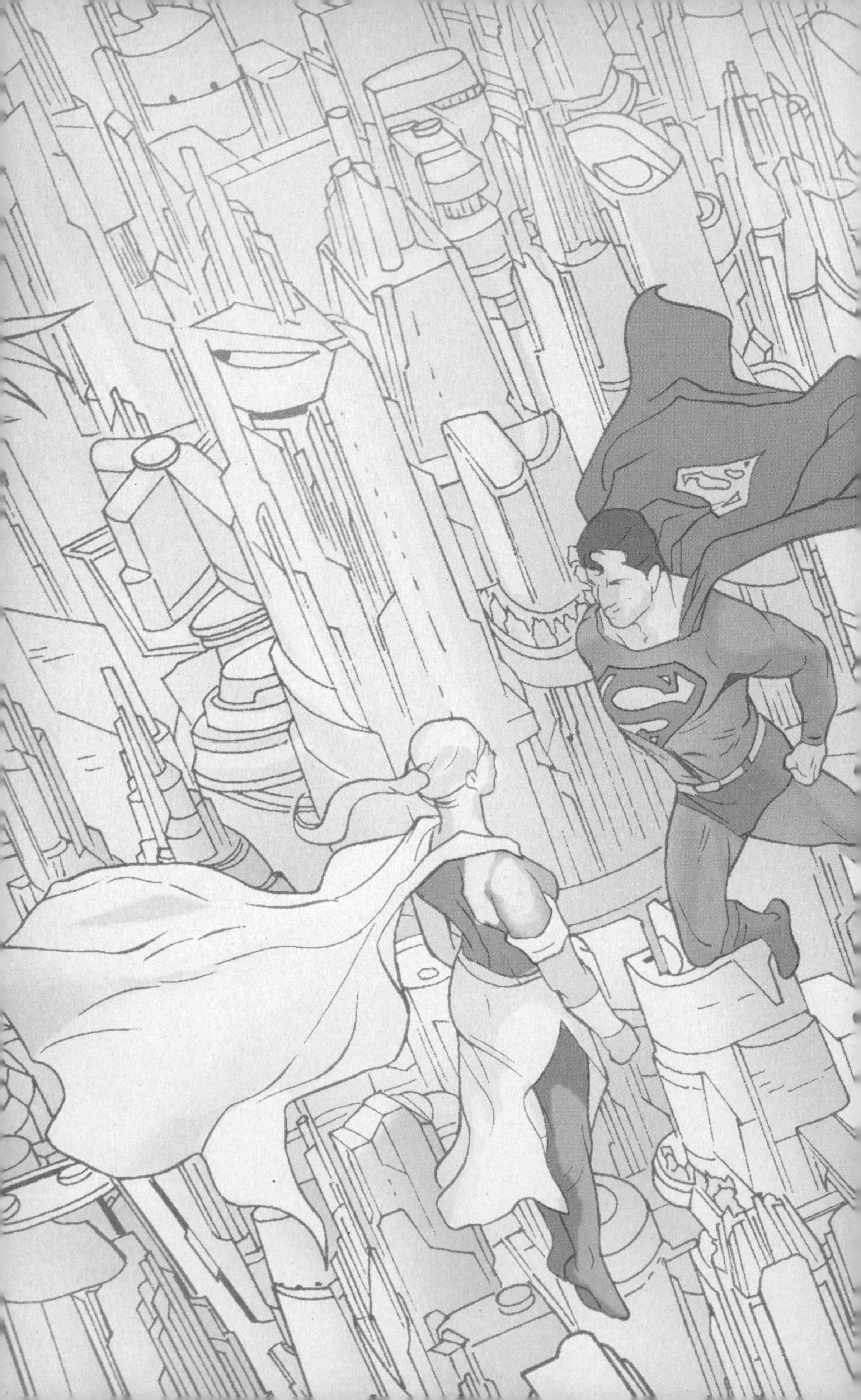

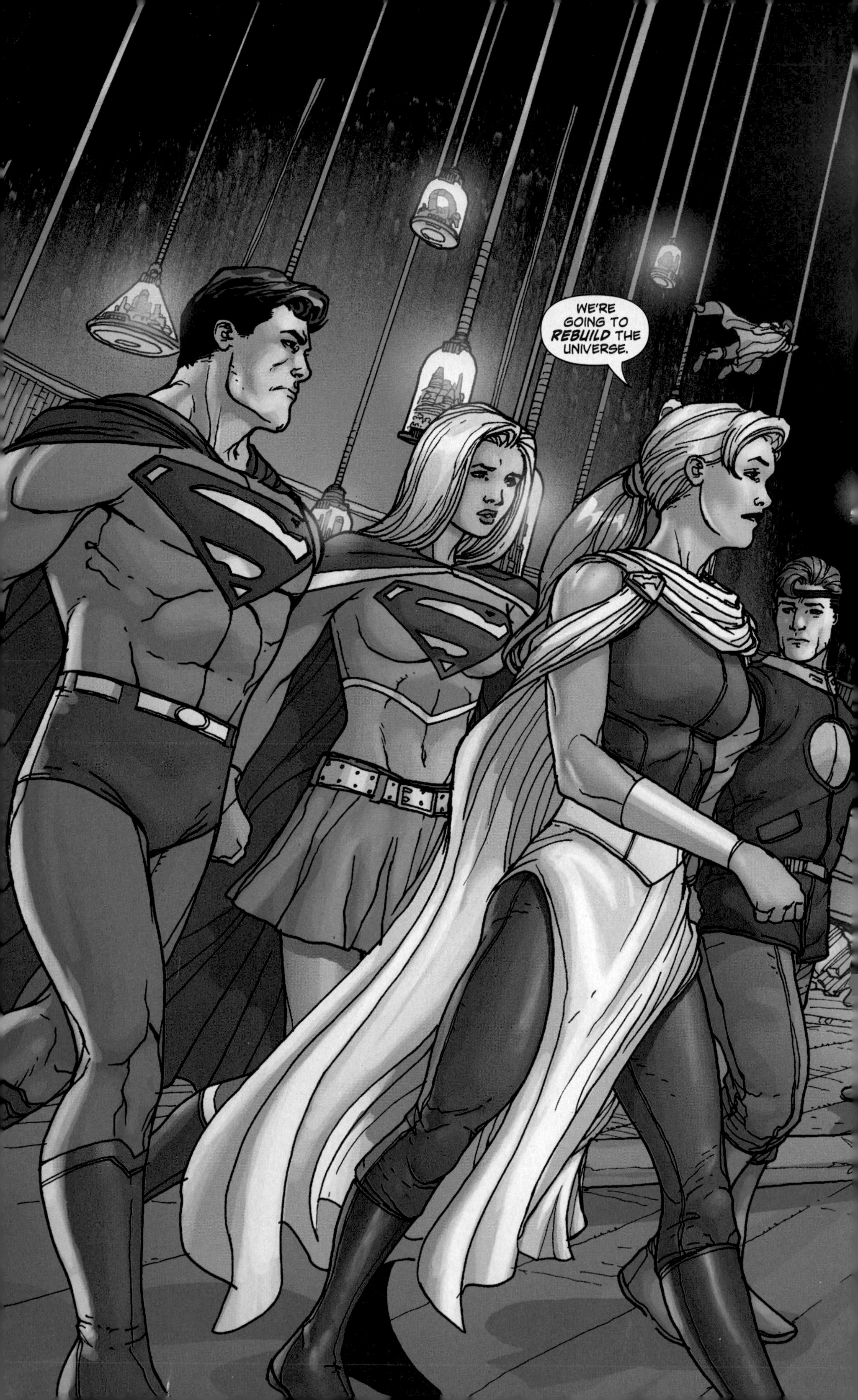
WE'RE GOING TO **REBUILD** THE UNIVERSE.

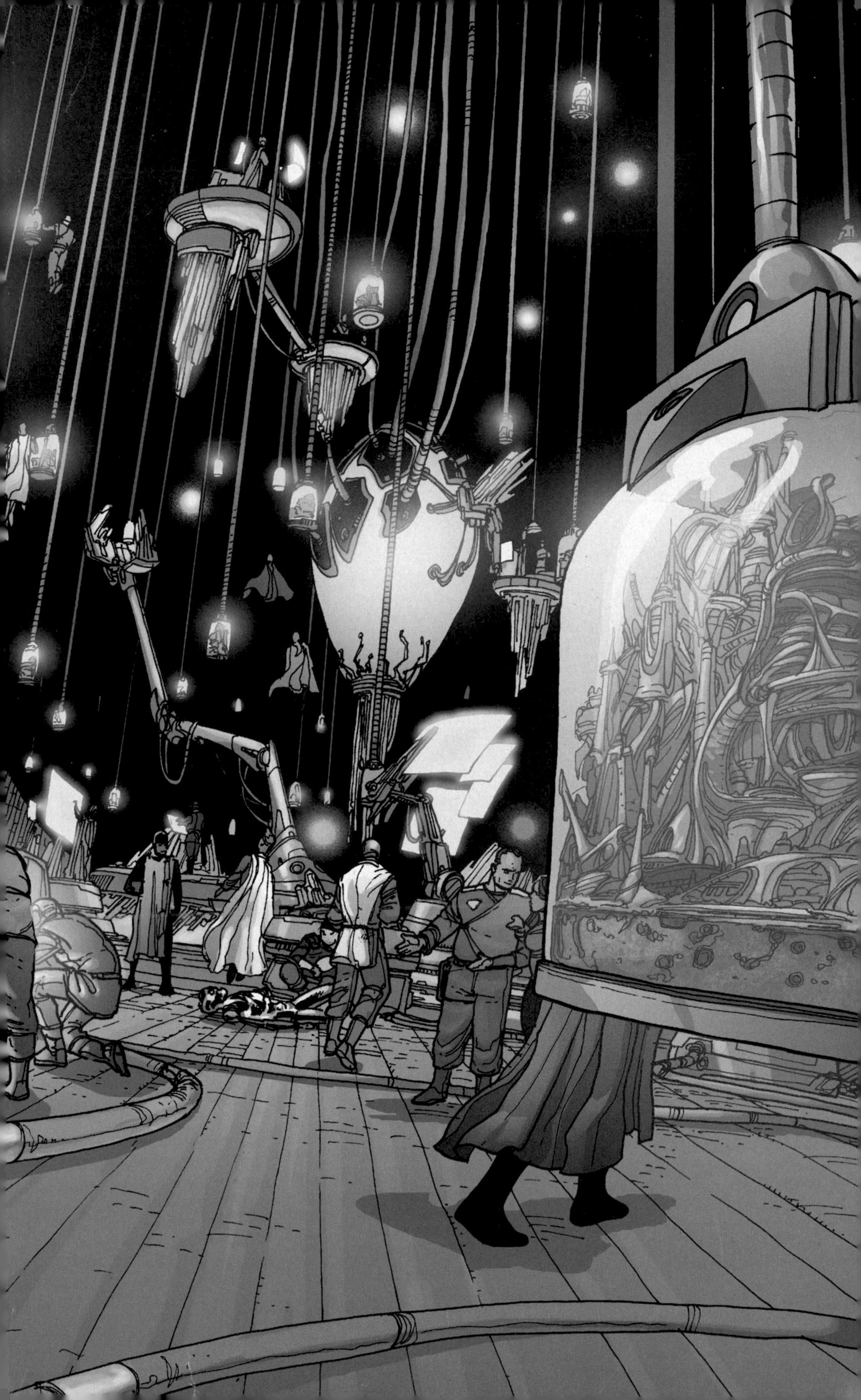

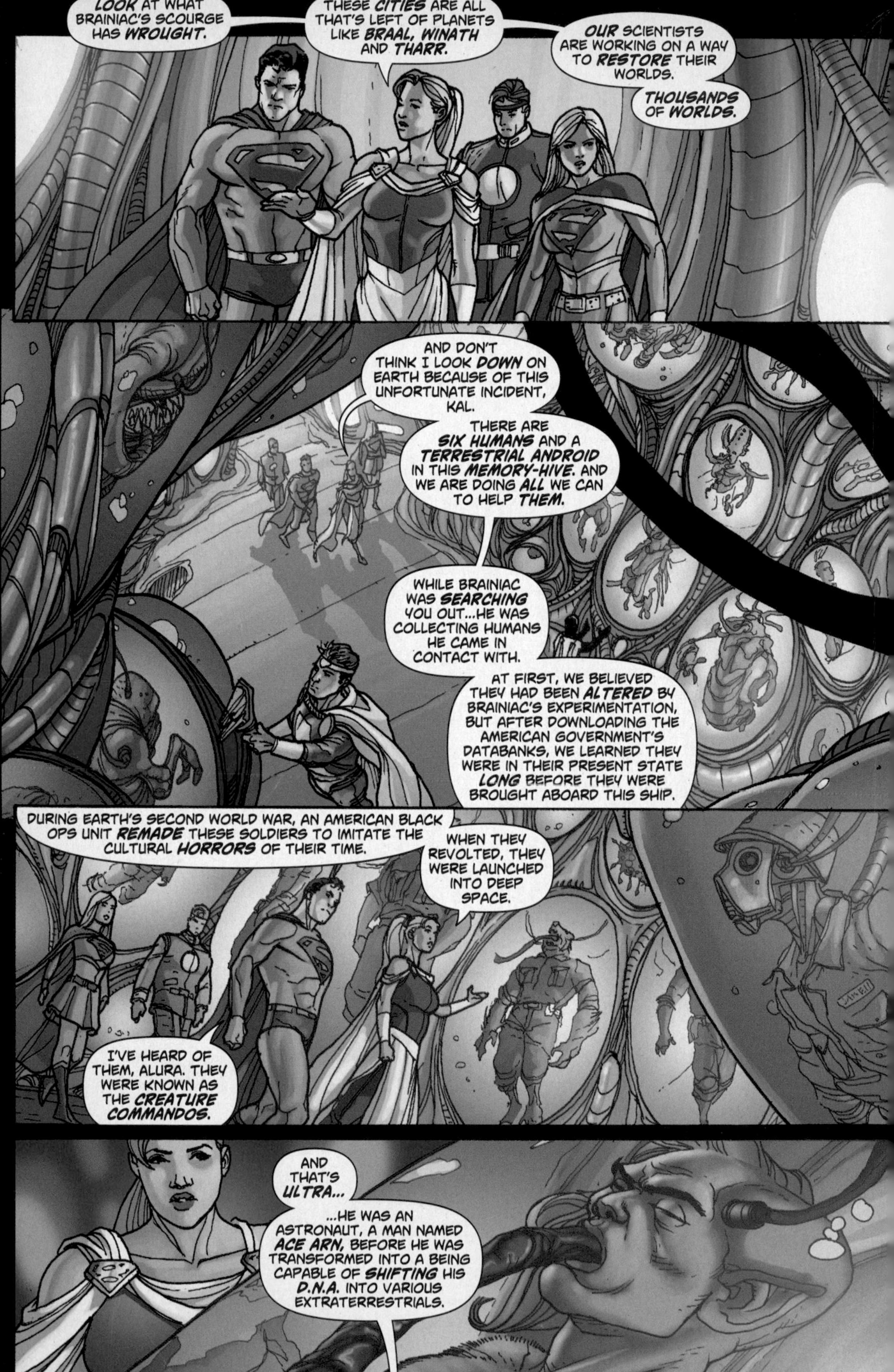
LOOK AT WHAT BRAINIAC'S SCOURGE HAS WROUGHT.
THESE CITIES ARE ALL THAT'S LEFT OF PLANETS LIKE BRAAL, WINATH AND THARR.
OUR SCIENTISTS ARE WORKING ON A WAY TO RESTORE THEIR WORLDS.
THOUSANDS OF WORLDS.
AND DON'T THINK I LOOK DOWN ON EARTH BECAUSE OF THIS UNFORTUNATE INCIDENT, KAL.
THERE ARE SIX HUMANS AND A TERRESTRIAL ANDROID IN THIS MEMORY-HIVE. AND WE ARE DOING ALL WE CAN TO HELP THEM.
WHILE BRAINIAC WAS SEARCHING YOU OUT...HE WAS COLLECTING HUMANS HE CAME IN CONTACT WITH.
AT FIRST, WE BELIEVED THEY HAD BEEN ALTERED BY BRAINIAC'S EXPERIMENTATION, BUT AFTER DOWNLOADING THE AMERICAN GOVERNMENT'S DATABANKS, WE LEARNED THEY WERE IN THEIR PRESENT STATE LONG BEFORE THEY WERE BROUGHT ABOARD THIS SHIP.
DURING EARTH'S SECOND WORLD WAR, AN AMERICAN BLACK OPS UNIT REMADE THESE SOLDIERS TO IMITATE THE CULTURAL HORRORS OF THEIR TIME.
WHEN THEY REVOLTED, THEY WERE LAUNCHED INTO DEEP SPACE.
I'VE HEARD OF THEM, ALURA. THEY WERE KNOWN AS THE CREATURE COMMANDOS.
AND THAT'S ULTRA...
...HE WAS AN ASTRONAUT, A MAN NAMED ACE ARN, BEFORE HE WAS TRANSFORMED INTO A BEING CAPABLE OF SHIFTING HIS D.N.A. INTO VARIOUS EXTRATERRESTRIALS.

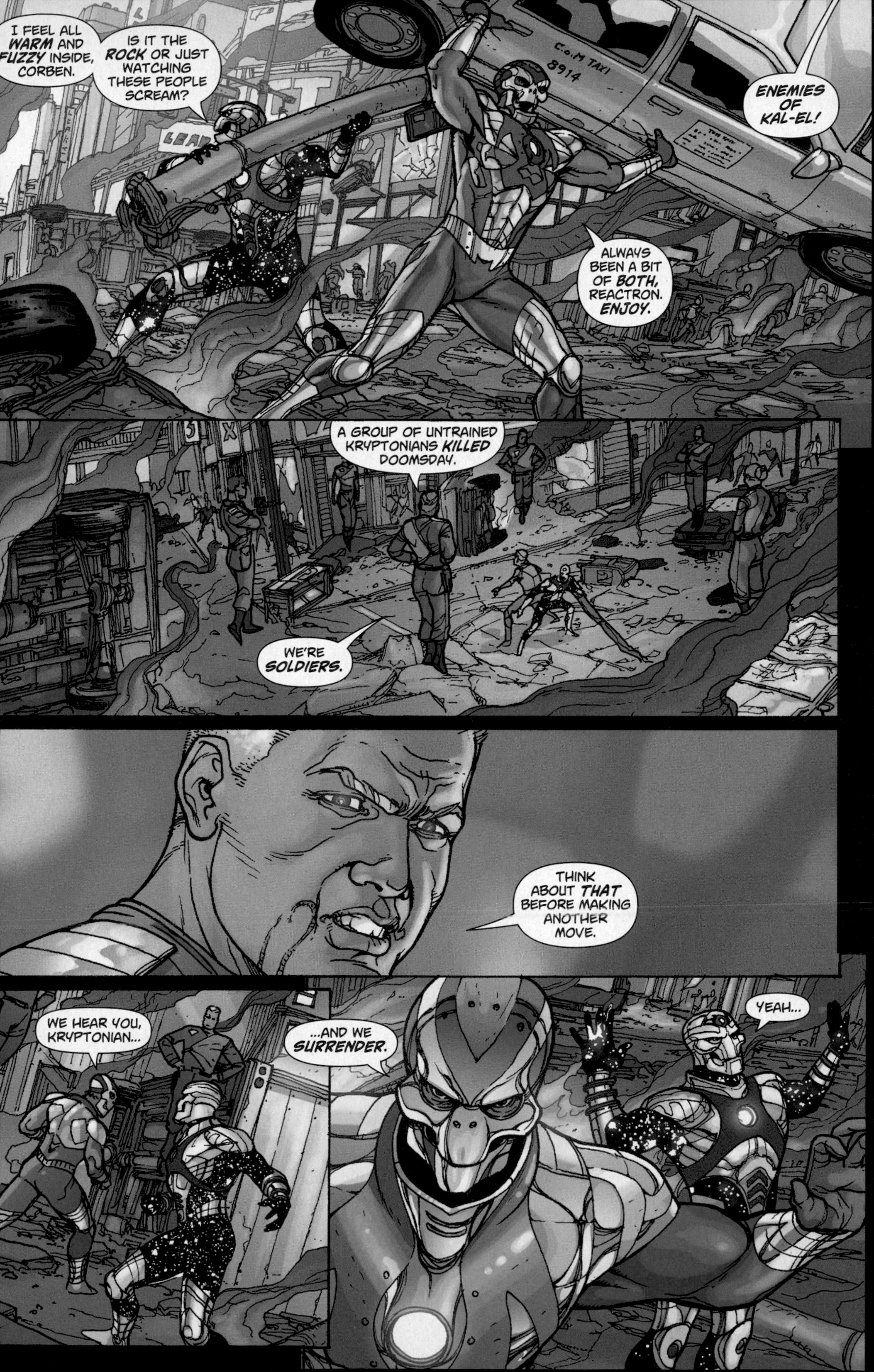
I FEEL ALL WARM AND FUZZY INSIDE, CORBEN.
IS IT THE ROCK OR JUST WATCHING THESE PEOPLE SCREAM?
ENEMIES OF KAL-EL!
ALWAYS BEEN A BIT OF BOTH, REACTRON. ENJOY.
A GROUP OF UNTRAINED KRYPTONIANS KILLED DOOMSDAY.
WE'RE SOLDIERS.
THINK ABOUT THAT BEFORE MAKING ANOTHER MOVE.
WE HEAR YOU, KRYPTONIAN...
...AND WE SURRENDER.
YEAH...

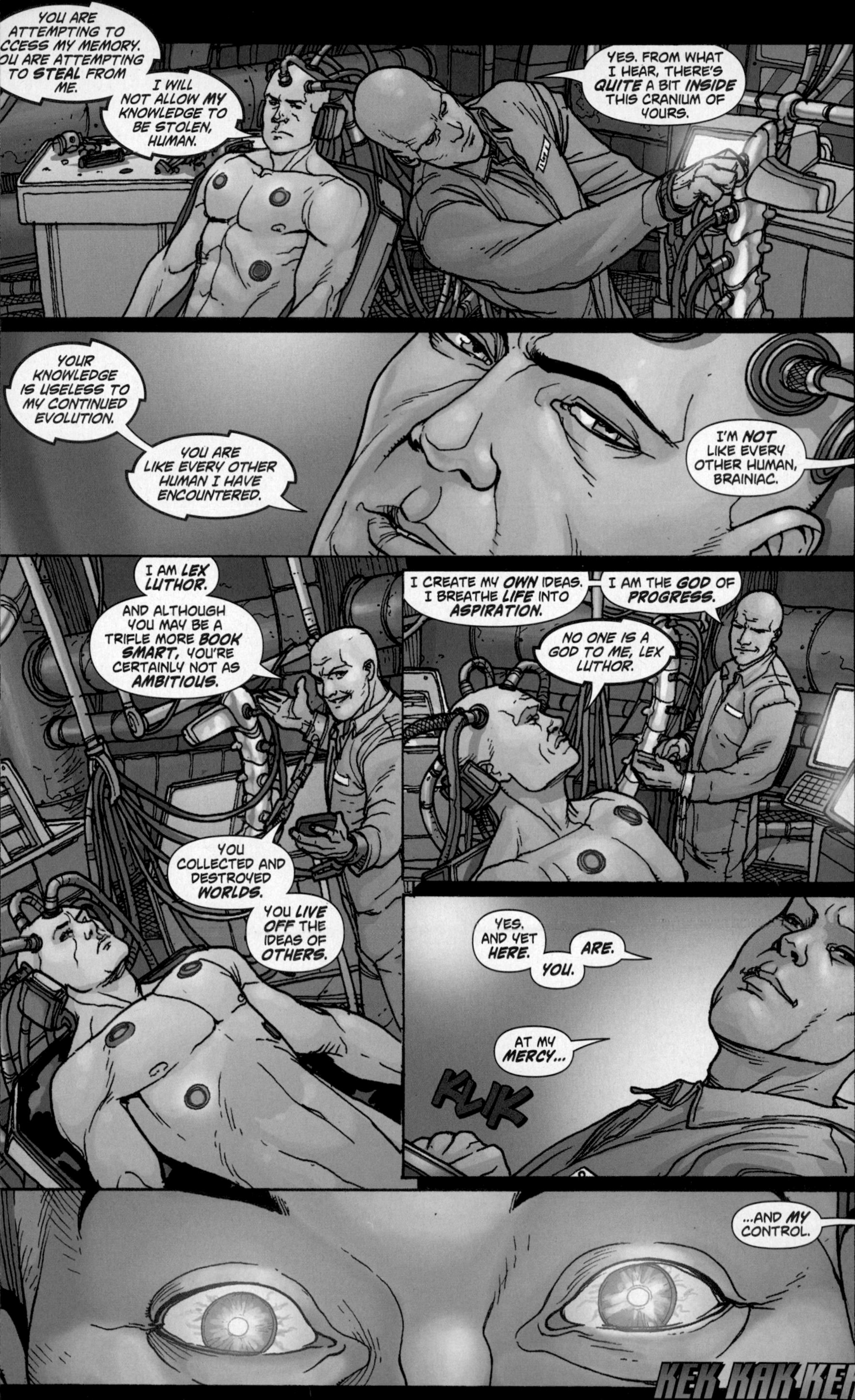

YOU ARE ATTEMPTING TO CCESS MY MEMORY. OU ARE ATTEMPTING TO STEAL FROM ME.
I WILL NOT ALLOW MY KNOWLEDGE TO BE STOLEN, HUMAN.
YES. FROM WHAT I HEAR, THERE'S QUITE A BIT INSIDE THIS CRANIUM OF YOURS.
YOUR KNOWLEDGE IS USELESS TO MY CONTINUED EVOLUTION.
YOU ARE LIKE EVERY OTHER HUMAN I HAVE ENCOUNTERED.
I'M NOT LIKE EVERY OTHER HUMAN, BRAINIAC.
I AM LEX LUTHOR.
AND ALTHOUGH YOU MAY BE A TRIFLE MORE BOOK SMART, YOU'RE CERTAINLY NOT AS AMBITIOUS.
YOU COLLECTED AND DESTROYED WORLDS.
YOU LIVE OFF THE IDEAS OF OTHERS.
I CREATE MY OWN IDEAS. I BREATHE LIFE INTO ASPIRATION.
I AM THE GOD OF PROGRESS.
NO ONE IS A GOD TO ME, LEX LUTHOR.
YES, AND YET HERE.
YOU.
ARE.
AT MY MERCY...
KLIK
...AND MY CONTROL.
KEK KAK KE

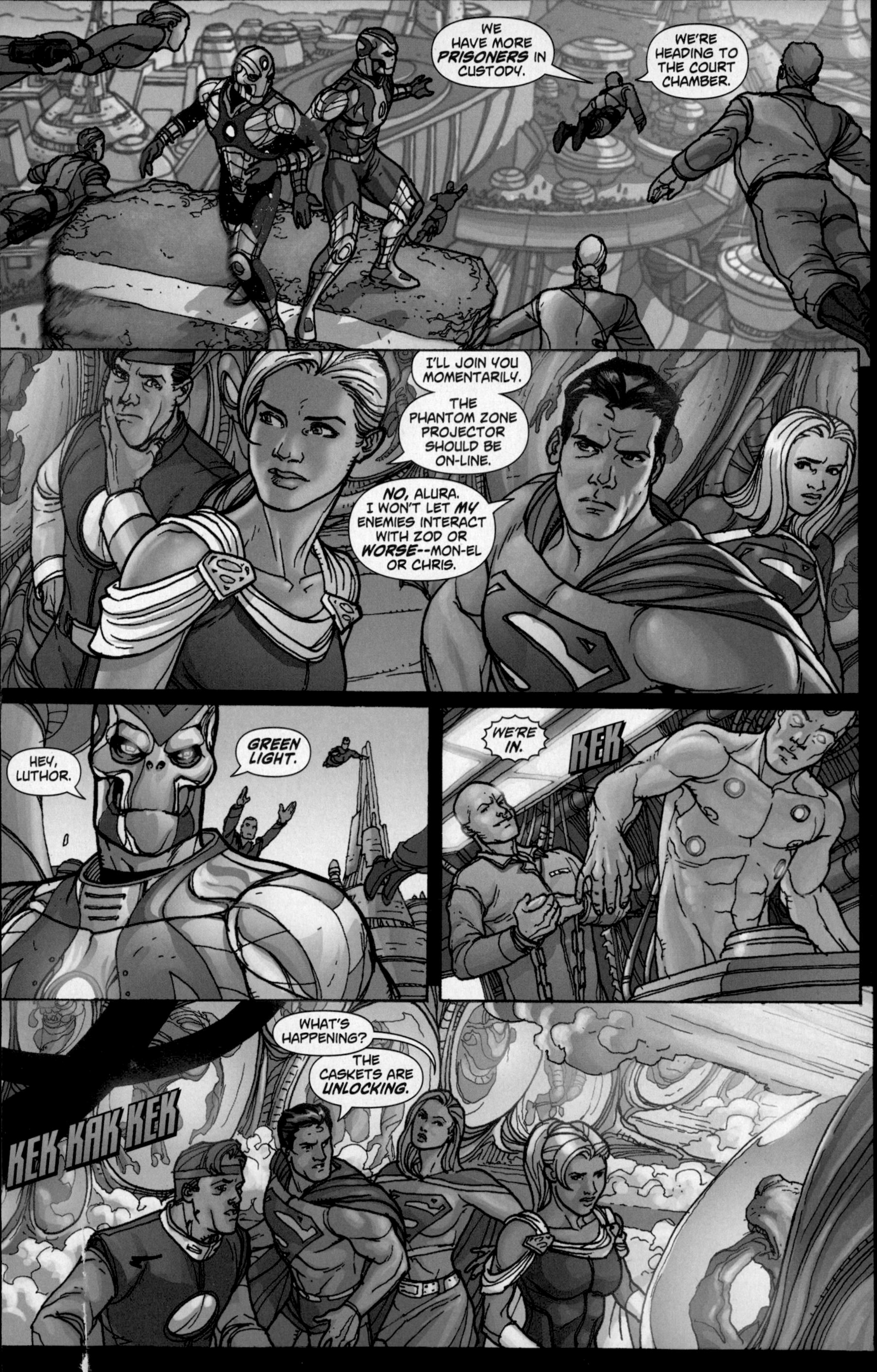
WE HAVE MORE PRISONERS IN CUSTODY.
WE'RE HEADING TO THE COURT CHAMBER.
I'LL JOIN YOU MOMENTARILY.
THE PHANTOM ZONE PROJECTOR SHOULD BE ON-LINE.
NO, ALURA. I WON'T LET MY ENEMIES INTERACT WITH ZOD OR WORSE--MON-EL OR CHRIS.
HEY, LUTHOR.
GREEN LIGHT.
WE'RE IN.
KEK
KEK KAK KEK
WHAT'S HAPPENING?
THE CASKETS ARE UNLOCKING.

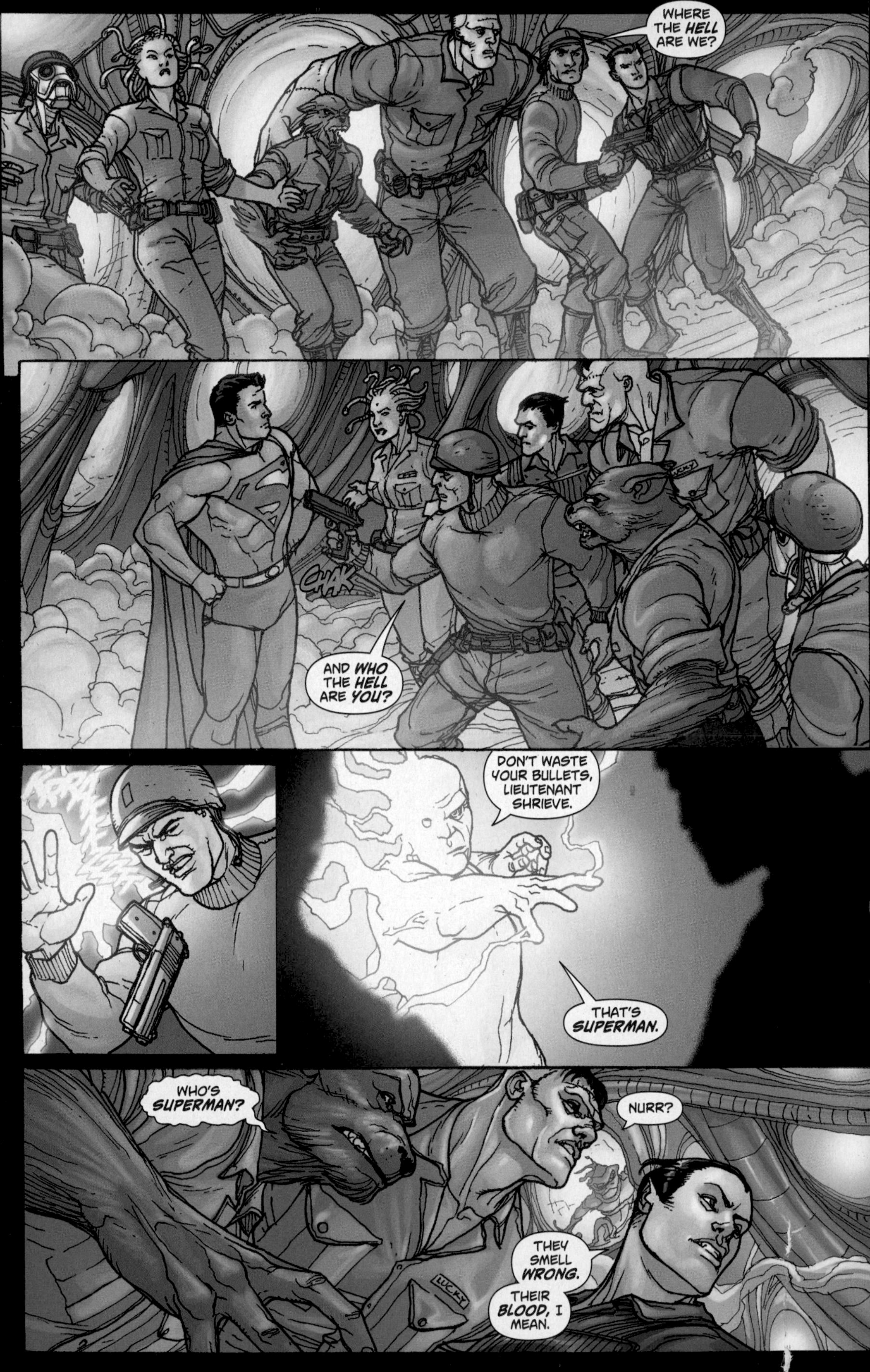
WHERE THE HELL ARE WE?
CHAK
AND WHO THE HELL ARE YOU?
DON'T WASTE YOUR BULLETS, LIEUTENANT SHRIEVE.
THAT'S SUPERMAN.
WHO'S SUPERMAN?
NURR?
THEY SMELL WRONG.
THEIR BLOOD, I MEAN.

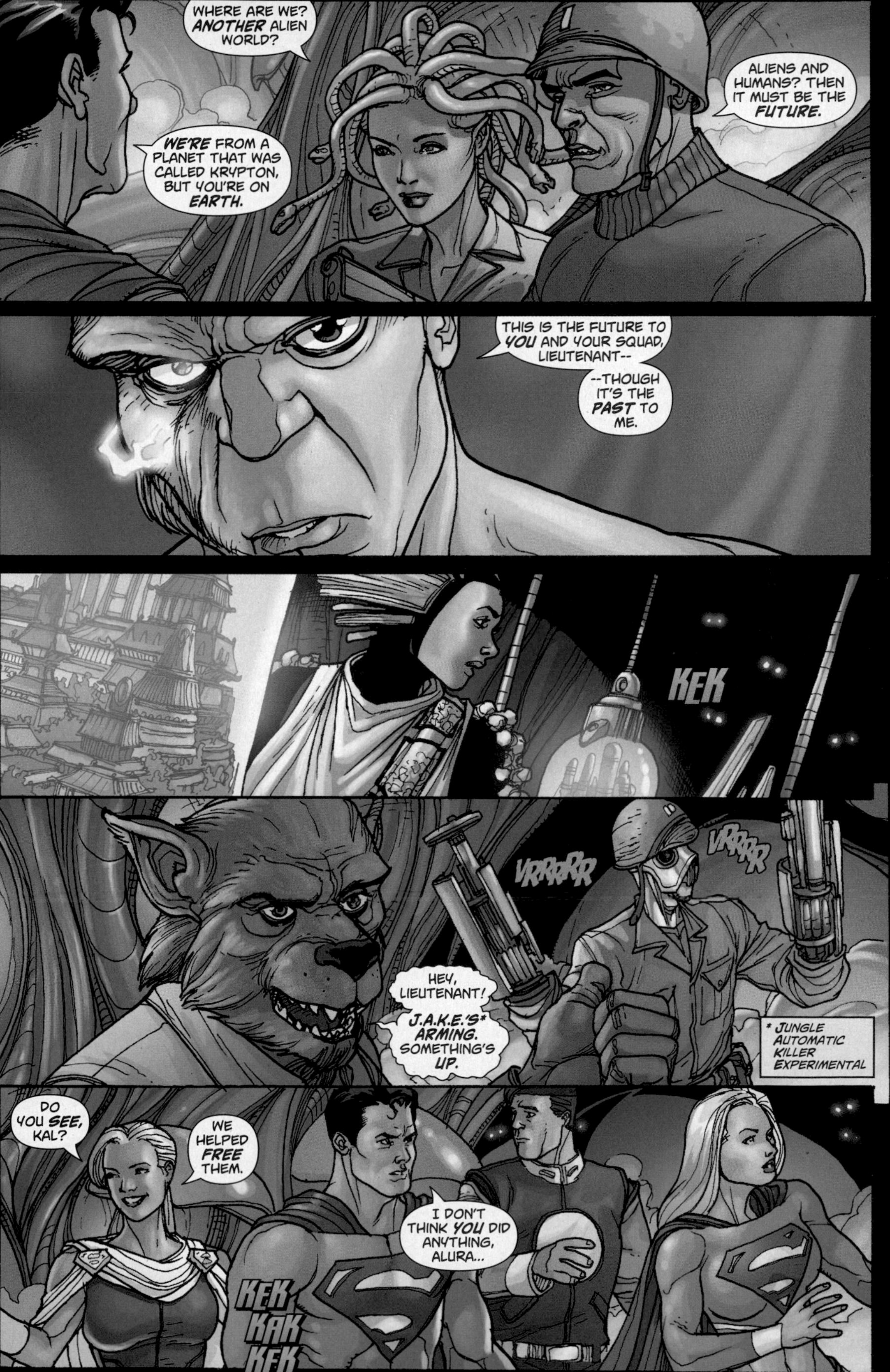
WHERE ARE WE? ANOTHER ALIEN WORLD?
ALIENS AND HUMANS? THEN IT MUST BE THE FUTURE.
WE'RE FROM A PLANET THAT WAS CALLED KRYPTON, BUT YOU'RE ON EARTH.
THIS IS THE FUTURE TO YOU AND YOUR SQUAD, LIEUTENANT--
--THOUGH IT'S THE PAST TO ME.
KEK
VRRRRR
VRRRR
HEY, LIEUTENANT!
J.A.K.E.'S* ARMING. SOMETHING'S UP.
* JUNGLE AUTOMATIC KILLER EXPERIMENTAL
DO YOU SEE, KAL?
WE HELPED FREE THEM.
I DON'T THINK YOU DID ANYTHING, ALURA...
KEK KAK KEK

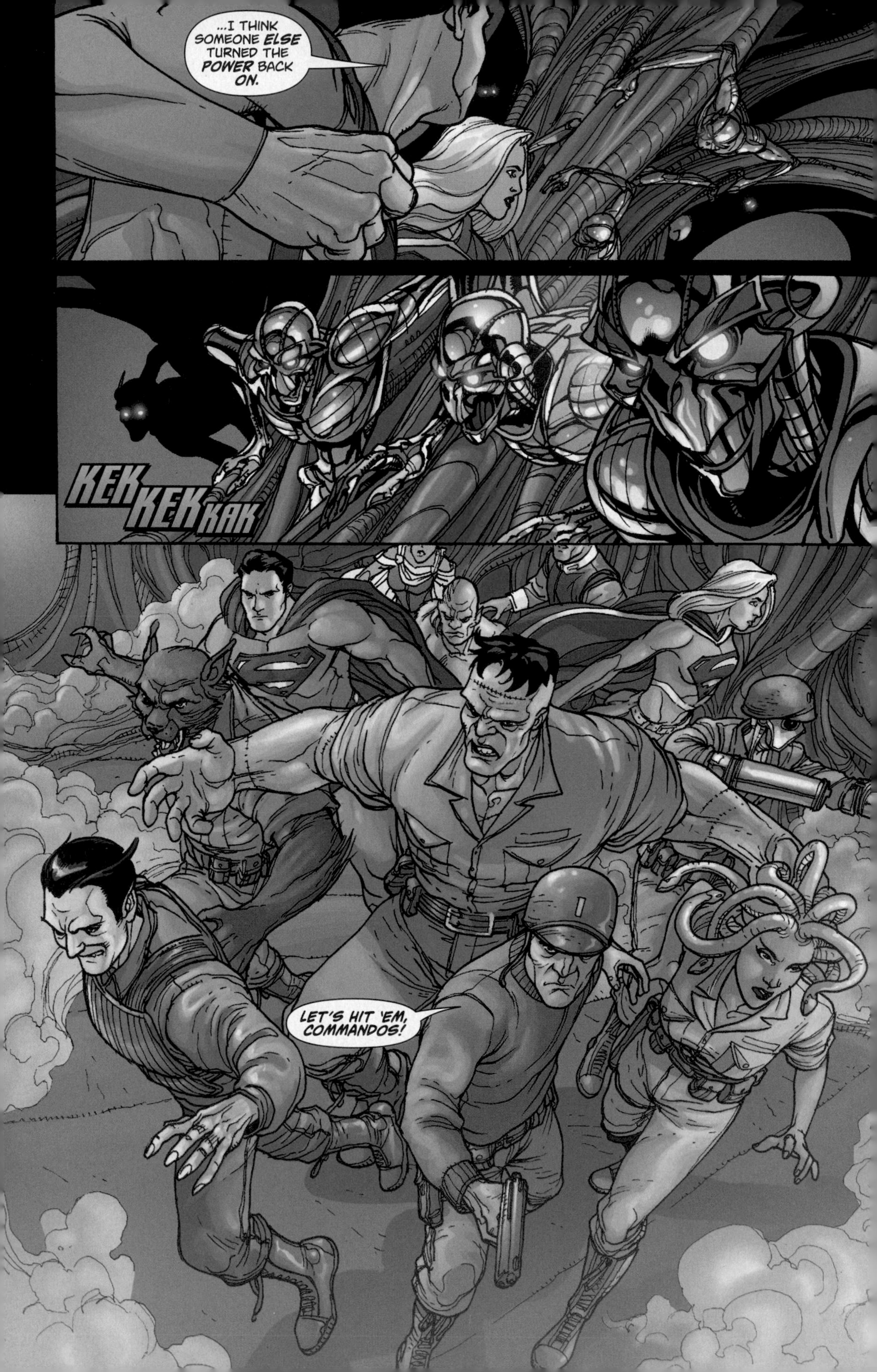
...I THINK SOMEONE ELSE TURNED THE POWER BACK ON.
KEK KEK KAK
LET'S HIT 'EM, COMMANDOS!

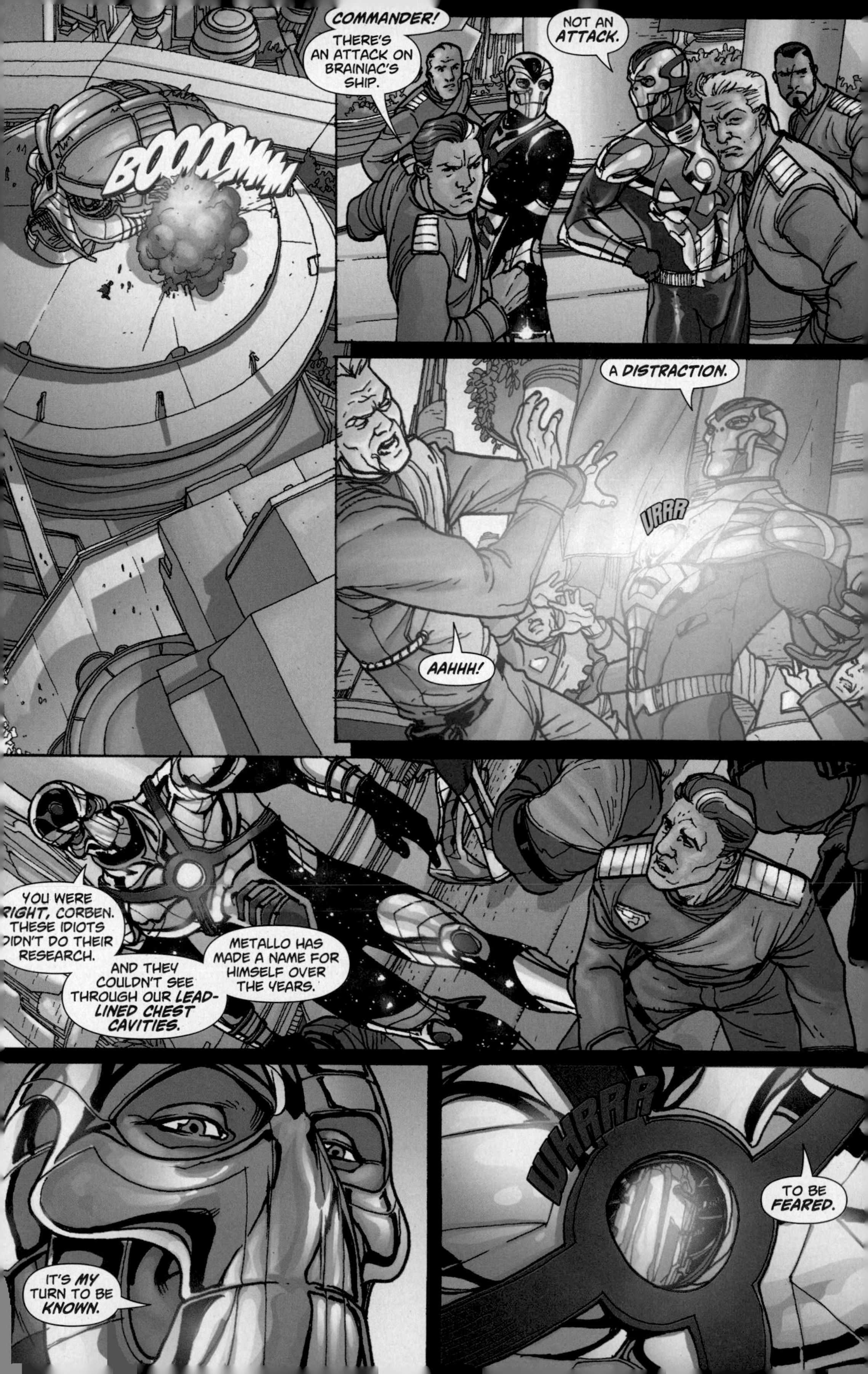
BOOOOMM
COMMANDER!
THERE'S AN ATTACK ON BRAINIAC'S SHIP.
NOT AN ATTACK.
A DISTRACTION.
URRR
AAHHH!
YOU WERE RIGHT, CORBEN. THESE IDIOTS DIDN'T DO THEIR RESEARCH.
AND THEY COULDN'T SEE THROUGH OUR LEAD-LINED CHEST CAVITIES.
METALLO HAS MADE A NAME FOR HIMSELF OVER THE YEARS.
IT'S MY TURN TO BE KNOWN.
UHRRR
TO BE FEARED.

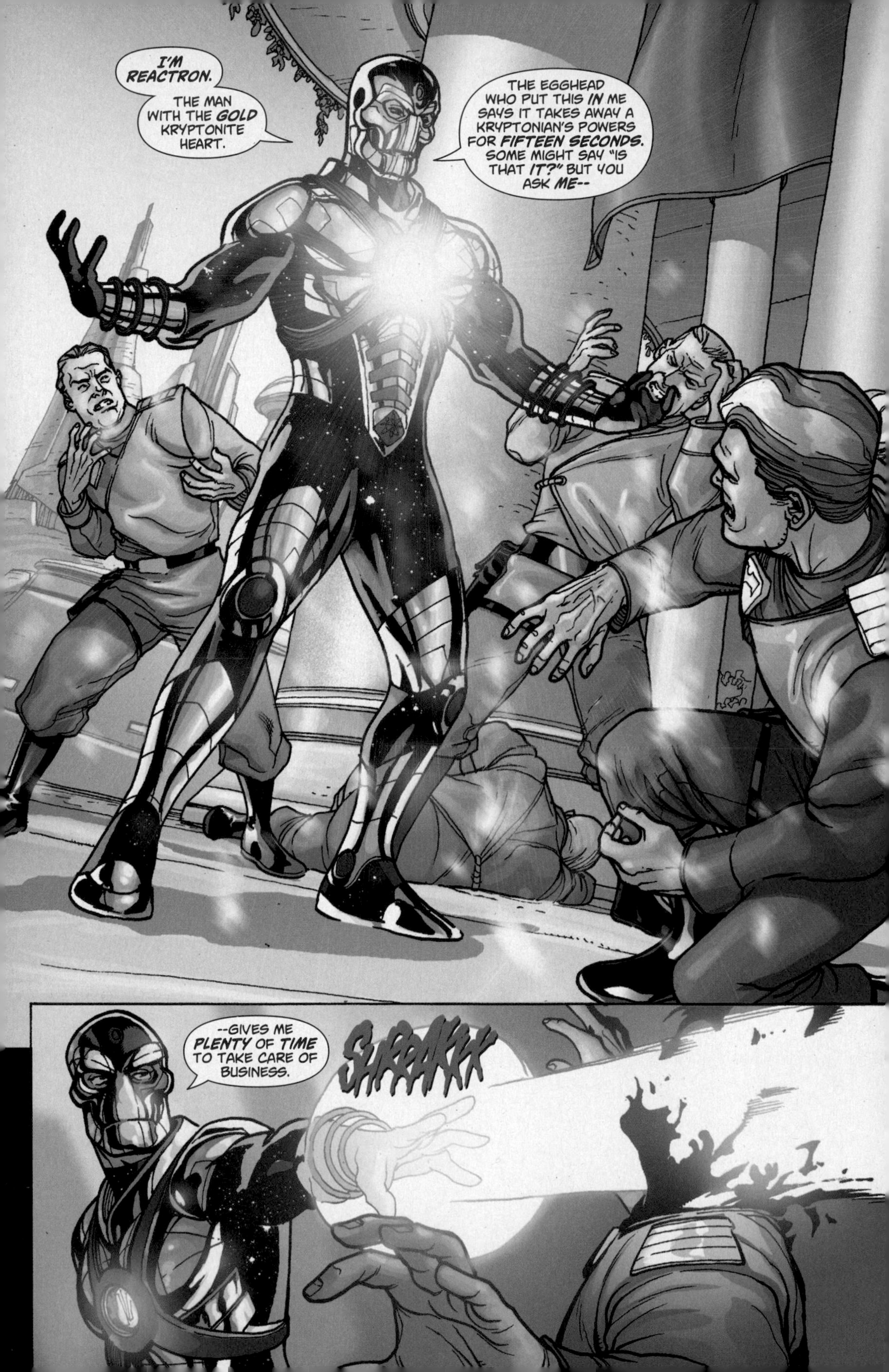
I'M REACTRON.
THE MAN WITH THE GOLD KRYPTONITE HEART.
THE EGGHEAD WHO PUT THIS IN ME SAYS IT TAKES AWAY A KRYPTONIAN'S POWERS FOR FIFTEEN SECONDS. SOME MIGHT SAY "IS THAT IT?" BUT YOU ASK ME--
--GIVES ME PLENTY OF TIME TO TAKE CARE OF BUSINESS.
SHRAKKK

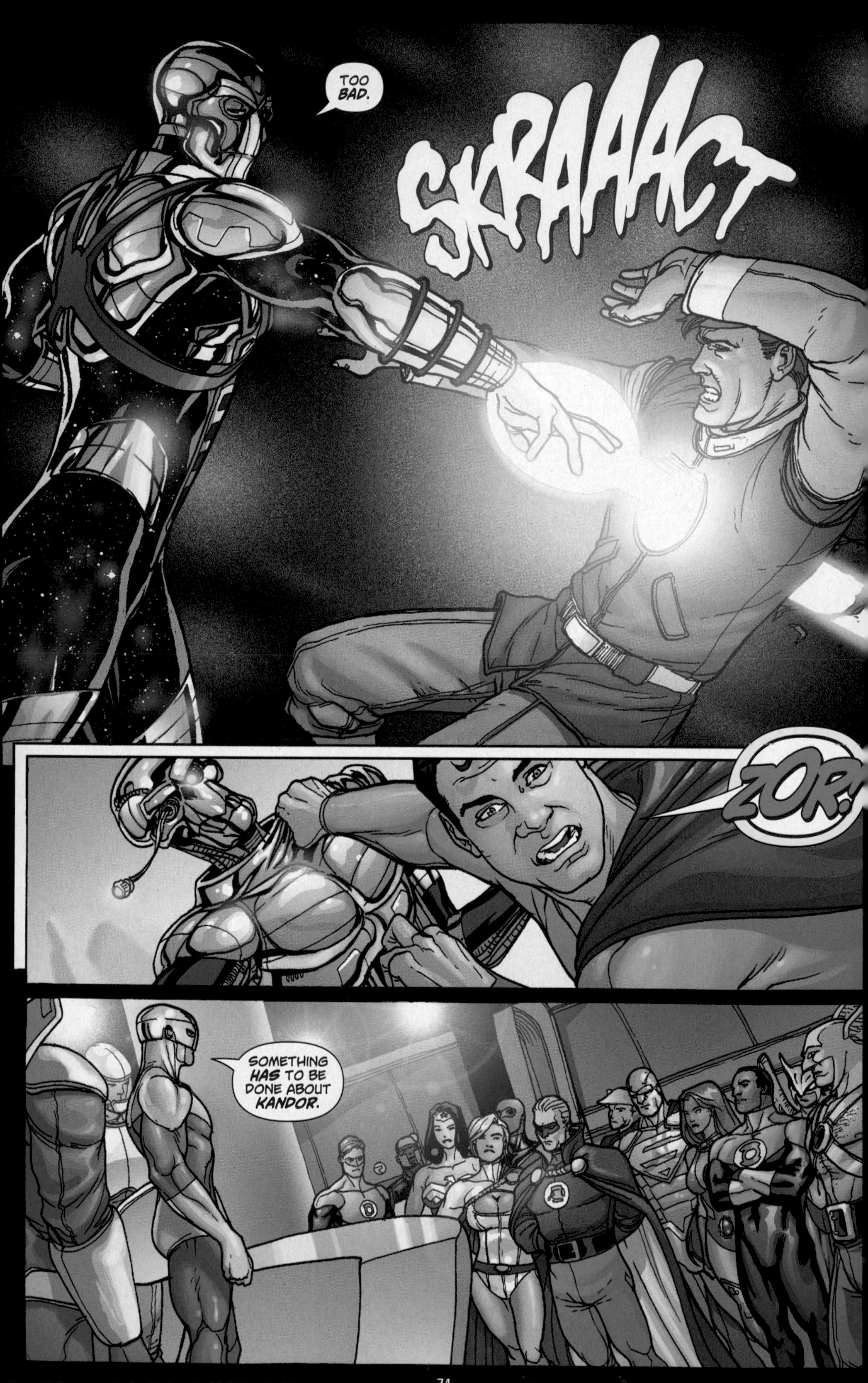
TOO BAD.
SKRAAACT
ZOR!
SOMETHING HAS TO BE DONE ABOUT KANDOR.

<DEATH IN THE HOUSE OF EL> SUPERGIRL 36 COVER ART BY **JOSHUA MIDDLETON**

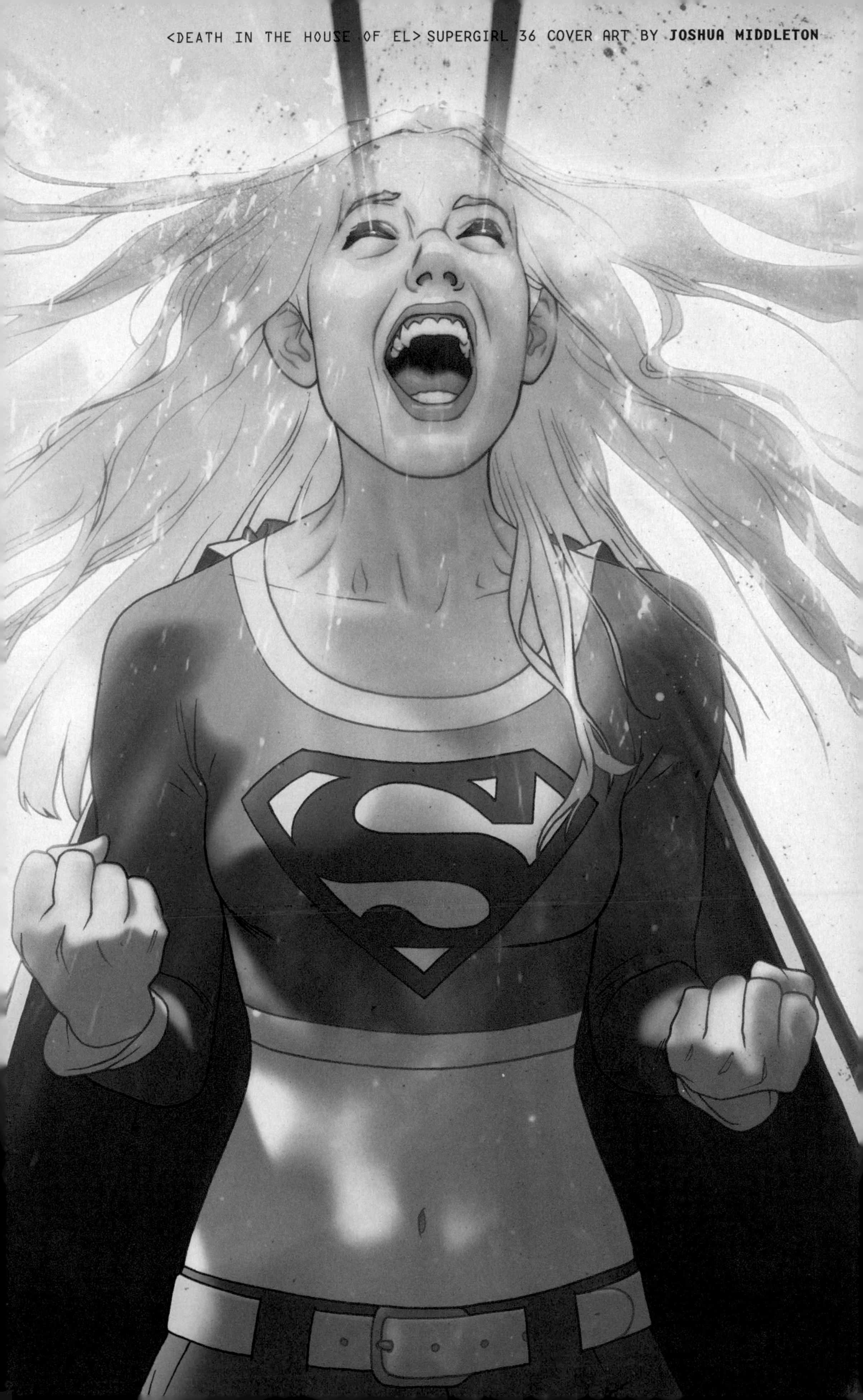

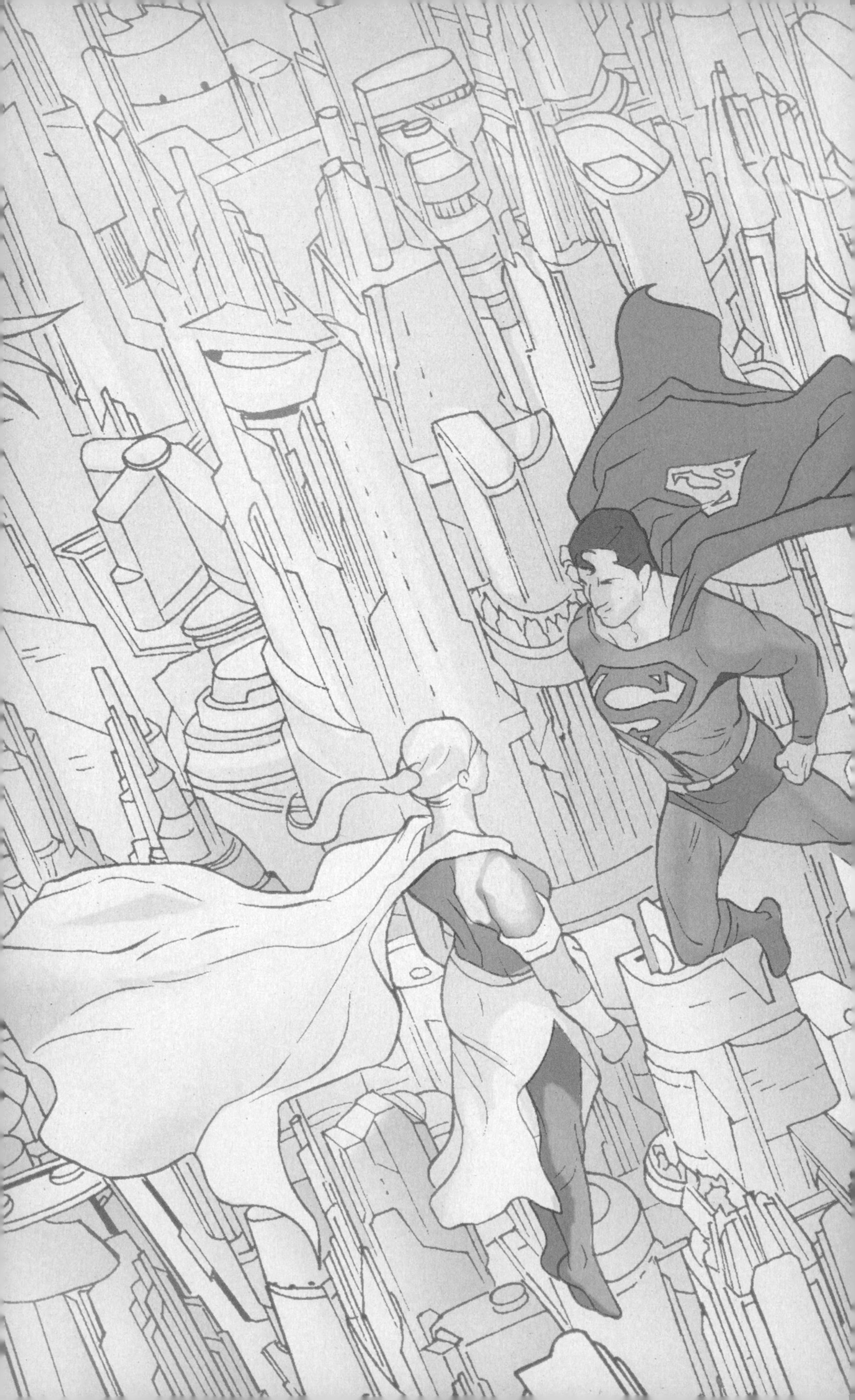

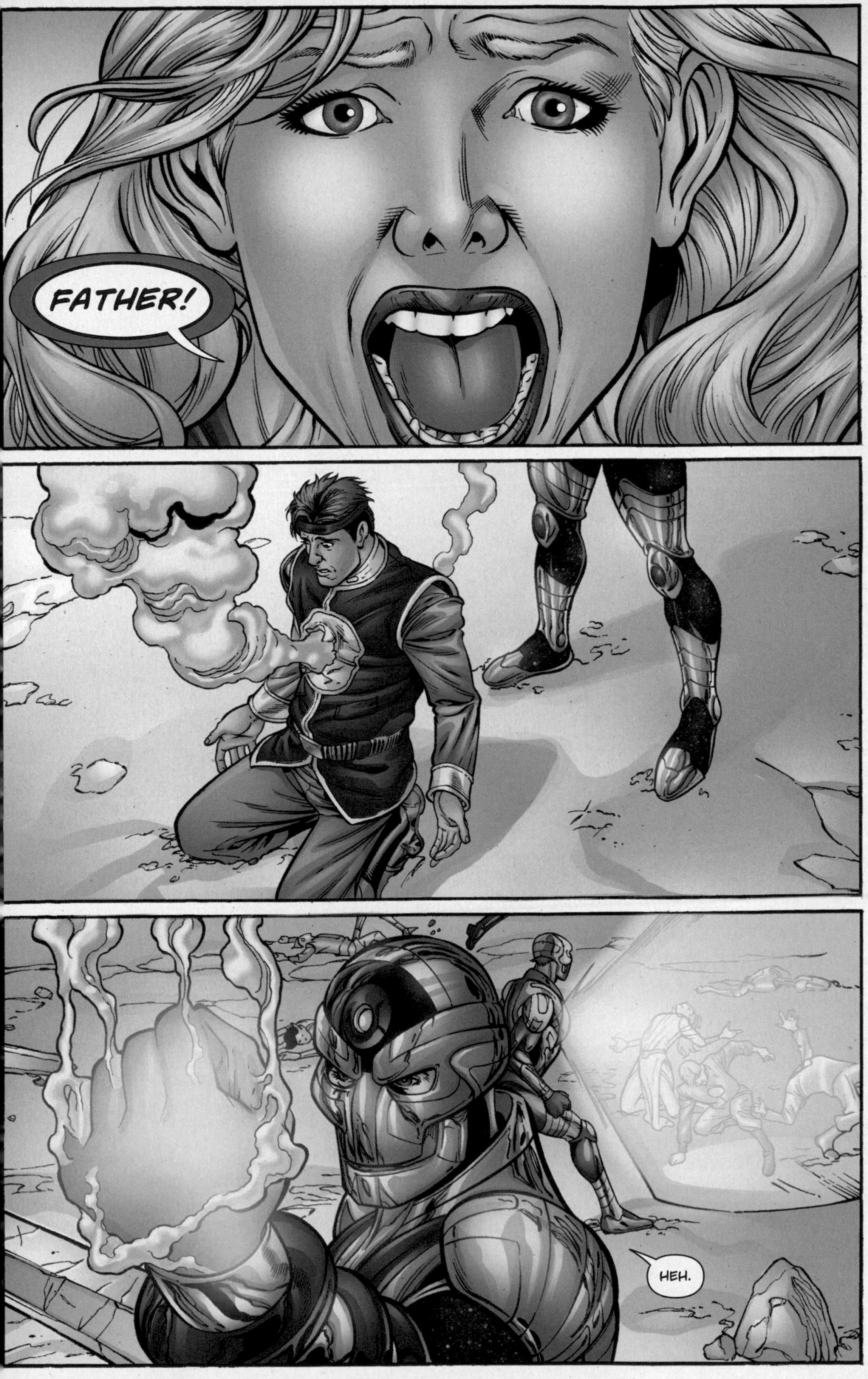
FATHER!
HEH.

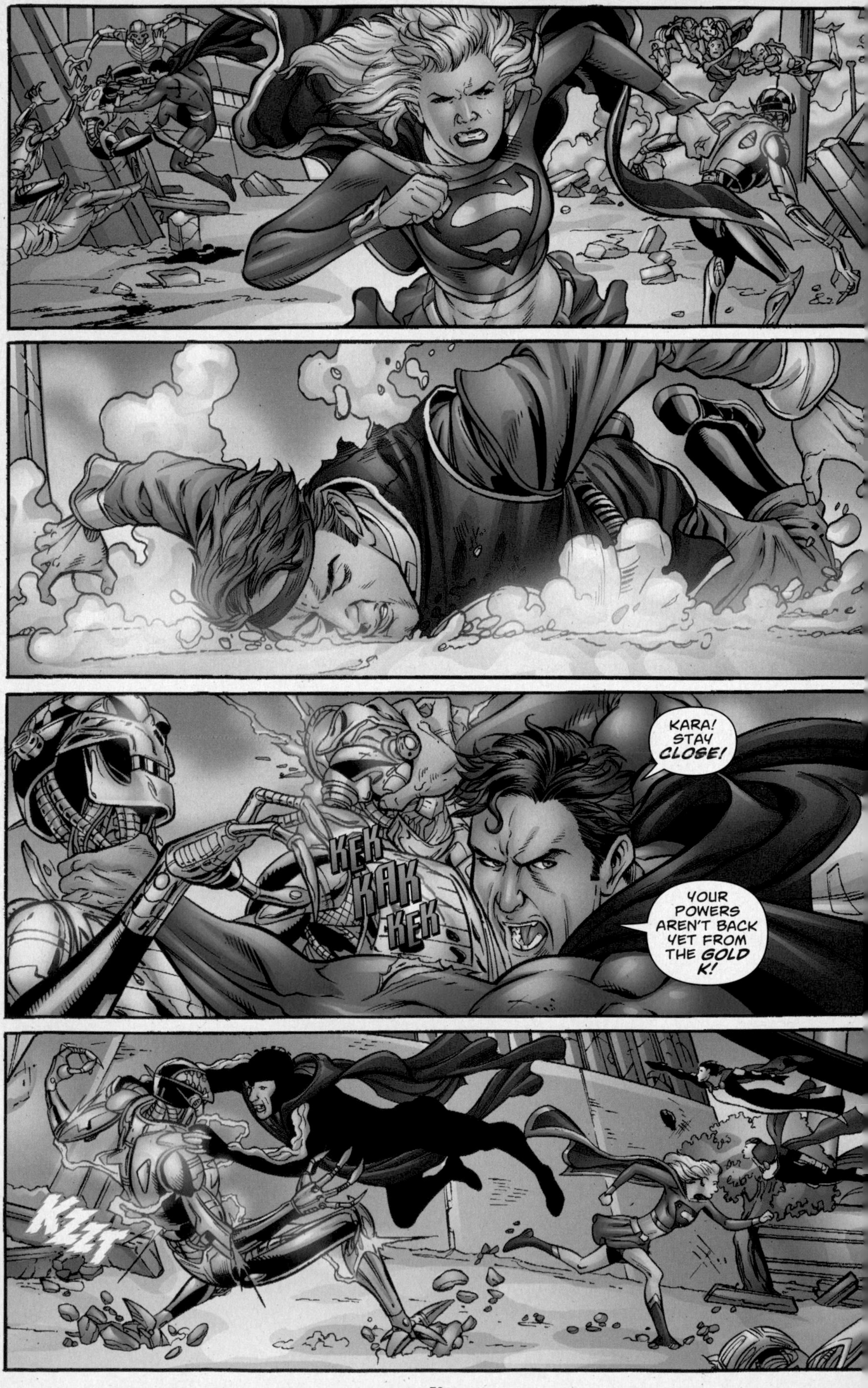
KARA! STAY CLOSE!
KEK KAK KEK
YOUR POWERS AREN'T BACK YET FROM THE GOLD K!
KZZZT

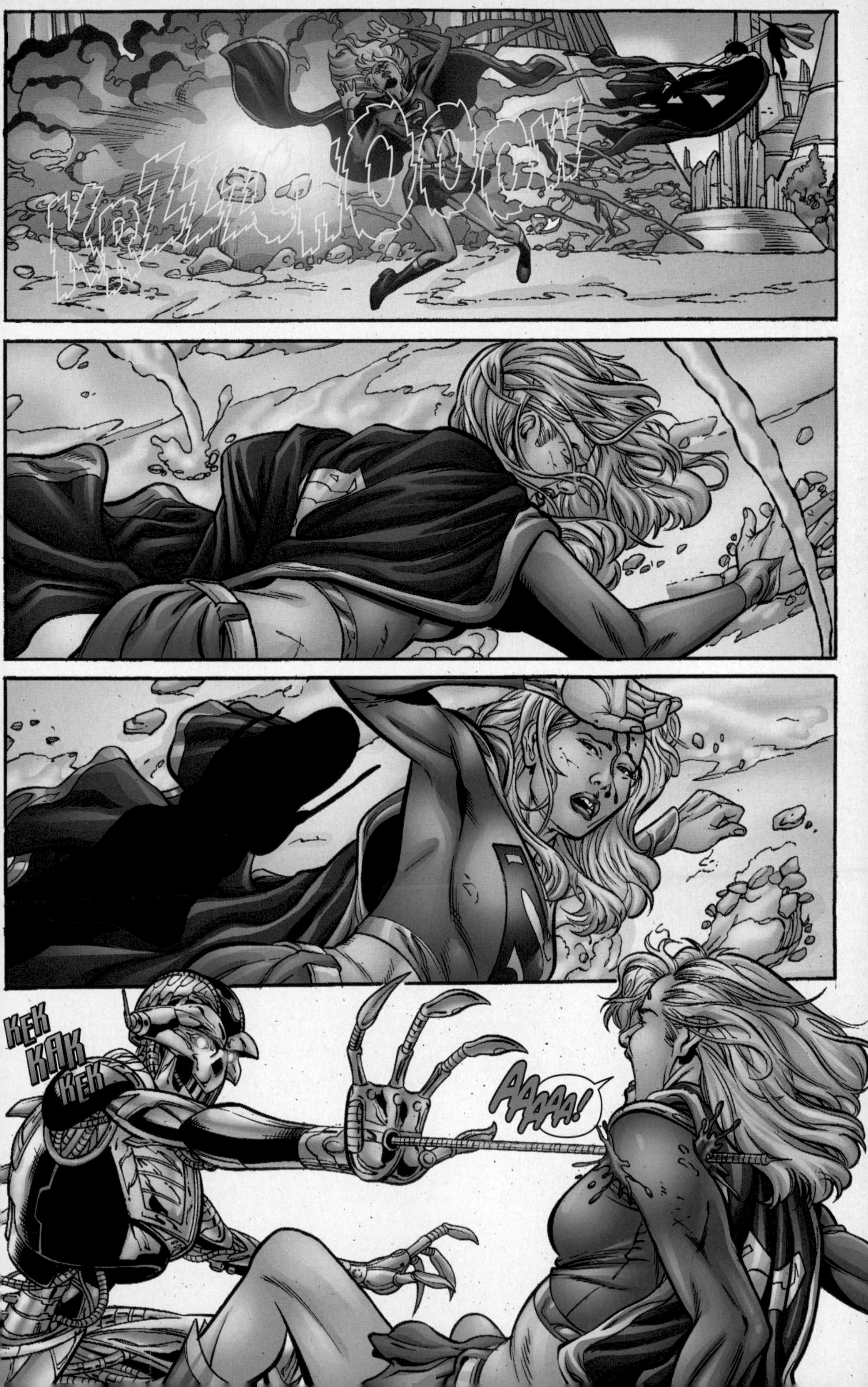
KEK
KAK
KEK
AAAAA!

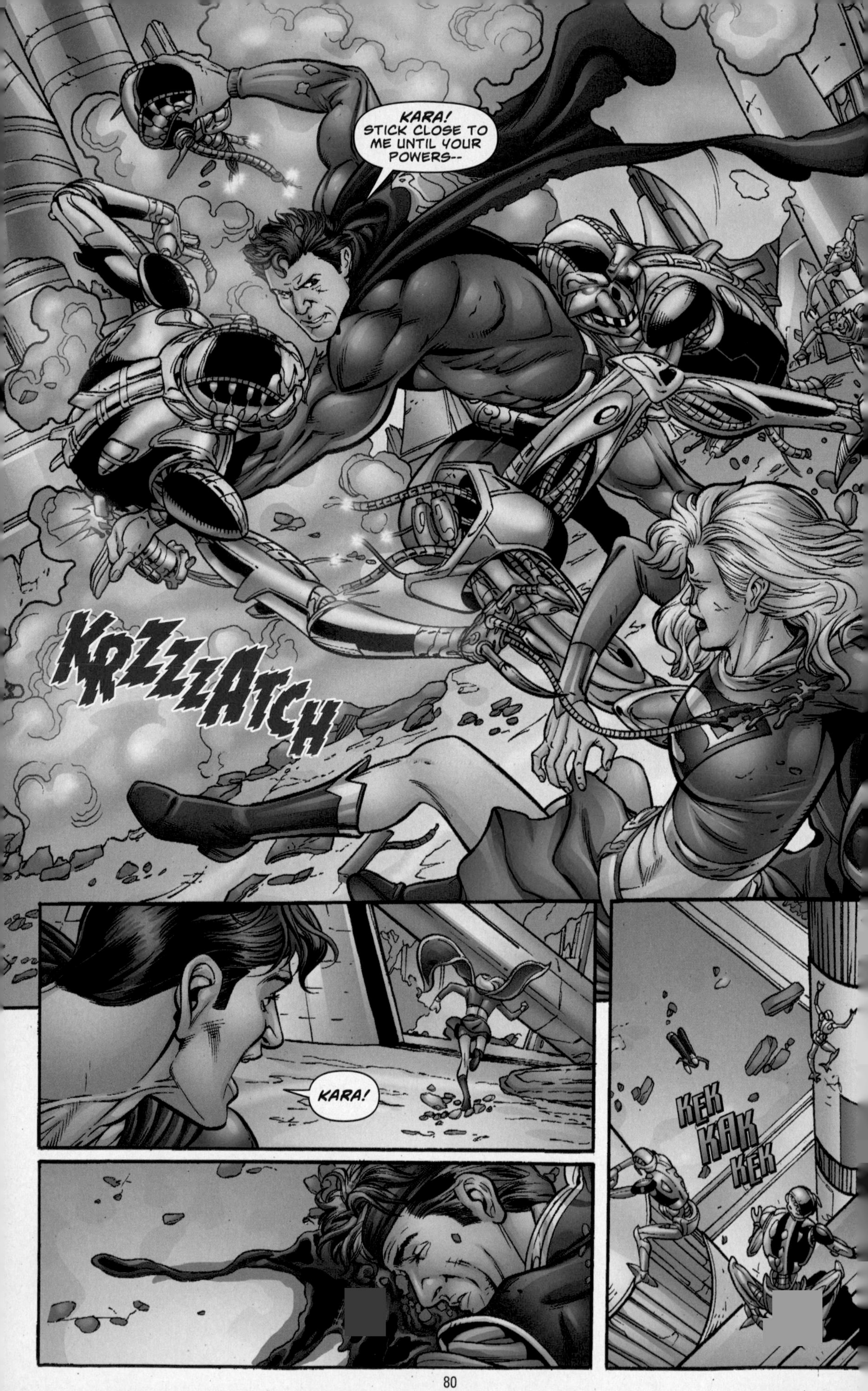
KARA! STICK CLOSE TO ME UNTIL YOUR POWERS--
KRZZZZATCH
KARA!
KEK KAK KEK

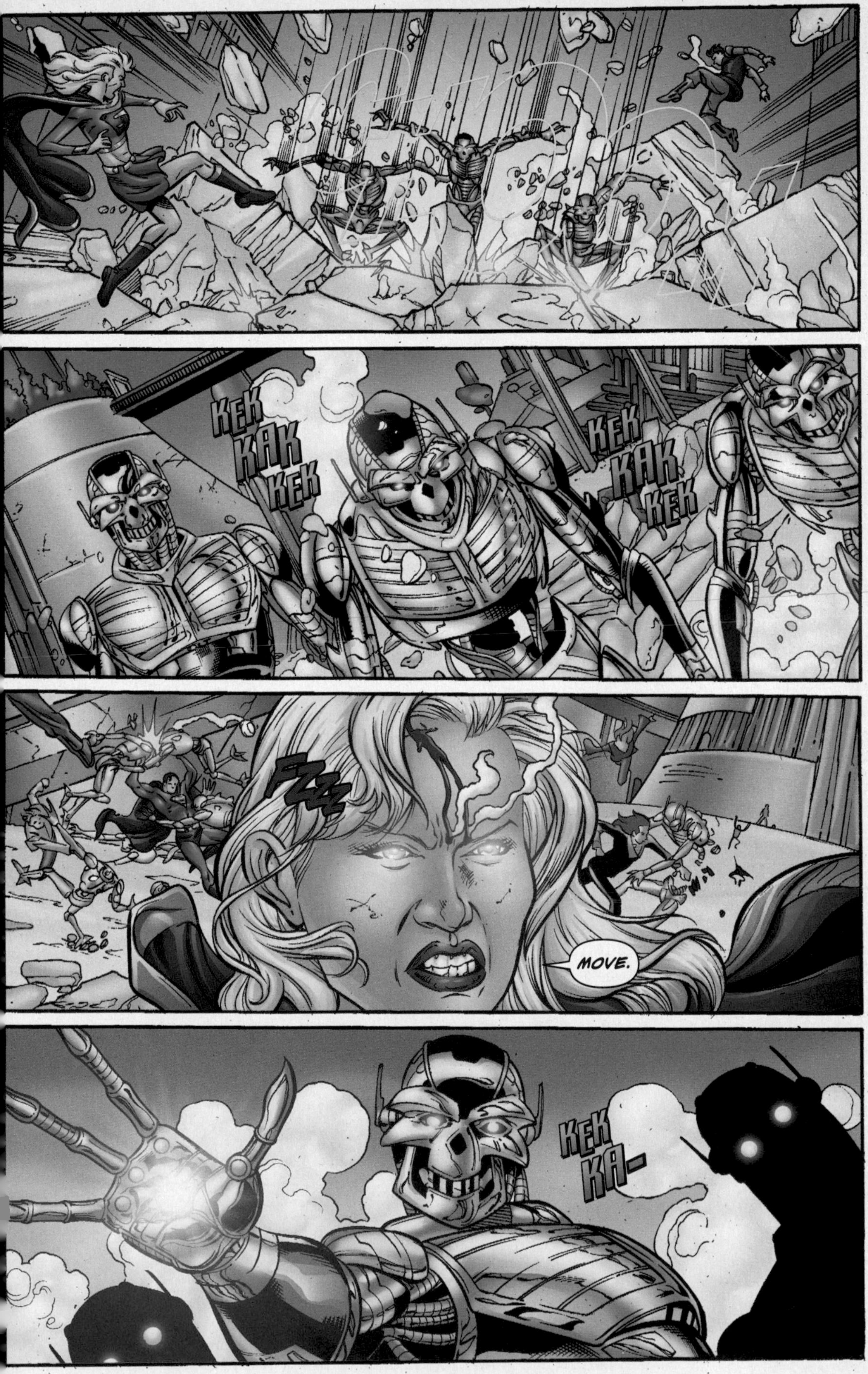
KEK
KAK
KEK
KEK
KAK
KEK
FZZZ
MOVE.
KEK
KA-

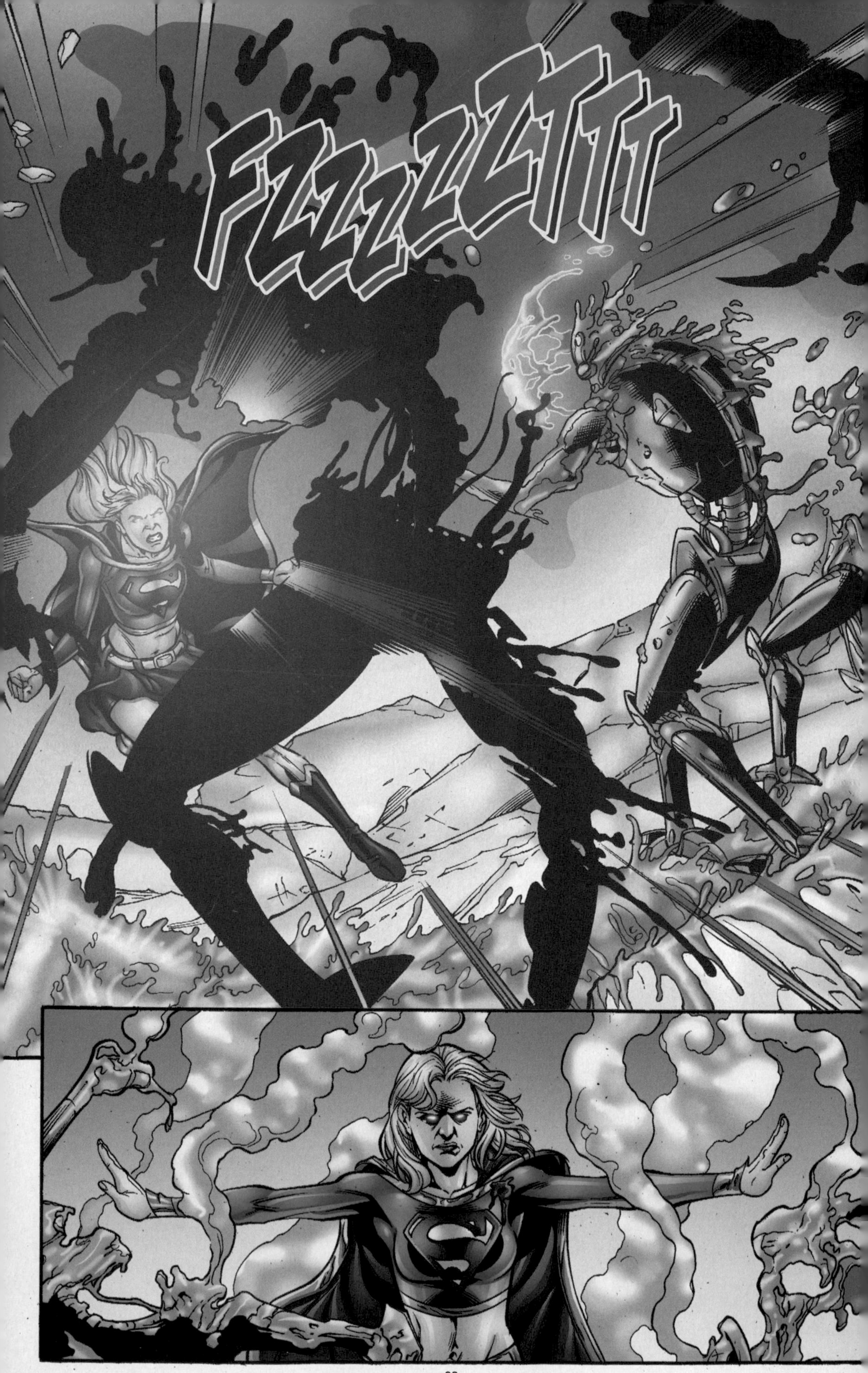
FZZZZZTTT

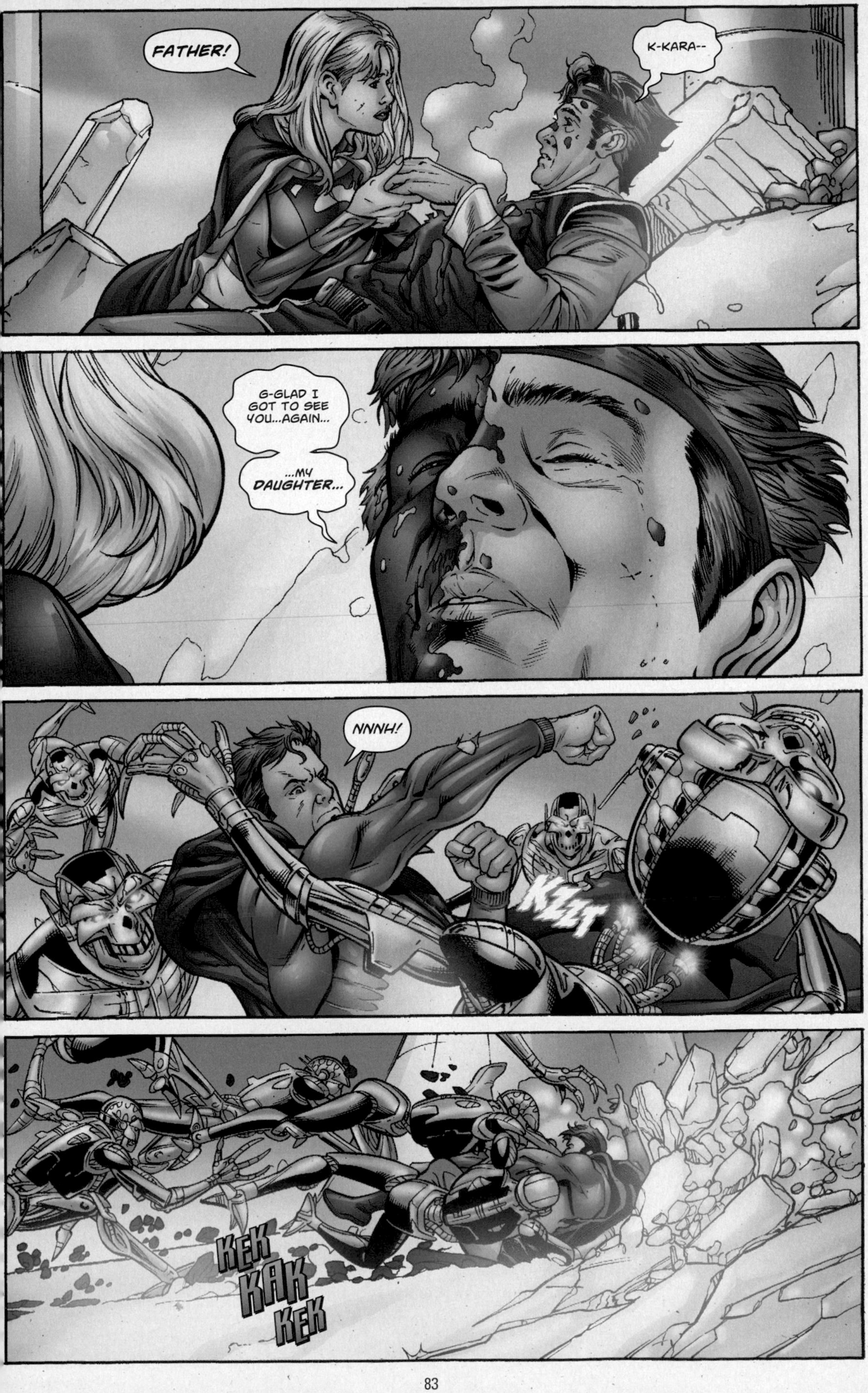
FATHER!
K-KARA--
G-GLAD I GOT TO SEE YOU...AGAIN...
...MY DAUGHTER...
NNNH!
KZZT
KEK KAK KEK

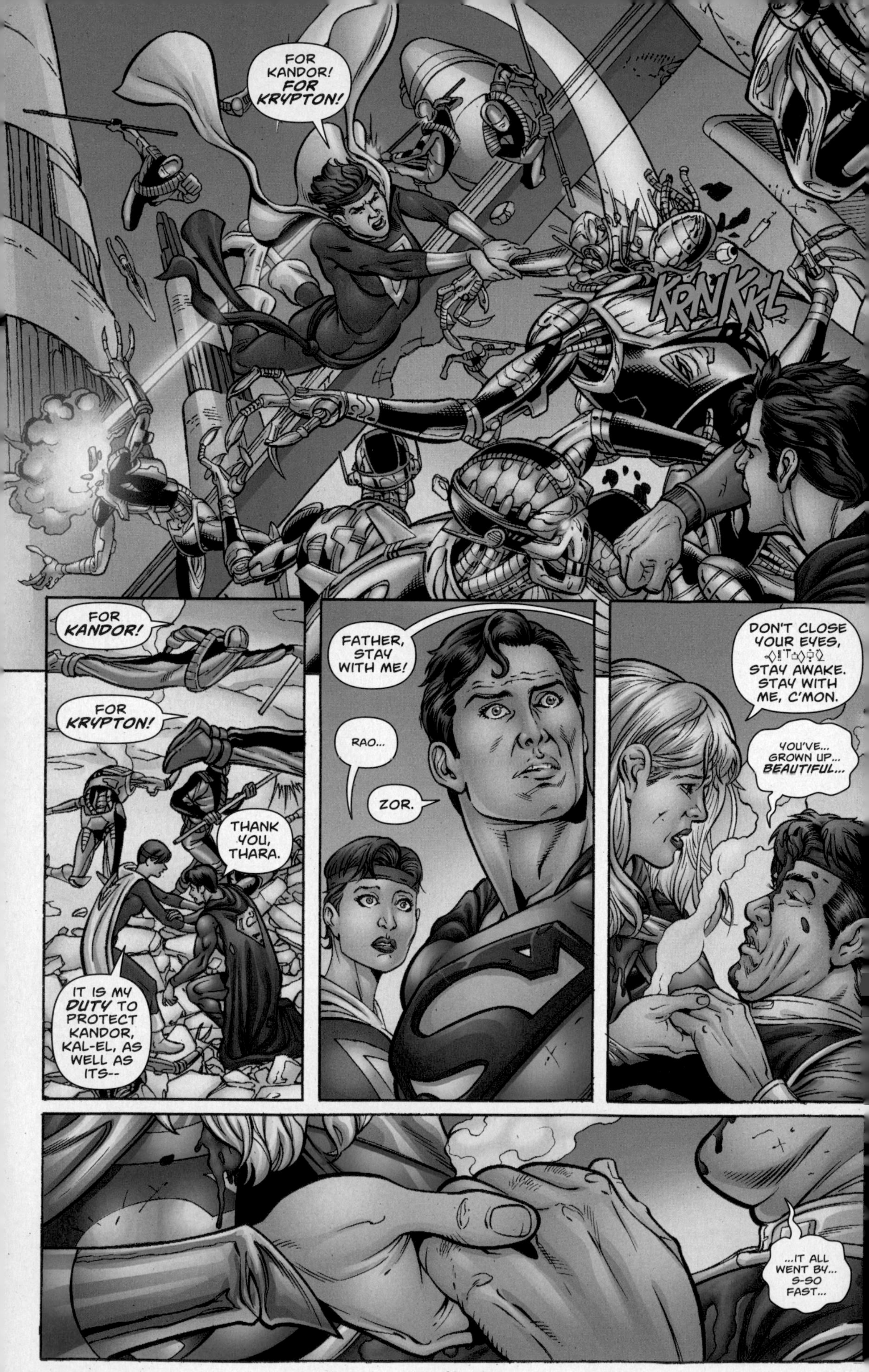
FOR KANDOR! FOR KRYPTON!
KRNKKL
FOR KANDOR!
FOR KRYPTON!
THANK YOU, THARA.
IT IS MY DUTY TO PROTECT KANDOR, KAL-EL, AS WELL AS ITS--
FATHER, STAY WITH ME!
RAO...
ZOR.
DON'T CLOSE YOUR EYES,
STAY AWAKE. STAY WITH ME, C'MON.
YOU'VE... GROWN UP... BEAUTIFUL...
...IT ALL WENT BY... S-SO FAST...

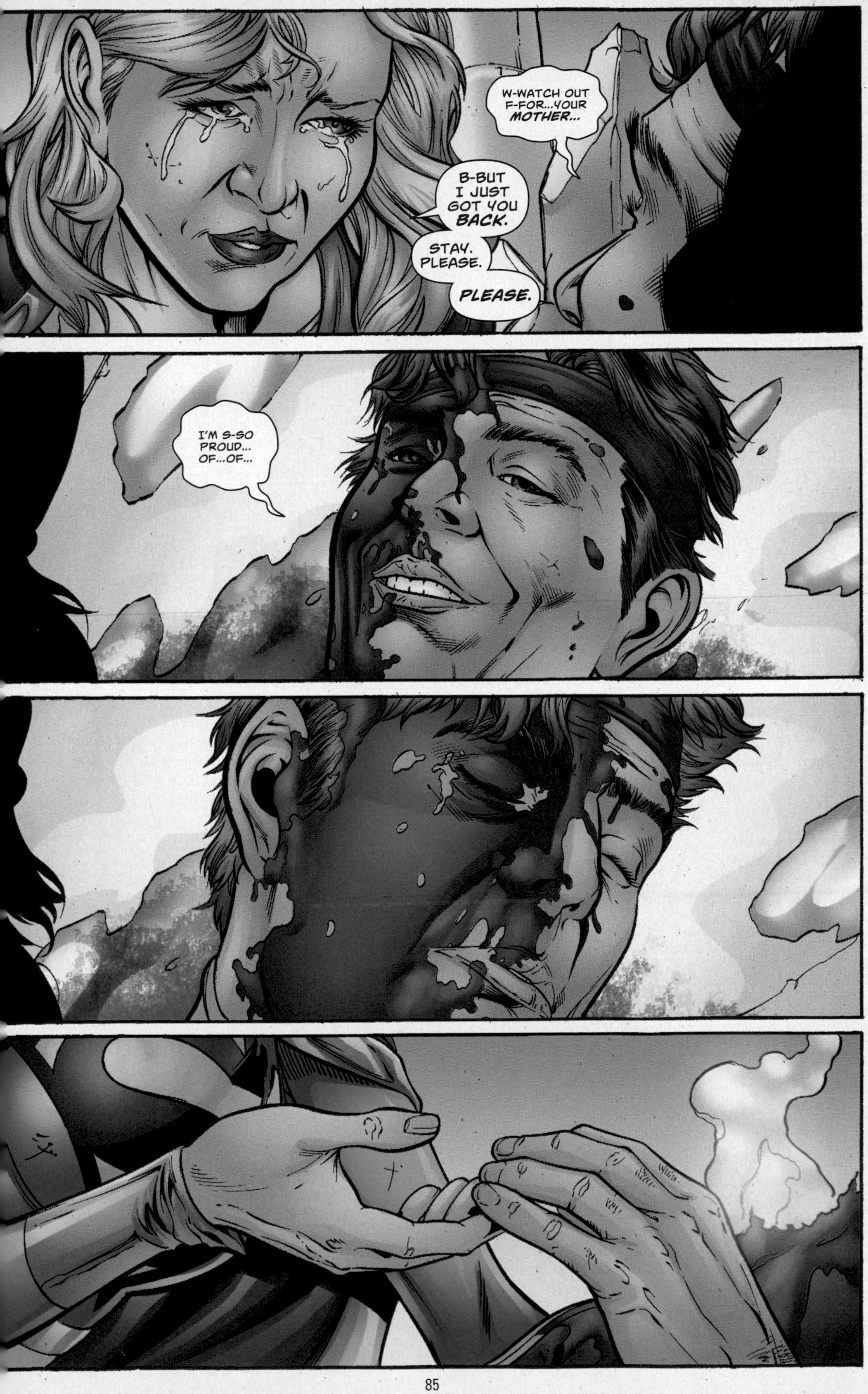
W-WATCH OUT F-FOR...YOUR MOTHER...
B-BUT I JUST GOT YOU BACK.
STAY. PLEASE.
PLEASE.
I'M S-SO PROUD... OF...OF...

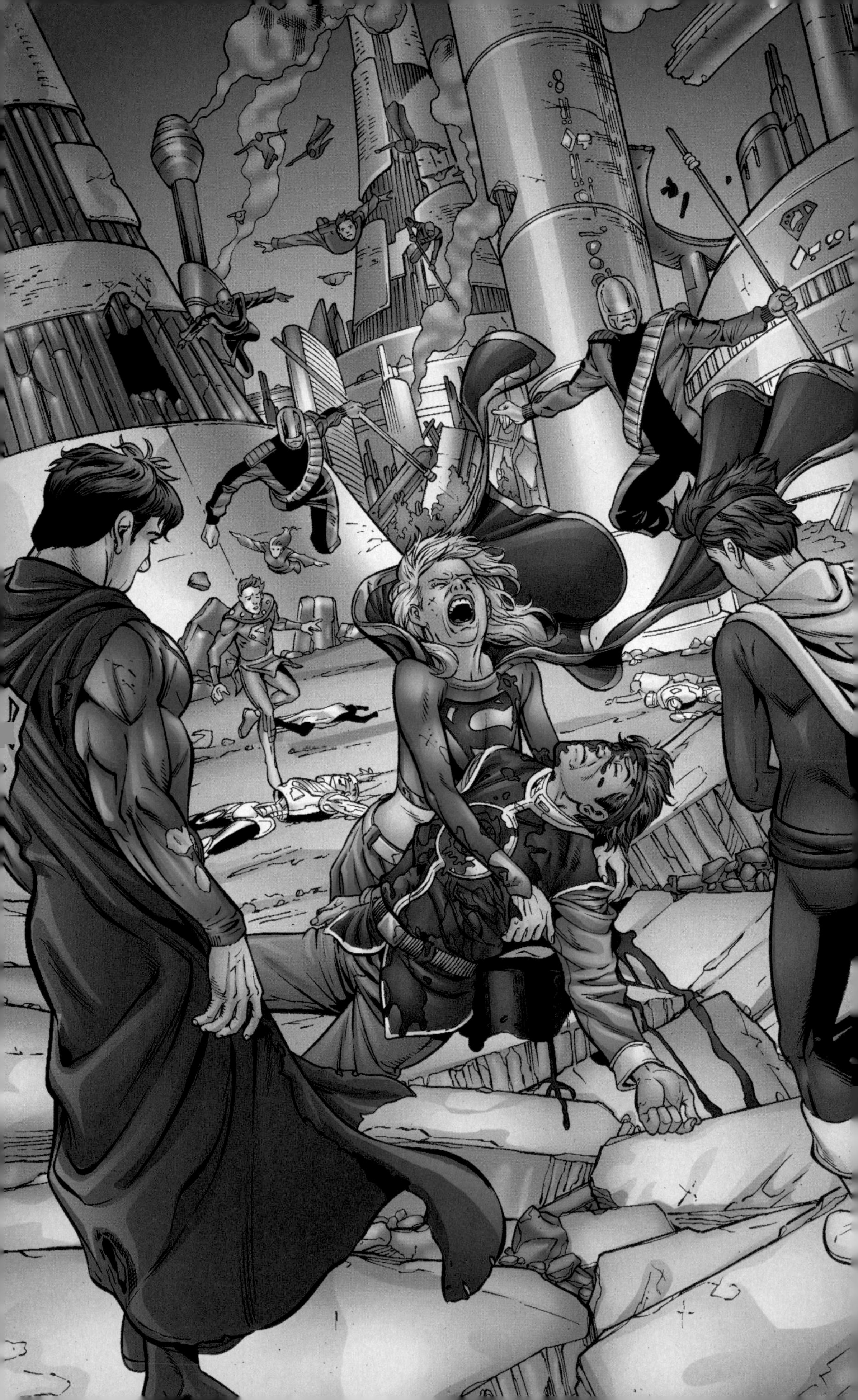

HELLO?!

I KNOW YOU BOYS ARE *UNPAID* INTERNS, BUT I'VE BEEN PAGING YOU THE LAST FIFTEEN MINUTES!

"SUPERGIRL: SCIENCE POLICE MURDERER?" IS DUE IN THE NEXT FIVE MINUTES, AND IF ONE OF YOU CAN'T GET MY EMAIL BACK UP, I'LL--

--OH.

IT CAN *WAIT*, CAT. WHILE YOU'VE BEEN REDEFINING THE WORD "LIBEL" WITH YOUR TRIPE, *REAL* NEWS HAPPENED.

--SUPERMAN ISSUED A STATEMENT THIS MORNING SAYING ZOR-EL, LEADER OF THE NEW KRYPTONIANS, WAS KILLED IN AN ATTACK ON KANDOR LATE YESTERDAY.

SUPERGIRL'S FATHER--?

WAS *KILLED.* YESTERDAY.

AND THE LAST THING SUPERGIRL *NEEDS* IS TO COME HOME AND FIND *MORE* OF YOUR *LIES* ON THE PLANET'S FRONT PAGE.

OH, IT'S NOT *ALL* A LIE, LANA. *SOMEBODY* UP THERE SHOULD BE HELD RESPONSIBLE FOR THE *DEATHS* OF CAPTAIN DuBARRY AND THE STRYKER'S ISLAND GUARDS.

BUT JUST WHAT DO *YOU* THINK THE GIRL OF STEEL NEEDS RIGHT *NOW*, LANA, BESIDES A *GOOD* LAWYER?

IN OTHER NEW KRYPTONIAN NEWS, THERE HAVE BEEN SEVERAL SIGHTINGS ACROSS THE WORLD OF A MYSTERIOUS NEW HERO.

JUST *WHO* IS THE WOMAN CALLING HERSELF *SUPERWOMAN?*

RIGHT NOW? WHAT *ALL* OF US NEED.

A *FRIEND.*

"ZOR WAS A SOURCE OF *HOPE*--"

88

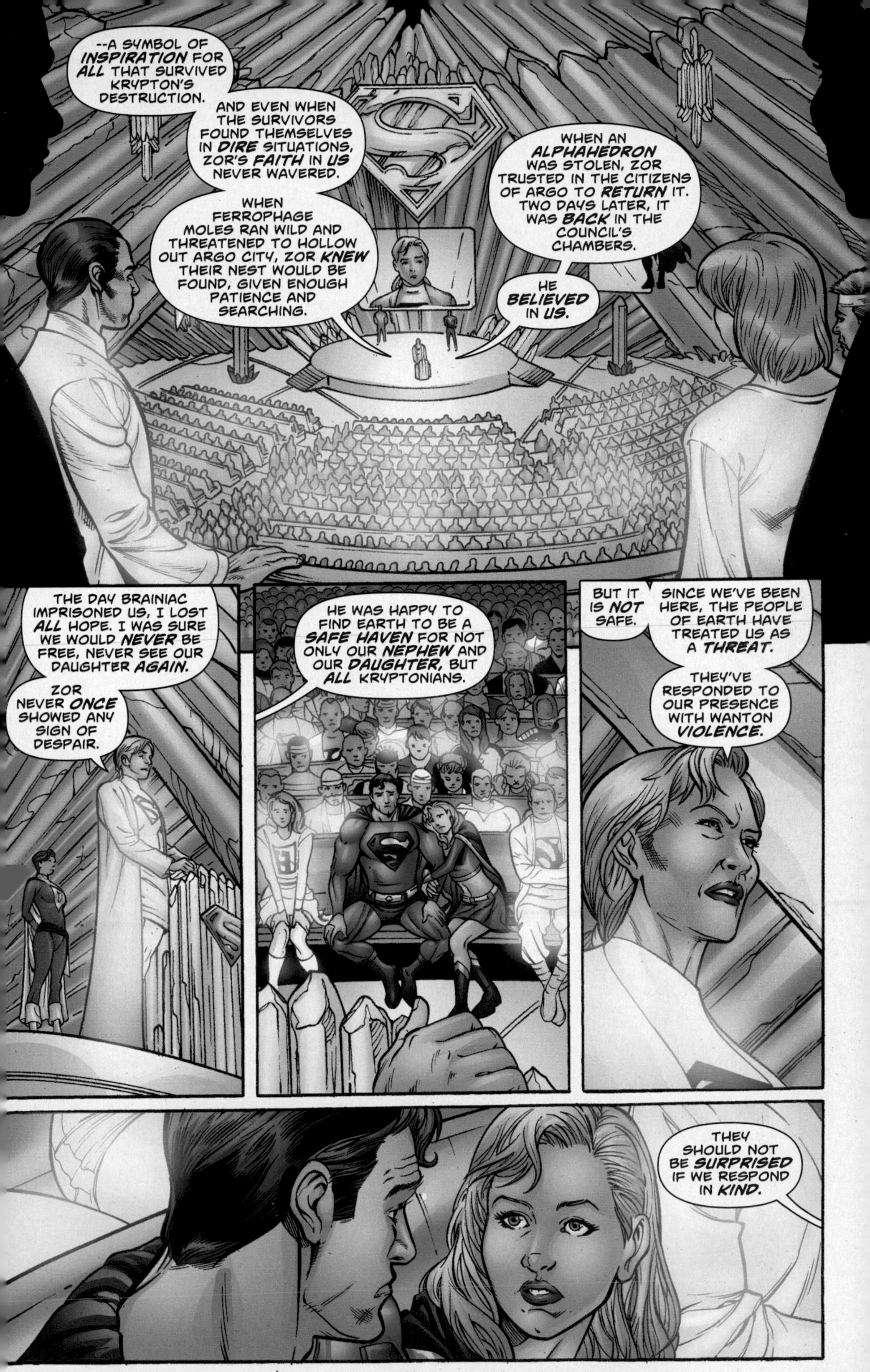
--A SYMBOL OF INSPIRATION FOR ALL THAT SURVIVED KRYPTON'S DESTRUCTION.
AND EVEN WHEN THE SURVIVORS FOUND THEMSELVES IN DIRE SITUATIONS, ZOR'S FAITH IN US NEVER WAVERED.
WHEN FERROPHAGE MOLES RAN WILD AND THREATENED TO HOLLOW OUT ARGO CITY, ZOR KNEW THEIR NEST WOULD BE FOUND, GIVEN ENOUGH PATIENCE AND SEARCHING.
WHEN AN ALPHAHEDRON WAS STOLEN, ZOR TRUSTED IN THE CITIZENS OF ARGO TO RETURN IT. TWO DAYS LATER, IT WAS BACK IN THE COUNCIL'S CHAMBERS.
HE BELIEVED IN US.
THE DAY BRAINIAC IMPRISONED US, I LOST ALL HOPE. I WAS SURE WE WOULD NEVER BE FREE, NEVER SEE OUR DAUGHTER AGAIN.
ZOR NEVER ONCE SHOWED ANY SIGN OF DESPAIR.
HE WAS HAPPY TO FIND EARTH TO BE A SAFE HAVEN FOR NOT ONLY OUR NEPHEW AND OUR DAUGHTER, BUT ALL KRYPTONIANS.
BUT IT IS NOT SAFE.
SINCE WE'VE BEEN HERE, THE PEOPLE OF EARTH HAVE TREATED US AS A THREAT.
THEY'VE RESPONDED TO OUR PRESENCE WITH WANTON VIOLENCE.
THEY SHOULD NOT BE SURPRISED IF WE RESPOND IN KIND.

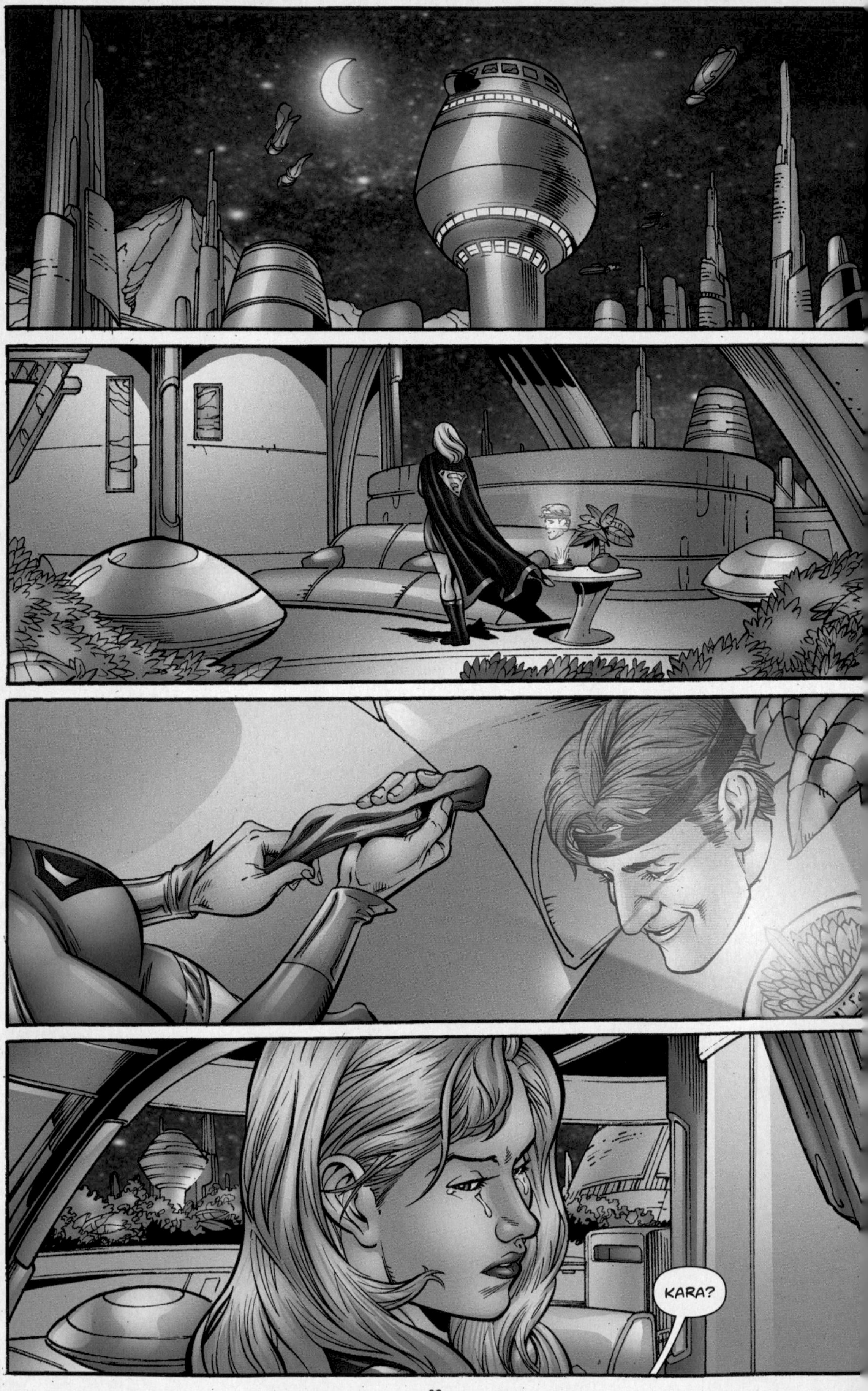
KARA?

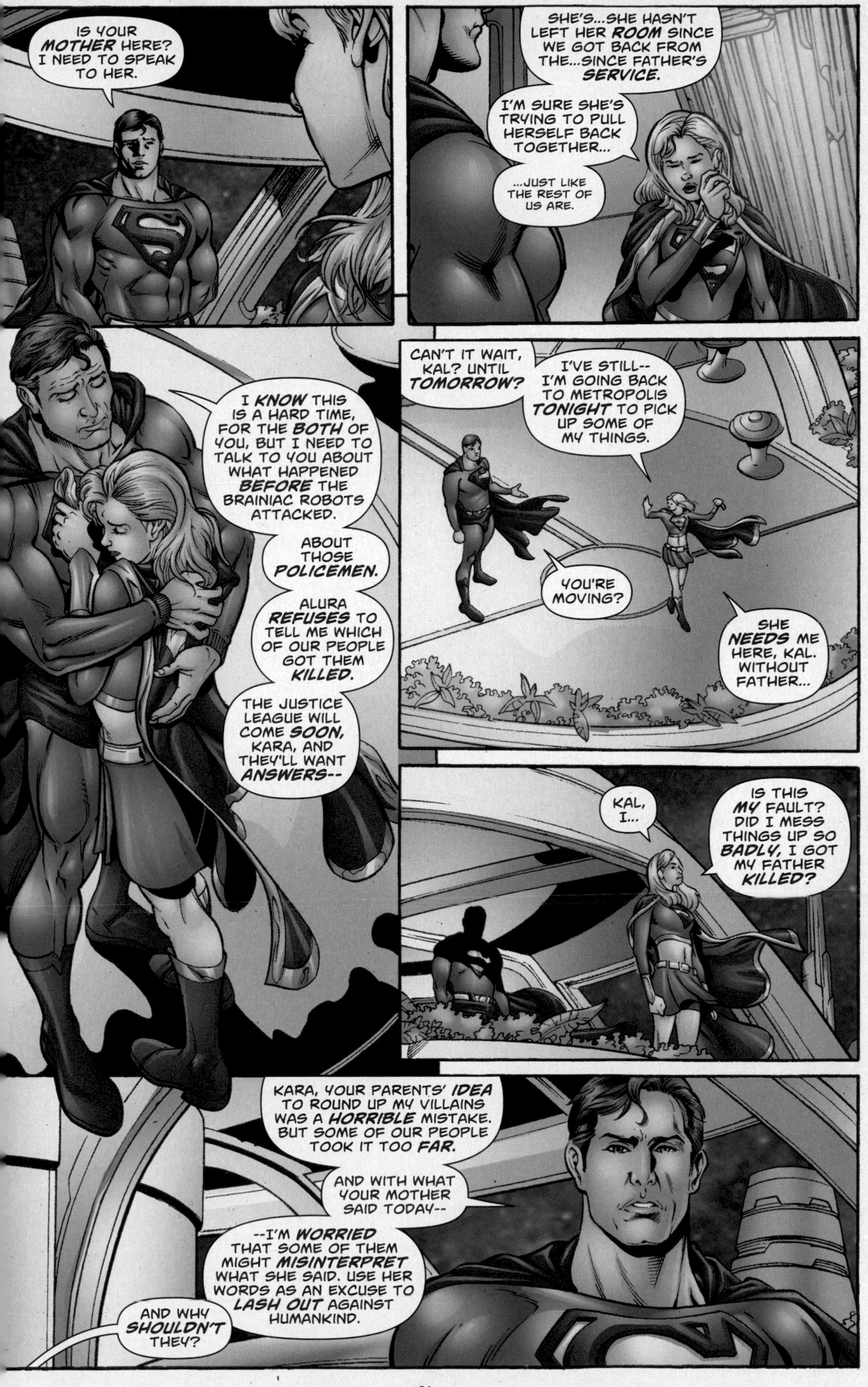
IS YOUR MOTHER HERE? I NEED TO SPEAK TO HER.
SHE'S...SHE HASN'T LEFT HER ROOM SINCE WE GOT BACK FROM THE...SINCE FATHER'S SERVICE.
I'M SURE SHE'S TRYING TO PULL HERSELF BACK TOGETHER...
...JUST LIKE THE REST OF US ARE.
I KNOW THIS IS A HARD TIME, FOR THE BOTH OF YOU, BUT I NEED TO TALK TO YOU ABOUT WHAT HAPPENED BEFORE THE BRAINIAC ROBOTS ATTACKED.
ABOUT THOSE POLICEMEN.
ALURA REFUSES TO TELL ME WHICH OF OUR PEOPLE GOT THEM KILLED.
THE JUSTICE LEAGUE WILL COME SOON, KARA, AND THEY'LL WANT ANSWERS--
CAN'T IT WAIT, KAL? UNTIL TOMORROW?
I'VE STILL-- I'M GOING BACK TO METROPOLIS TONIGHT TO PICK UP SOME OF MY THINGS.
YOU'RE MOVING?
SHE NEEDS ME HERE, KAL. WITHOUT FATHER...
KAL, I...
IS THIS MY FAULT? DID I MESS THINGS UP SO BADLY, I GOT MY FATHER KILLED?
KARA, YOUR PARENTS' IDEA TO ROUND UP MY VILLAINS WAS A HORRIBLE MISTAKE. BUT SOME OF OUR PEOPLE TOOK IT TOO FAR.
AND WITH WHAT YOUR MOTHER SAID TODAY--
--I'M WORRIED THAT SOME OF THEM MIGHT MISINTERPRET WHAT SHE SAID. USE HER WORDS AS AN EXCUSE TO LASH OUT AGAINST HUMANKIND.
AND WHY SHOULDN'T THEY?

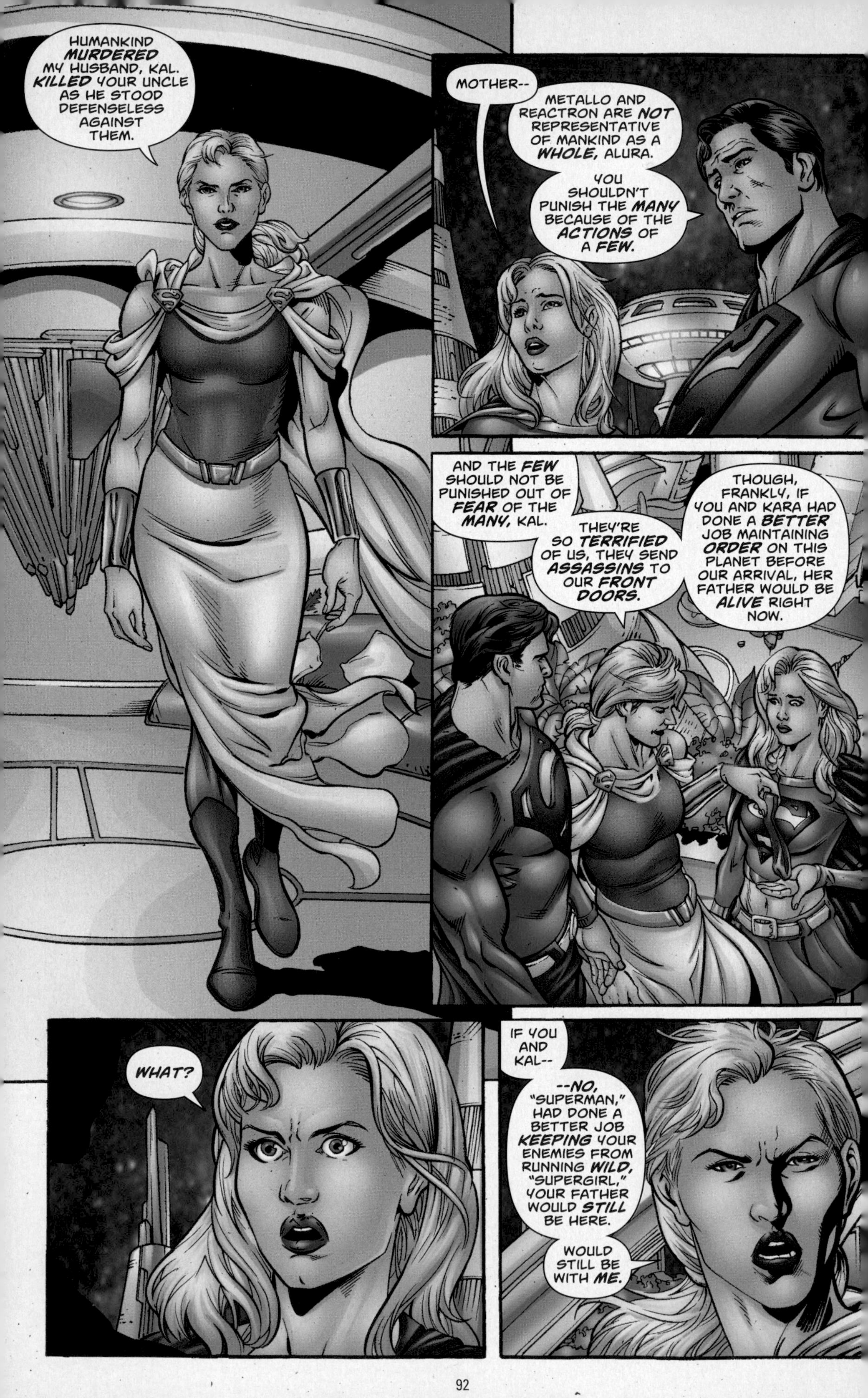
HUMANKIND MURDERED MY HUSBAND, KAL. KILLED YOUR UNCLE AS HE STOOD DEFENSELESS AGAINST THEM.
MOTHER--
METALLO AND REACTRON ARE NOT REPRESENTATIVE OF MANKIND AS A WHOLE, ALURA.
YOU SHOULDN'T PUNISH THE MANY BECAUSE OF THE ACTIONS OF A FEW.
AND THE FEW SHOULD NOT BE PUNISHED OUT OF FEAR OF THE MANY, KAL.
THEY'RE SO TERRIFIED OF US, THEY SEND ASSASSINS TO OUR FRONT DOORS.
THOUGH, FRANKLY, IF YOU AND KARA HAD DONE A BETTER JOB MAINTAINING ORDER ON THIS PLANET BEFORE OUR ARRIVAL, HER FATHER WOULD BE ALIVE RIGHT NOW.
WHAT?
IF YOU AND KAL--
--NO, "SUPERMAN," HAD DONE A BETTER JOB KEEPING YOUR ENEMIES FROM RUNNING WILD, "SUPERGIRL," YOUR FATHER WOULD STILL BE HERE.
WOULD STILL BE WITH ME.

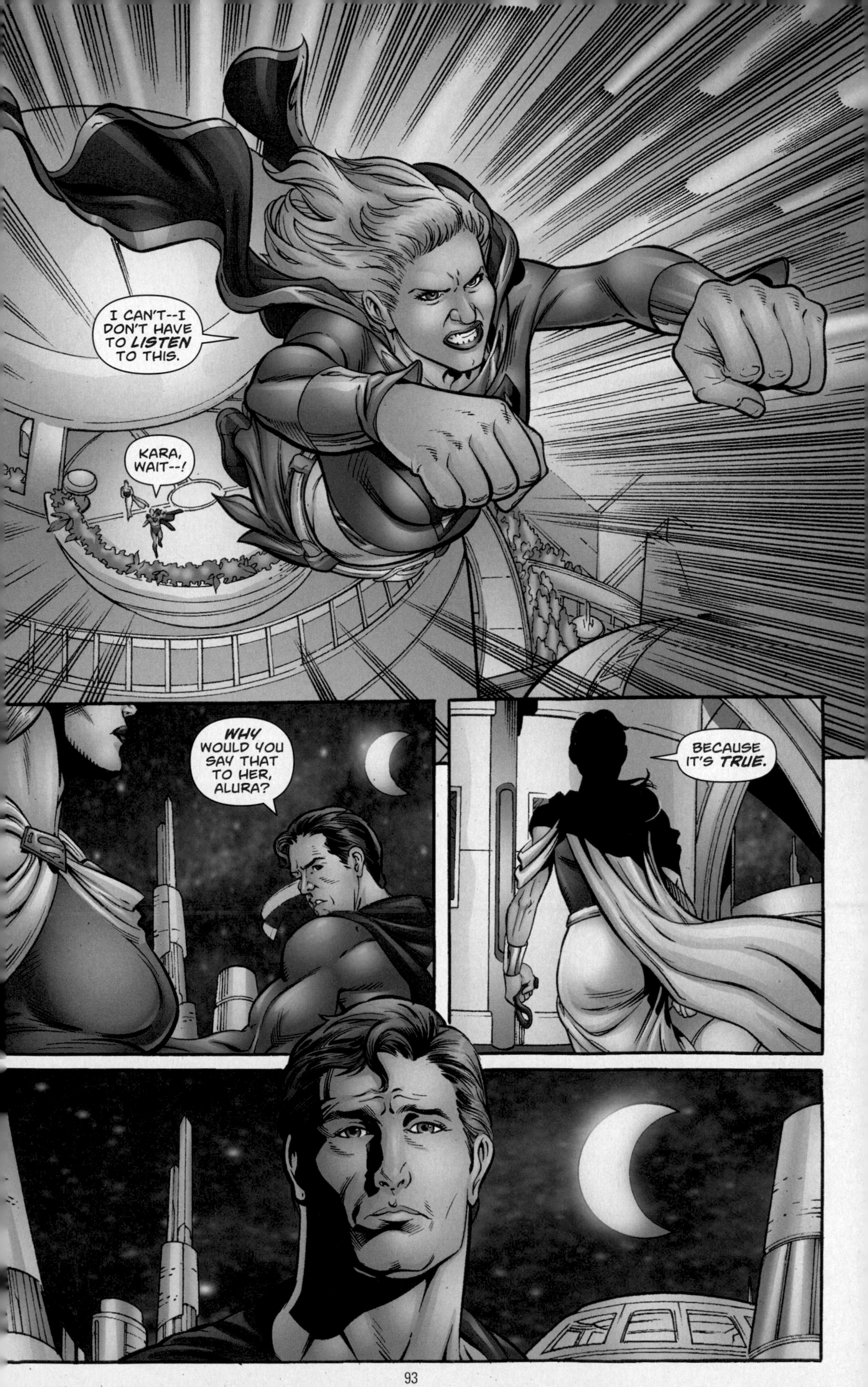
I CAN'T--I DON'T HAVE TO LISTEN TO THIS.
KARA, WAIT--!
WHY WOULD YOU SAY THAT TO HER, ALURA?
BECAUSE IT'S TRUE.

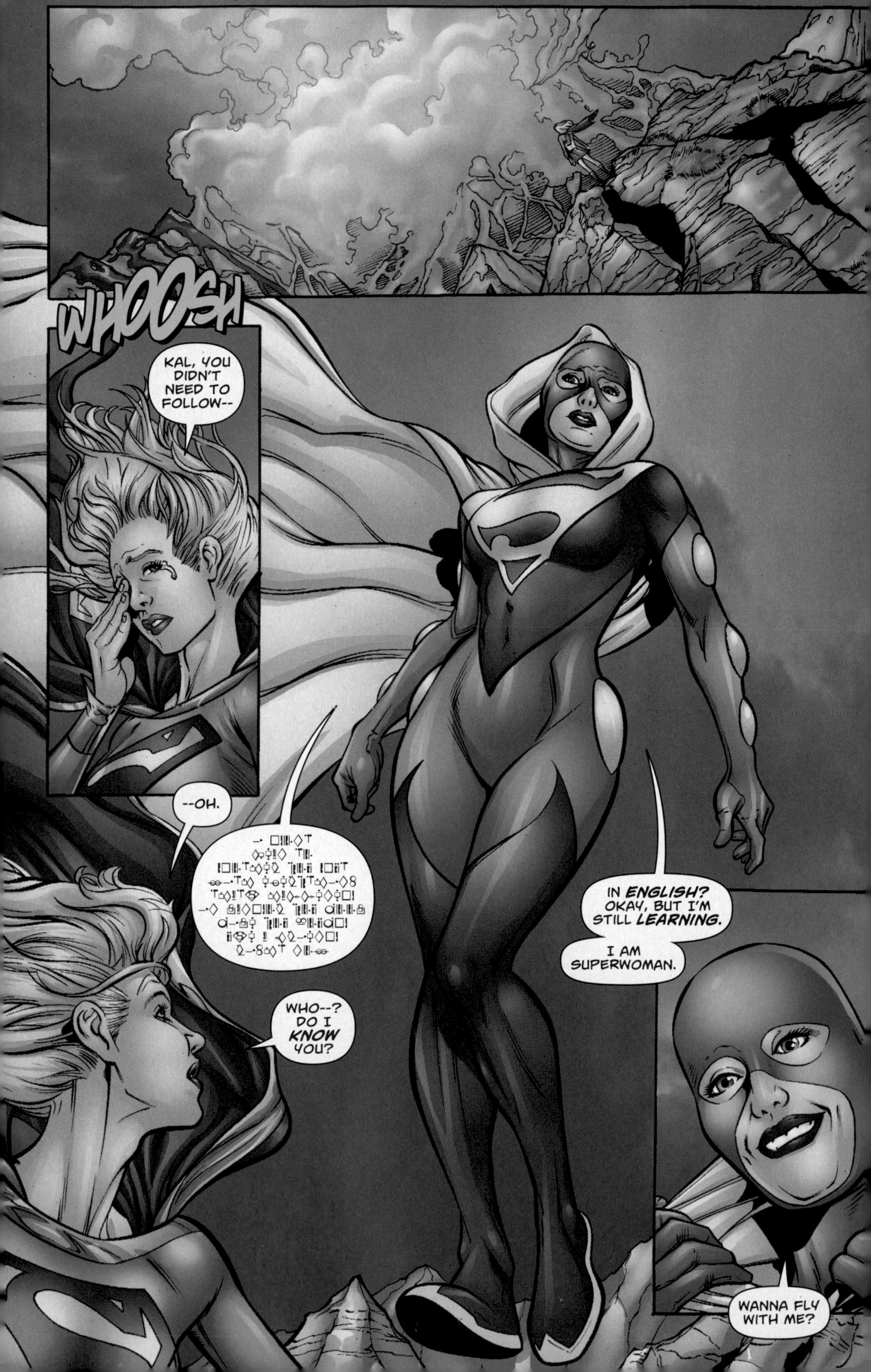
WHOOSH
KAL, YOU DIDN'T NEED TO FOLLOW--
--OH.
WHO--? DO I KNOW YOU?
IN ENGLISH? OKAY, BUT I'M STILL LEARNING.
I AM SUPERWOMAN.
WANNA FLY WITH ME?

...JUST CAN'T BELIEVE SHE THINKS IT'S *MY* FAULT.

I AM REALLY... WHAT'S THE WORD? 𝕾⊟⊡⊡⫶?

IT'S *"SORRY."*

I AM...*SORRY*, KARA. YOU DO KNOW YOUR MOTHER IS *WRONG*, THOUGH, RIGHT?

"SHE *CANNOT* BLAME YOU, OR *ANYONE* IN *KANDOR* FOR YOUR FATHER'S DEATH."

VH--!

UST LIKE SHE NEEDS TO REMEMBER SHE ESN'T *CONTROL* THE ANDORIAN PEOPLE."

"--WHAT WERE THEY GOING TO *DO* WITH THEM?"

S *BAD*. WHY ULD ALURA'S CURITY TEAM HAVE THE UEPRINTS TO THE *WHITE HOUSE?*

WHEN WE TOOK ON THESE IDENTITIES TO *STOP* ZOD'S FOLLOWERS, NIGHTWING--

RIGHT NOW, I THINK SHE'S HAVING TROUBLE CONTROLLING *HERSELF.*

--I DIDN'T THINK WE'D BE USING THEM TO FIGHT THE *GOOD* GUYS.

BUT WHAT I *REALLY* WANT TO KNOW IS--

I SAW HER AT YOUR FATHER'S *SERVICE*, KARA.

FWOOOSH

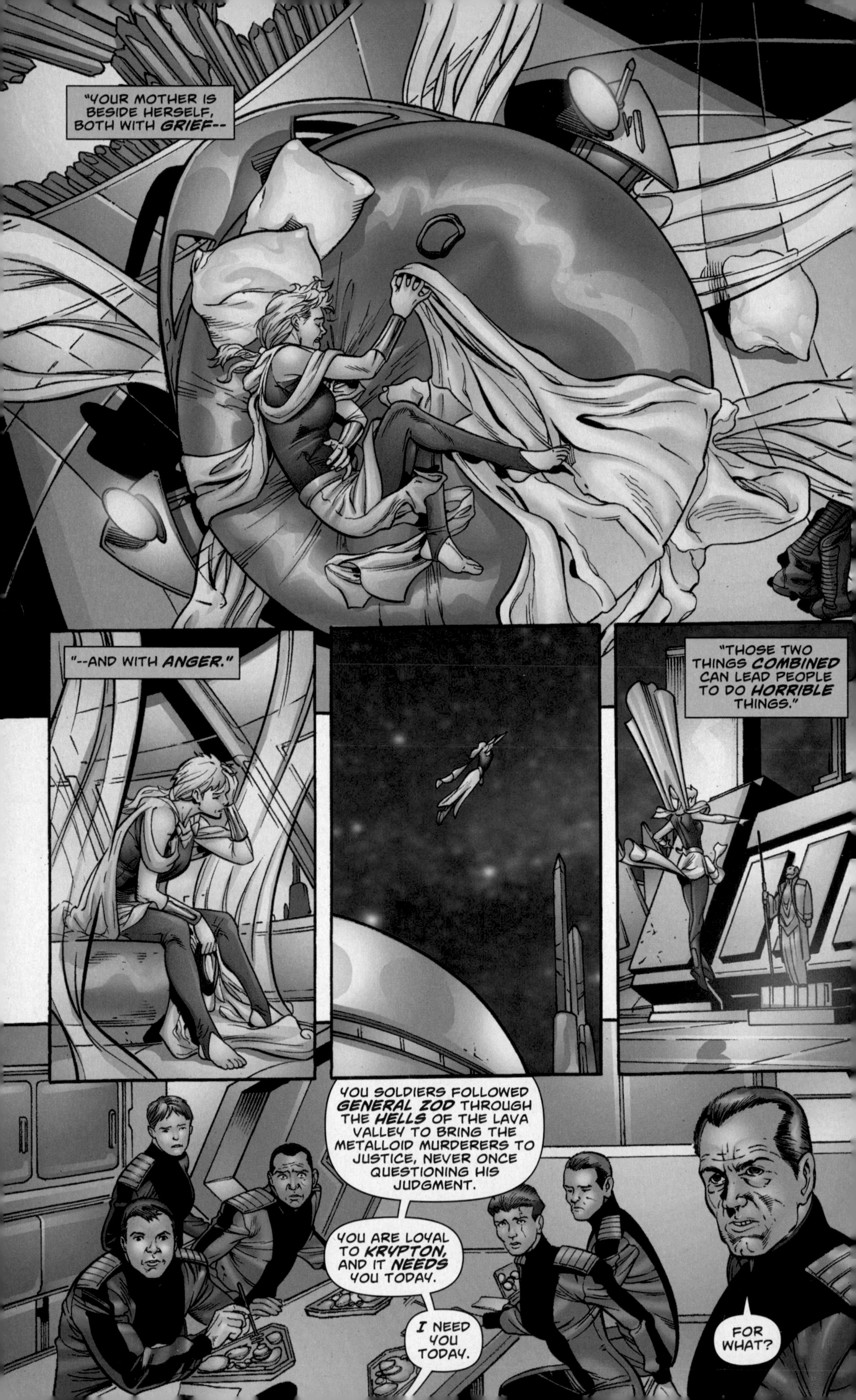
"YOUR MOTHER IS BESIDE HERSELF, BOTH WITH GRIEF--
"--AND WITH ANGER."
"THOSE TWO THINGS COMBINED CAN LEAD PEOPLE TO DO HORRIBLE THINGS."
YOU SOLDIERS FOLLOWED GENERAL ZOD THROUGH THE HELLS OF THE LAVA VALLEY TO BRING THE METALLOID MURDERERS TO JUSTICE, NEVER ONCE QUESTIONING HIS JUDGMENT.
YOU ARE LOYAL TO KRYPTON, AND IT NEEDS YOU TODAY.
I NEED YOU TODAY.
FOR WHAT?

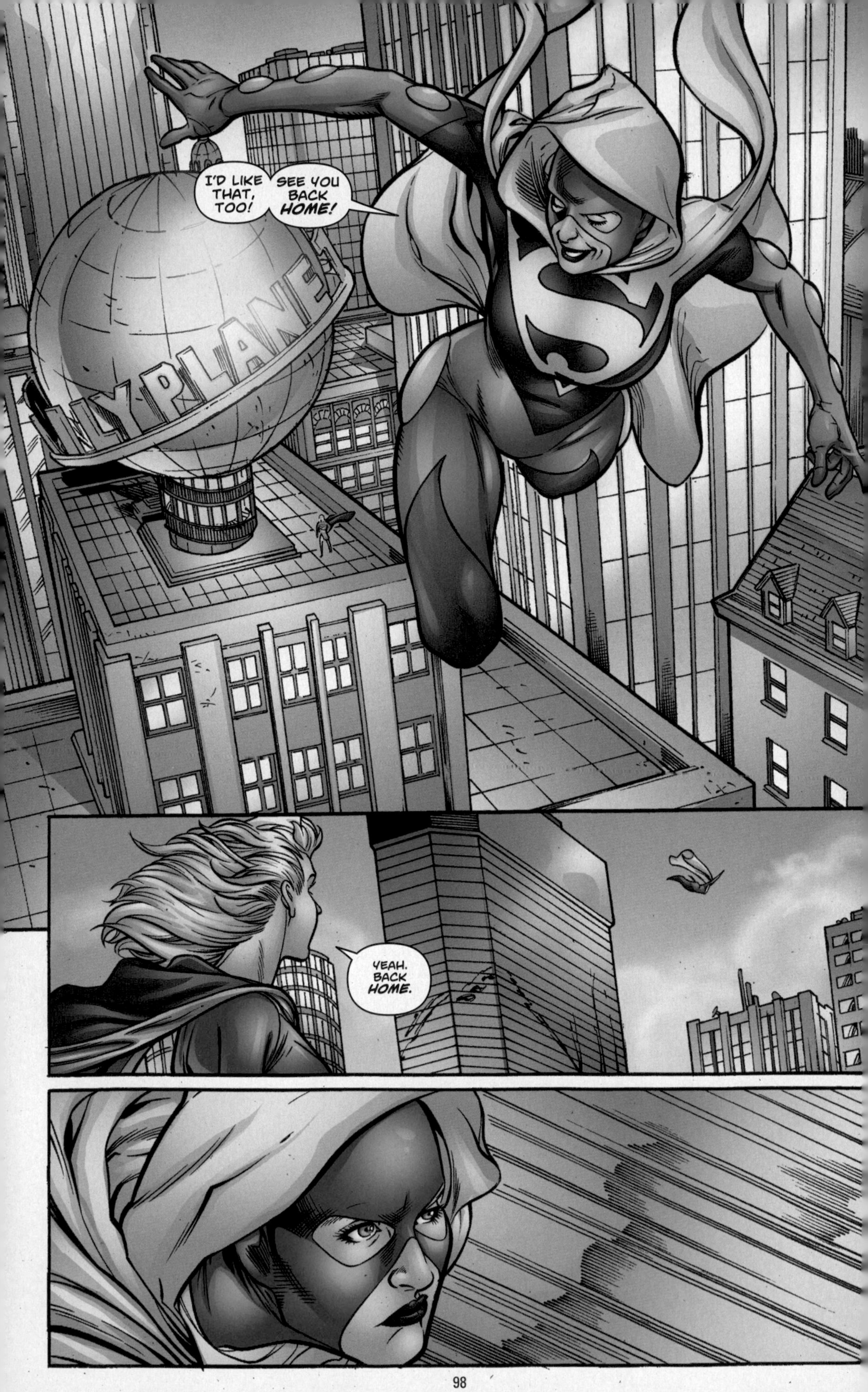
I'D LIKE THAT, TOO!
SEE YOU BACK HOME!
YEAH. BACK HOME.

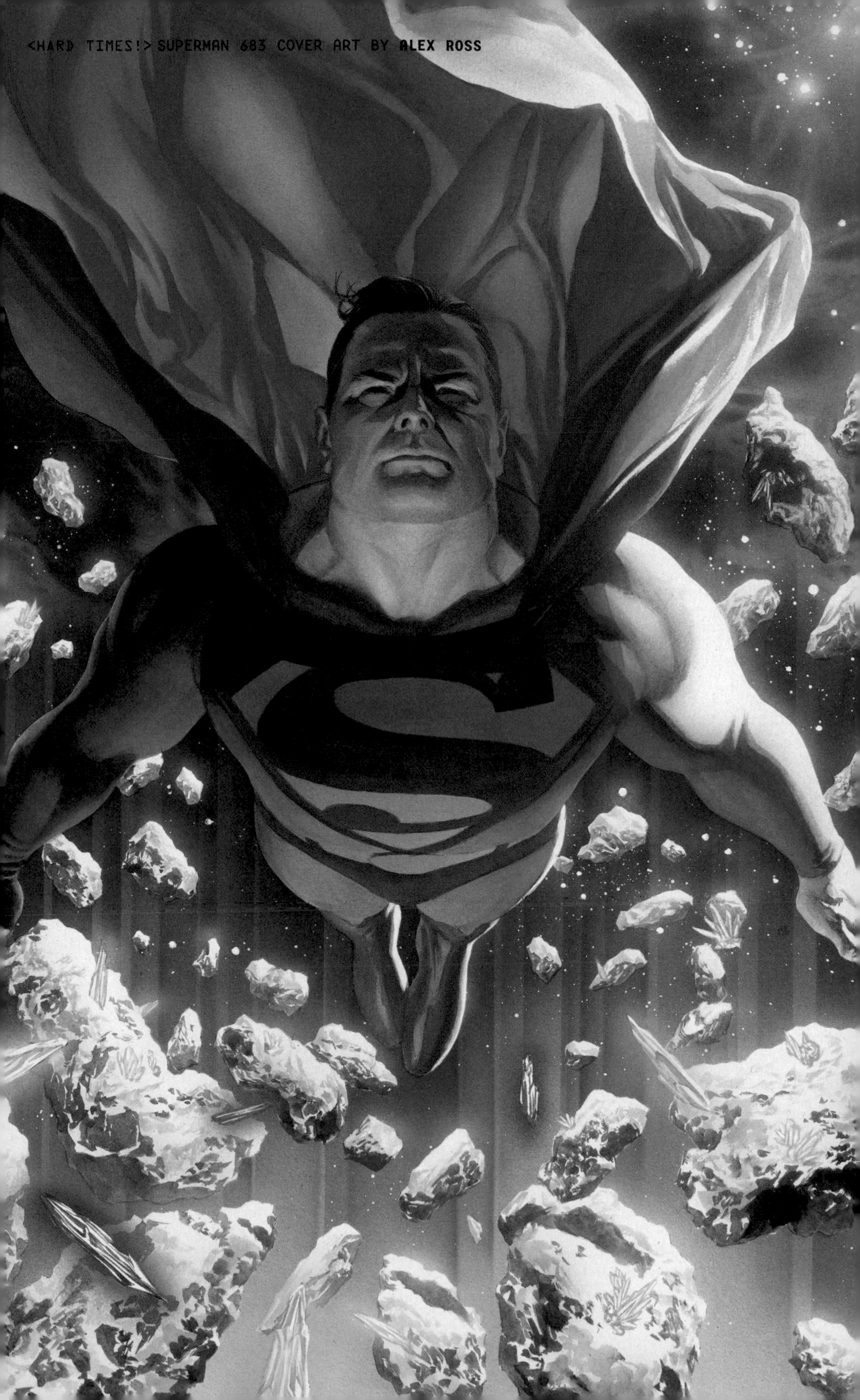

<HARD TIMES!> SUPERMAN 683 COVER ART BY ALEX ROSS

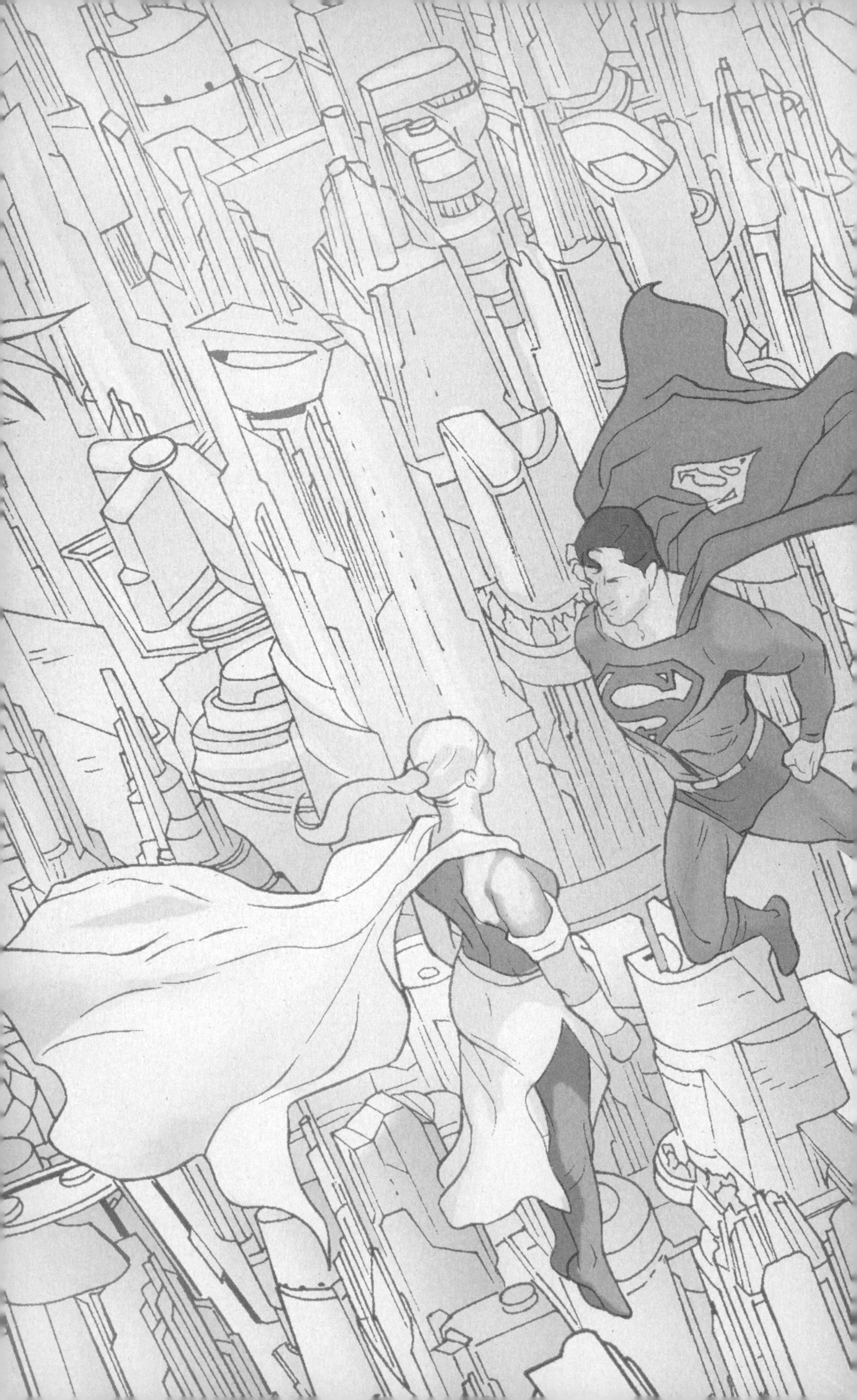

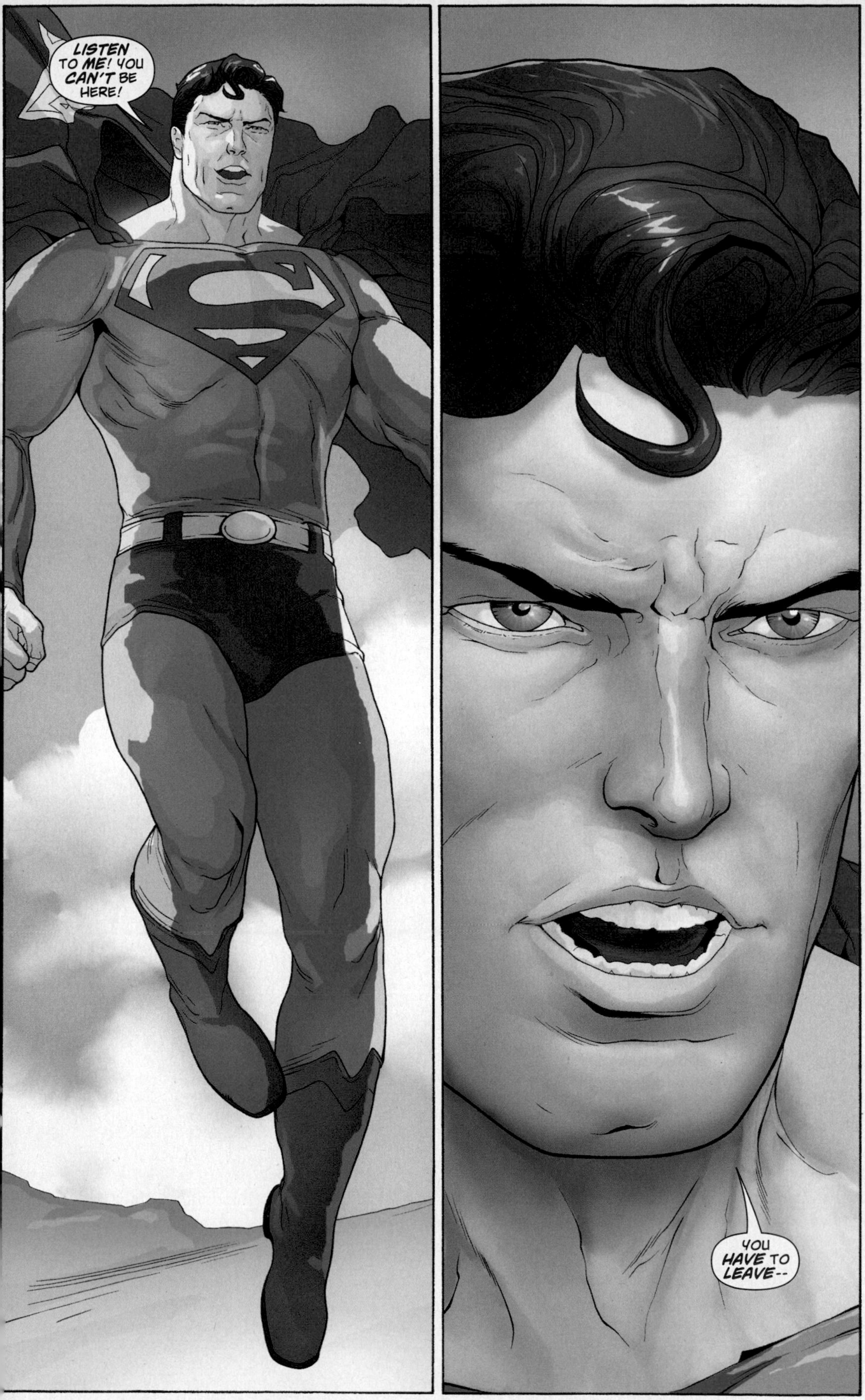
LISTEN TO ME! YOU CAN'T BE HERE!
YOU HAVE TO LEAVE--

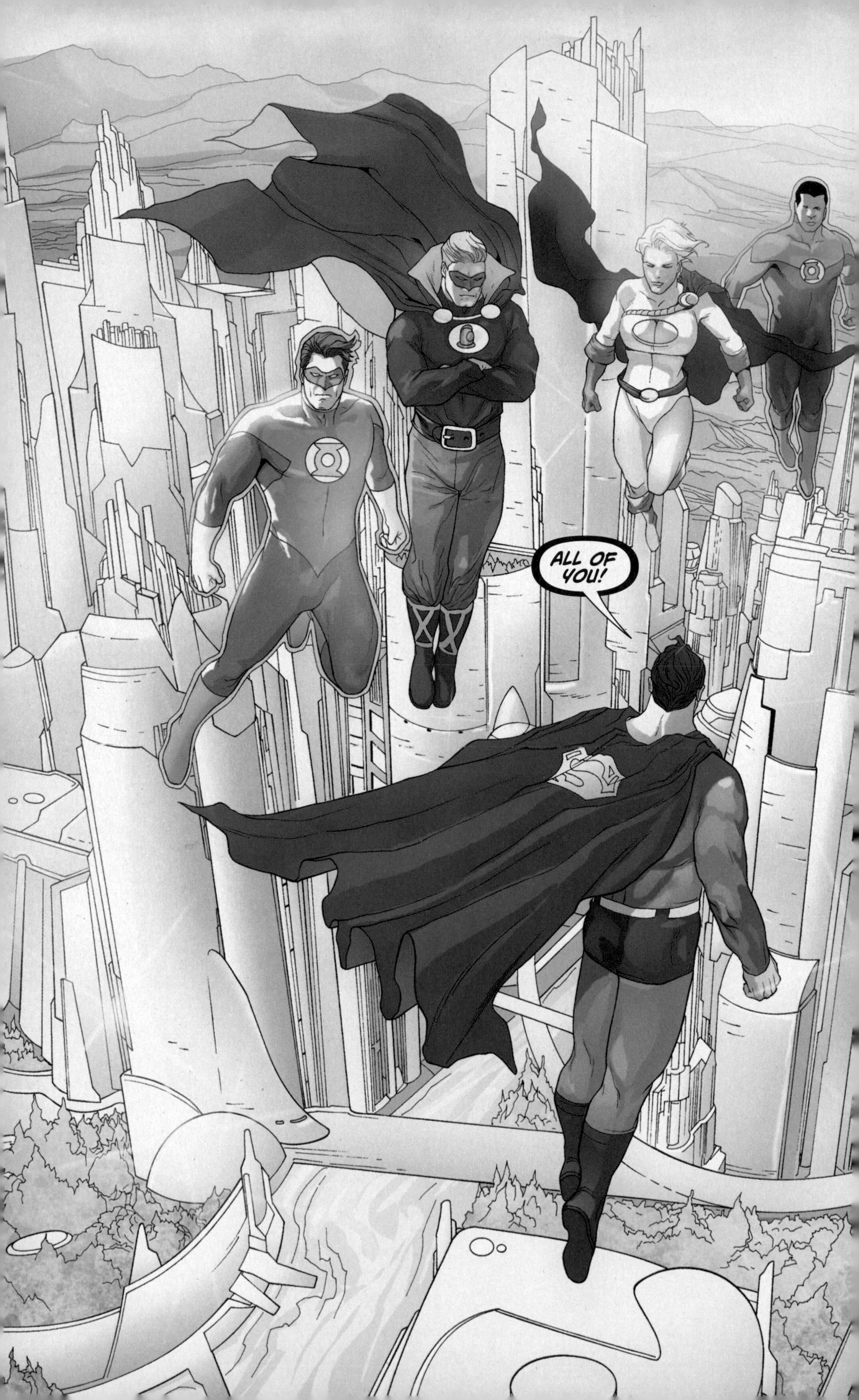
ALL OF YOU!

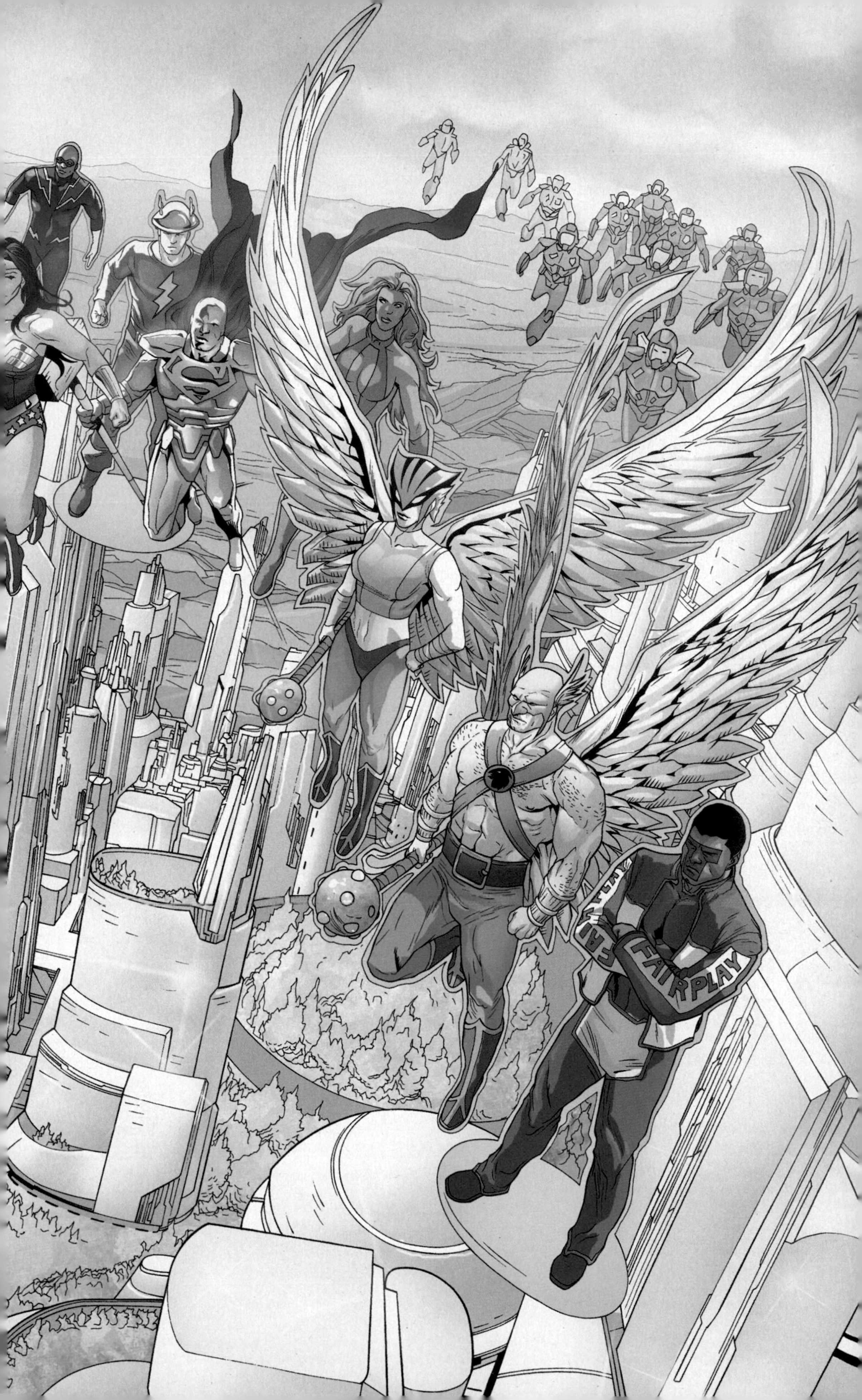
FAIRPLAY

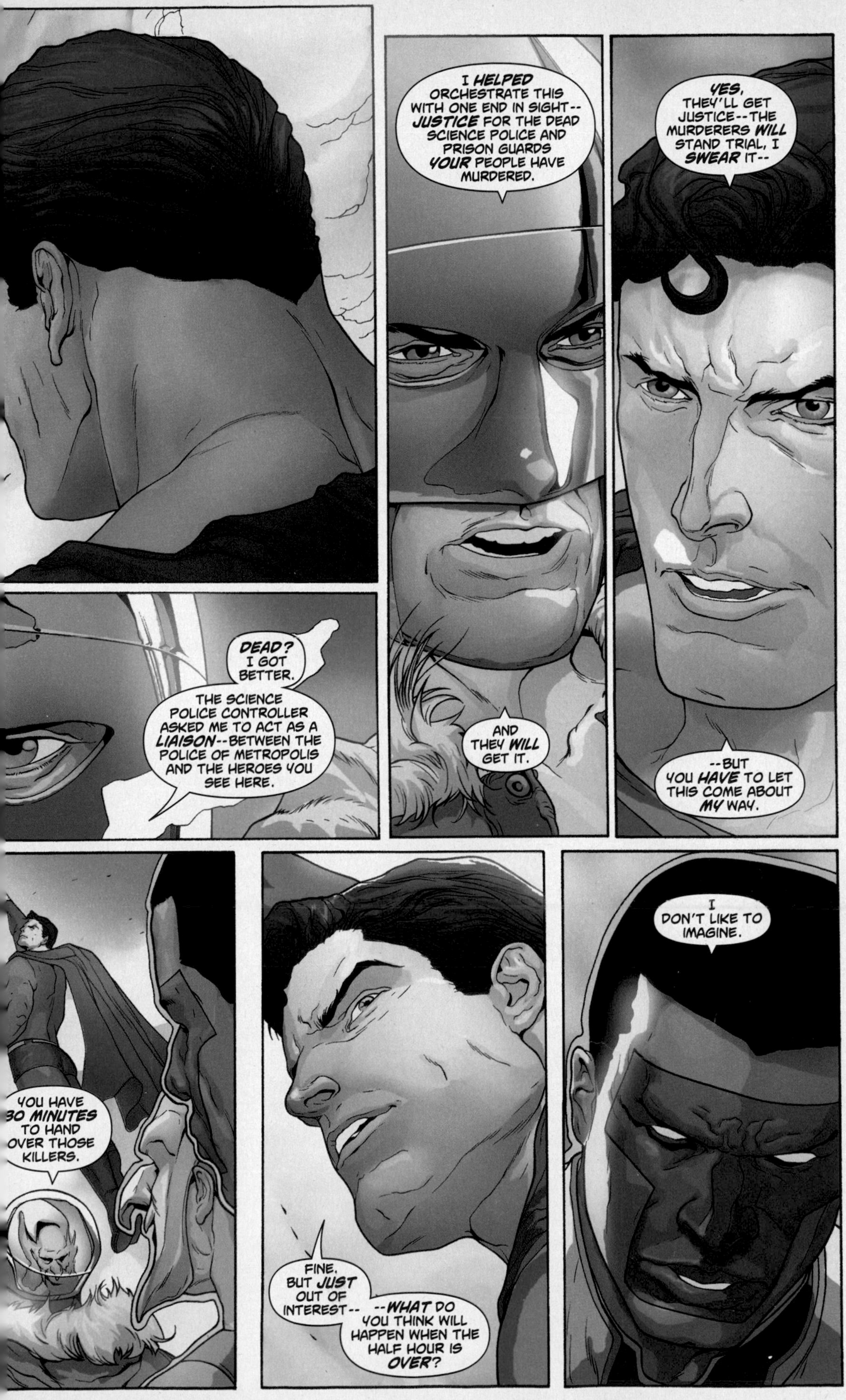
I HELPED ORCHESTRATE THIS WITH ONE END IN SIGHT-- JUSTICE FOR THE DEAD SCIENCE POLICE AND PRISON GUARDS YOUR PEOPLE HAVE MURDERED.
YES, THEY'LL GET JUSTICE--THE MURDERERS WILL STAND TRIAL, I SWEAR IT--
DEAD? I GOT BETTER.
THE SCIENCE POLICE CONTROLLER ASKED ME TO ACT AS A LIAISON--BETWEEN THE POLICE OF METROPOLIS AND THE HEROES YOU SEE HERE.
AND THEY WILL GET IT.
--BUT YOU HAVE TO LET THIS COME ABOUT MY WAY.
YOU HAVE 30 MINUTES TO HAND OVER THOSE KILLERS.
FINE. BUT JUST OUT OF INTEREST--
--WHAT DO YOU THINK WILL HAPPEN WHEN THE HALF HOUR IS OVER?
I DON'T LIKE TO IMAGINE.

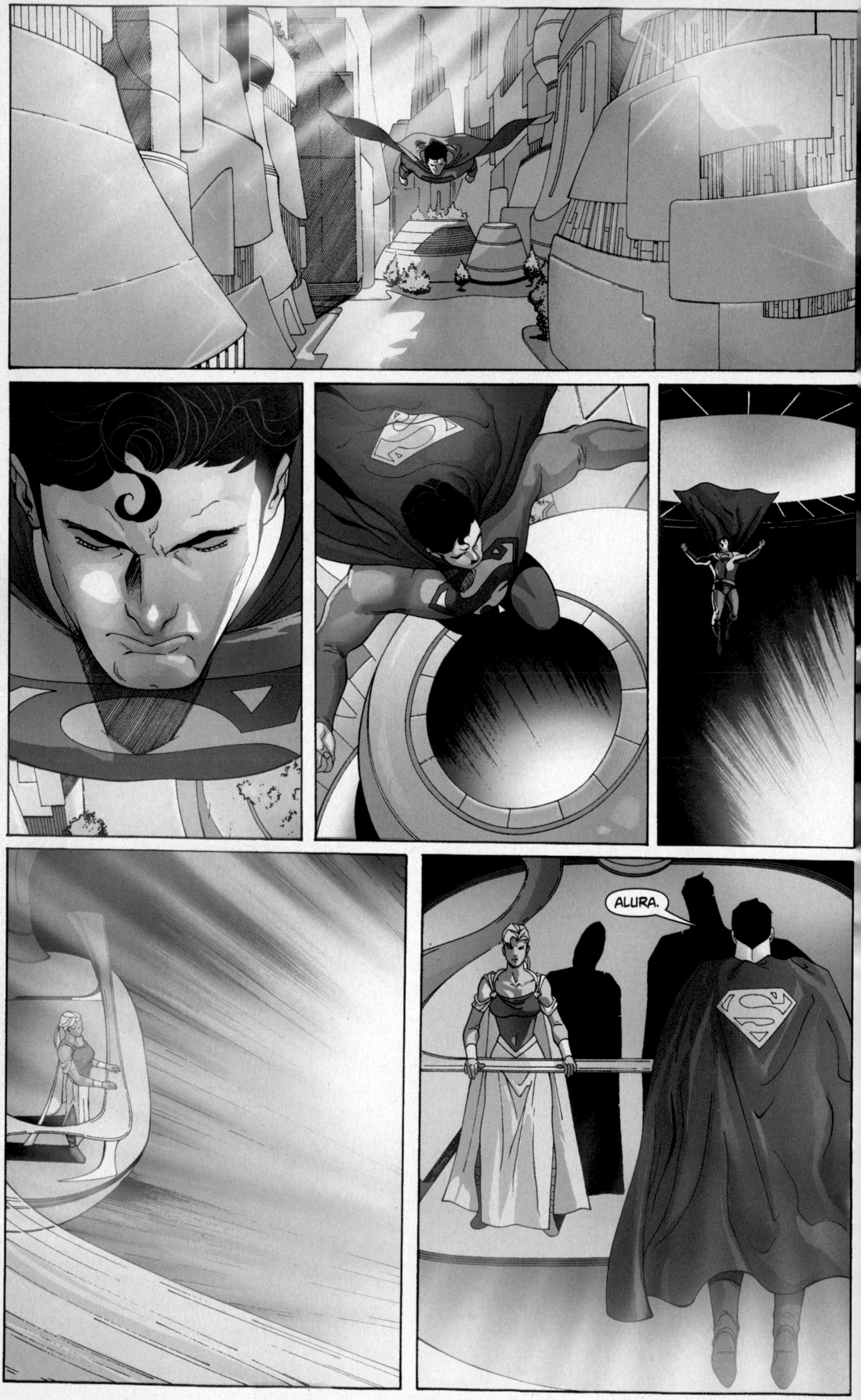
ALURA.

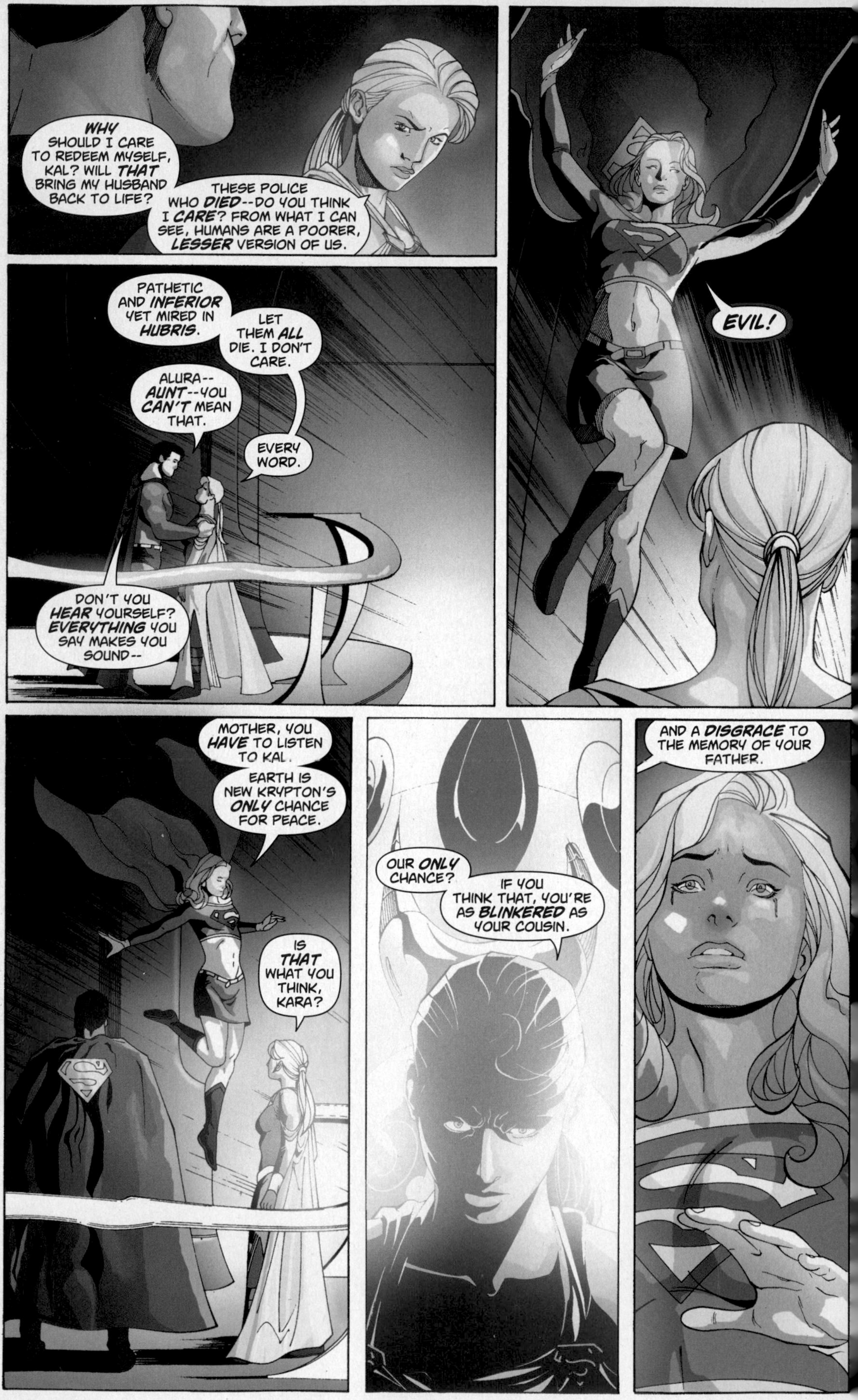
WHY SHOULD I CARE TO REDEEM MYSELF, KAL? WILL THAT BRING MY HUSBAND BACK TO LIFE?
THESE POLICE WHO DIED--DO YOU THINK I CARE? FROM WHAT I CAN SEE, HUMANS ARE A POORER, LESSER VERSION OF US.
PATHETIC AND INFERIOR YET MIRED IN HUBRIS.
LET THEM ALL DIE. I DON'T CARE.
ALURA-- AUNT--YOU CAN'T MEAN THAT.
EVERY WORD.
DON'T YOU HEAR YOURSELF? EVERYTHING YOU SAY MAKES YOU SOUND--
EVIL!
MOTHER, YOU HAVE TO LISTEN TO KAL.
EARTH IS NEW KRYPTON'S ONLY CHANCE FOR PEACE.
IS THAT WHAT YOU THINK, KARA?
OUR ONLY CHANCE?
IF YOU THINK THAT, YOU'RE AS BLINKERED AS YOUR COUSIN.
AND A DISGRACE TO THE MEMORY OF YOUR FATHER.

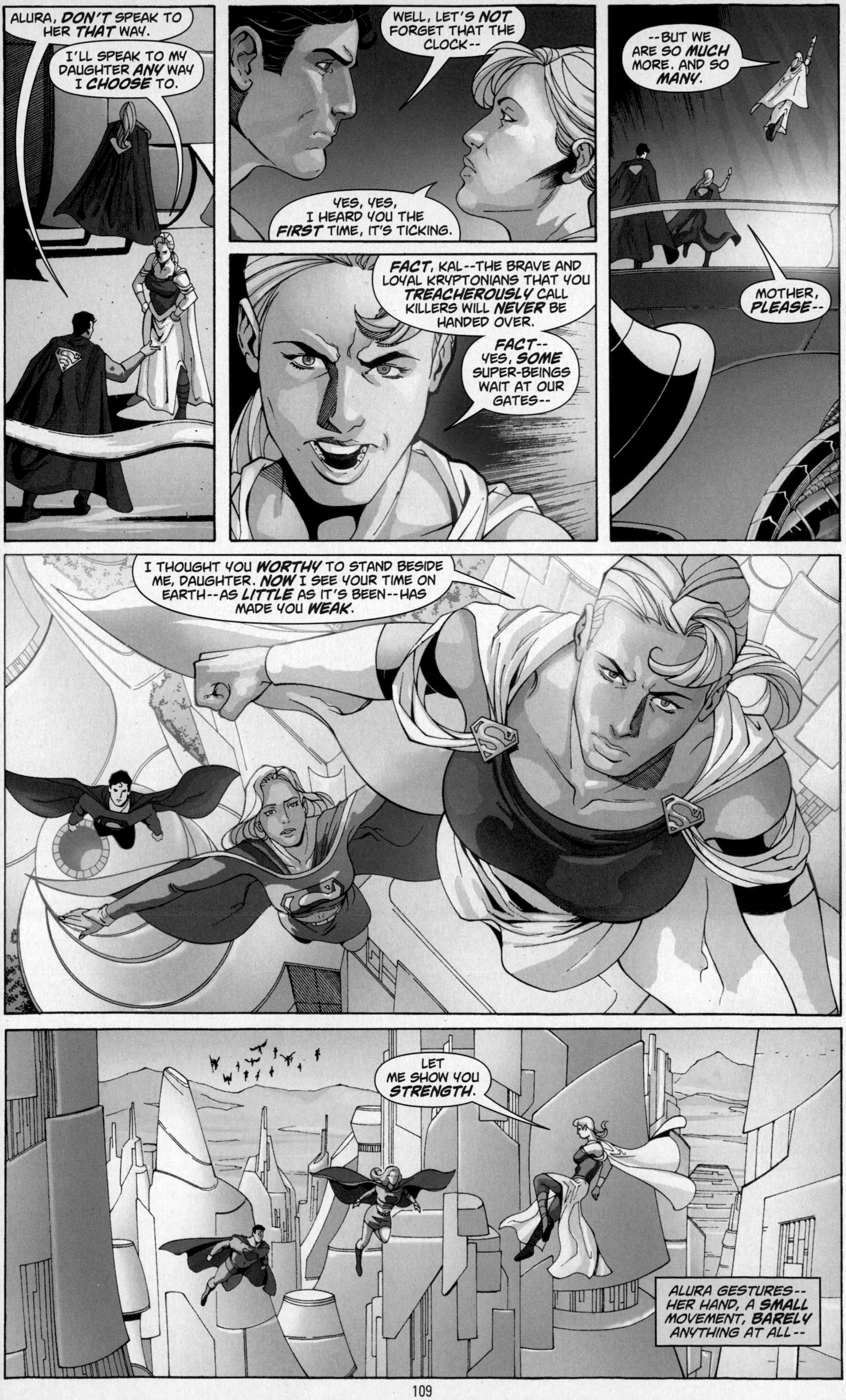
ALURA, DON'T SPEAK TO HER THAT WAY.
I'LL SPEAK TO MY DAUGHTER ANY WAY I CHOOSE TO.
WELL, LET'S NOT FORGET THAT THE CLOCK--
YES, YES, I HEARD YOU THE FIRST TIME, IT'S TICKING.
FACT, KAL--THE BRAVE AND LOYAL KRYPTONIANS THAT YOU TREACHEROUSLY CALL KILLERS WILL NEVER BE HANDED OVER.
FACT-- YES, SOME SUPER-BEINGS WAIT AT OUR GATES--
--BUT WE ARE SO MUCH MORE. AND SO MANY.
MOTHER, PLEASE--
I THOUGHT YOU WORTHY TO STAND BESIDE ME, DAUGHTER. NOW I SEE YOUR TIME ON EARTH--AS LITTLE AS IT'S BEEN--HAS MADE YOU WEAK.
LET ME SHOW YOU STRENGTH.
ALURA GESTURES-- HER HAND, A SMALL MOVEMENT, BARELY ANYTHING AT ALL--

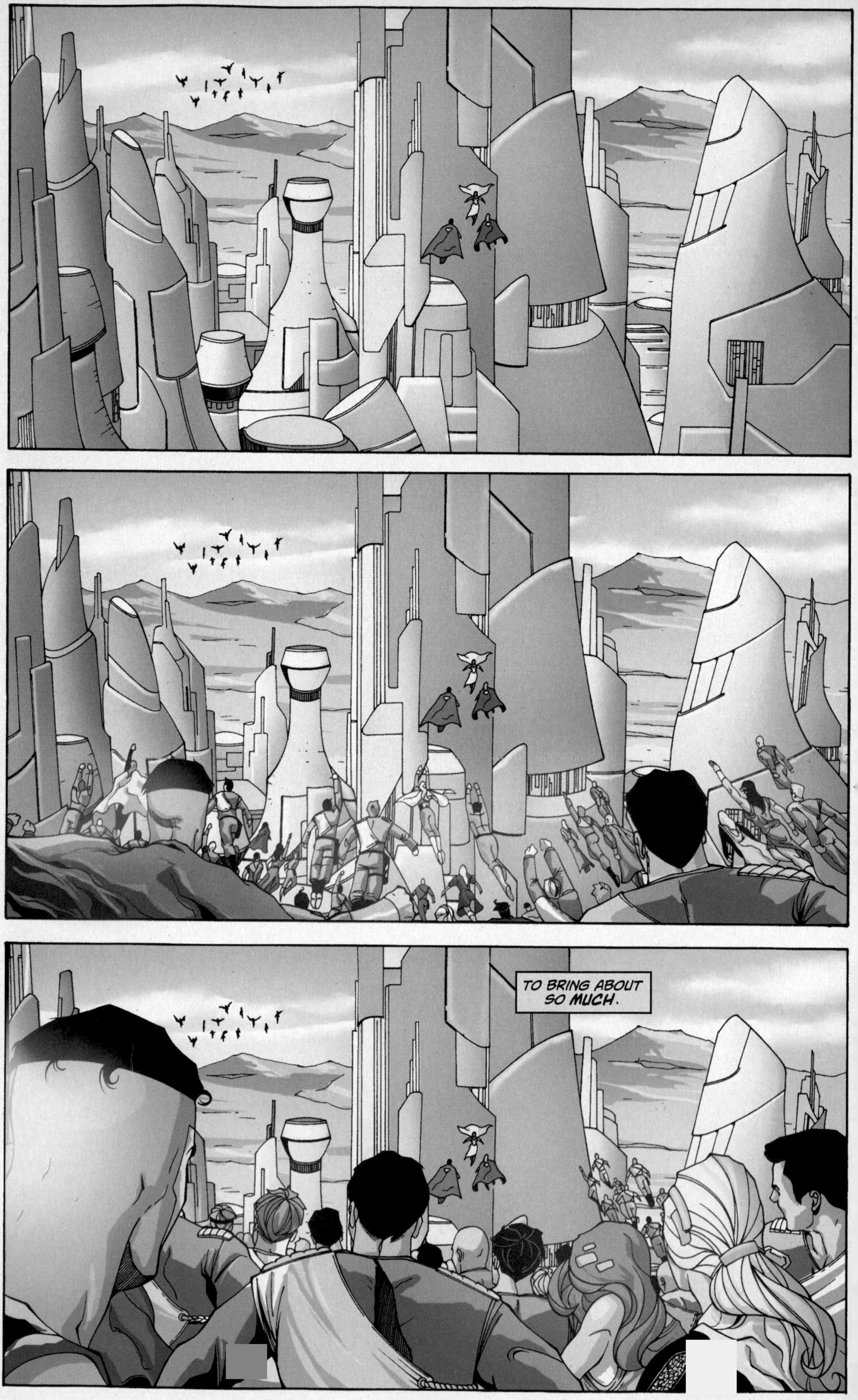
TO BRING ABOUT SO MUCH.

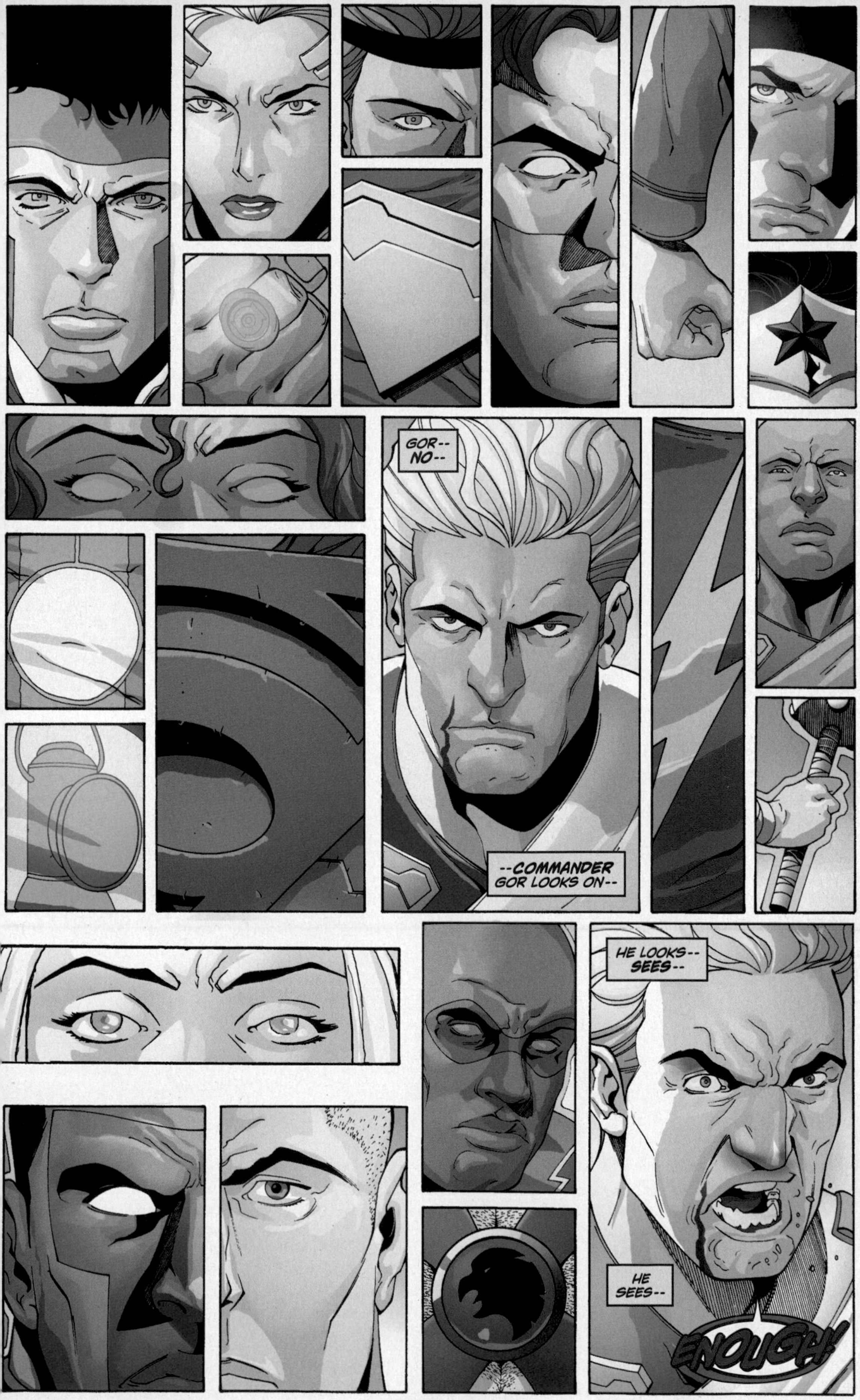
GOR--
NO--
--COMMANDER
GOR LOOKS ON--
HE LOOKS--
SEES--
HE
SEES--
ENOUGH!

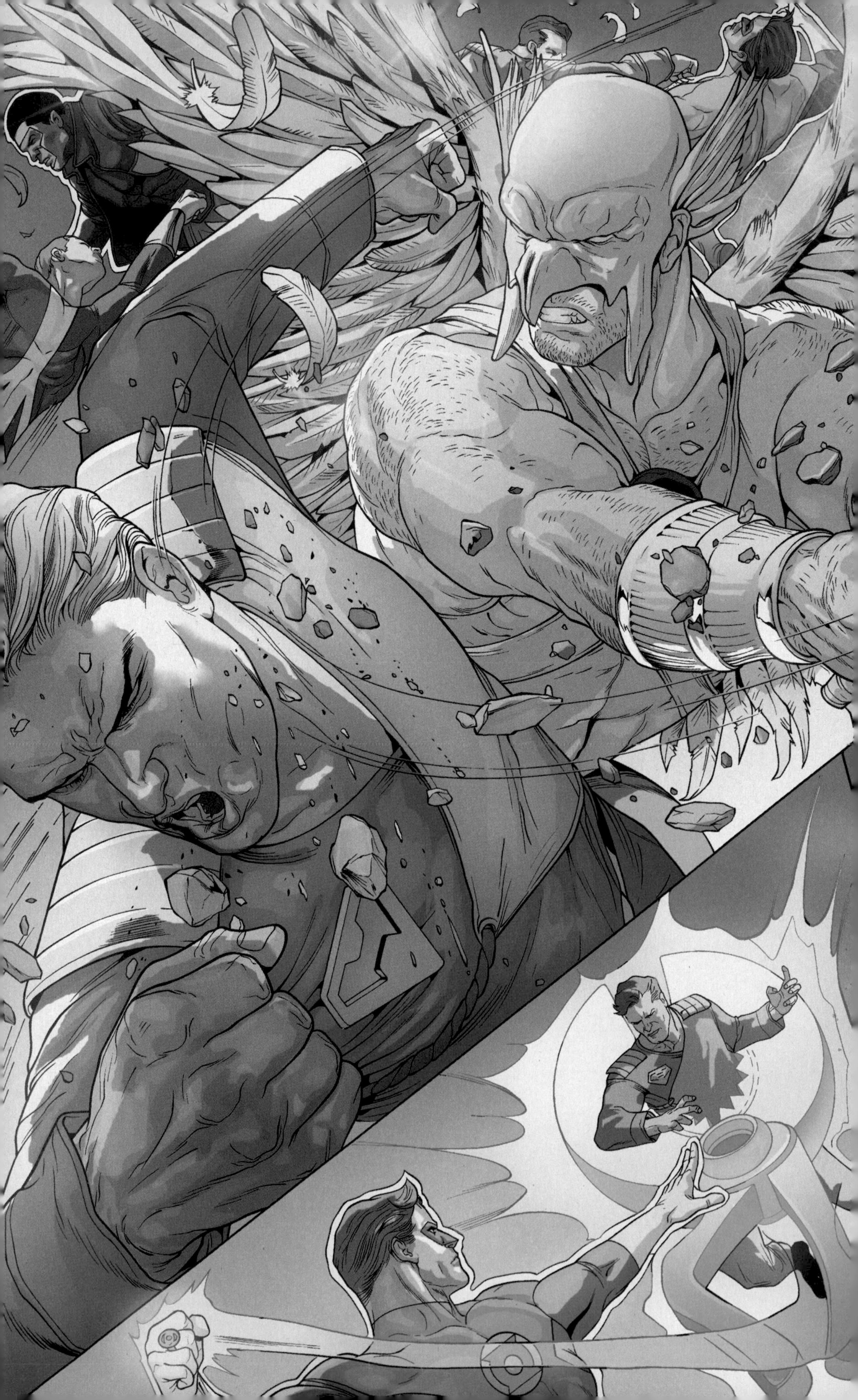

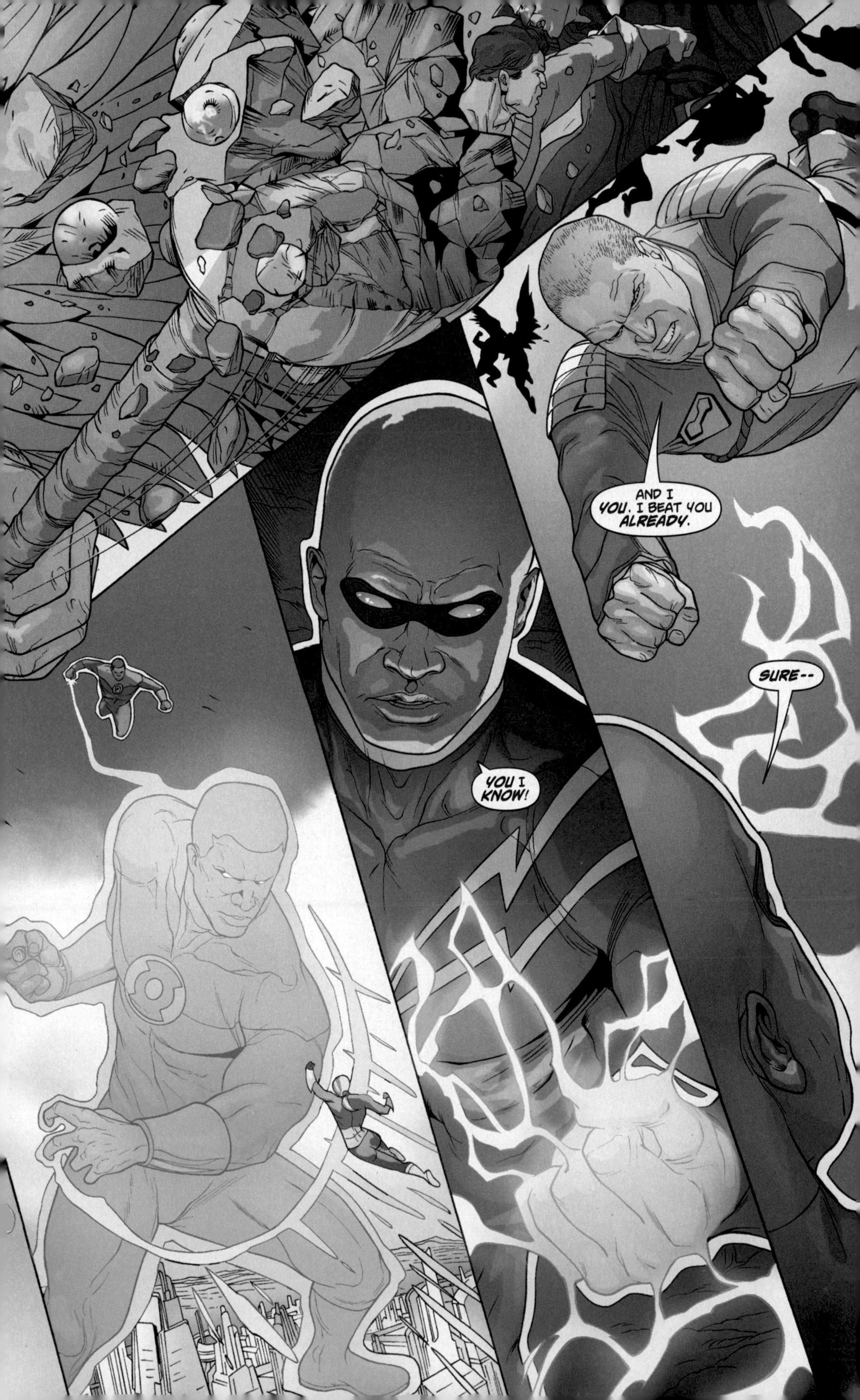
AND I
YOU. I BEAT YOU
ALREADY.
YOU I
KNOW!
SURE--

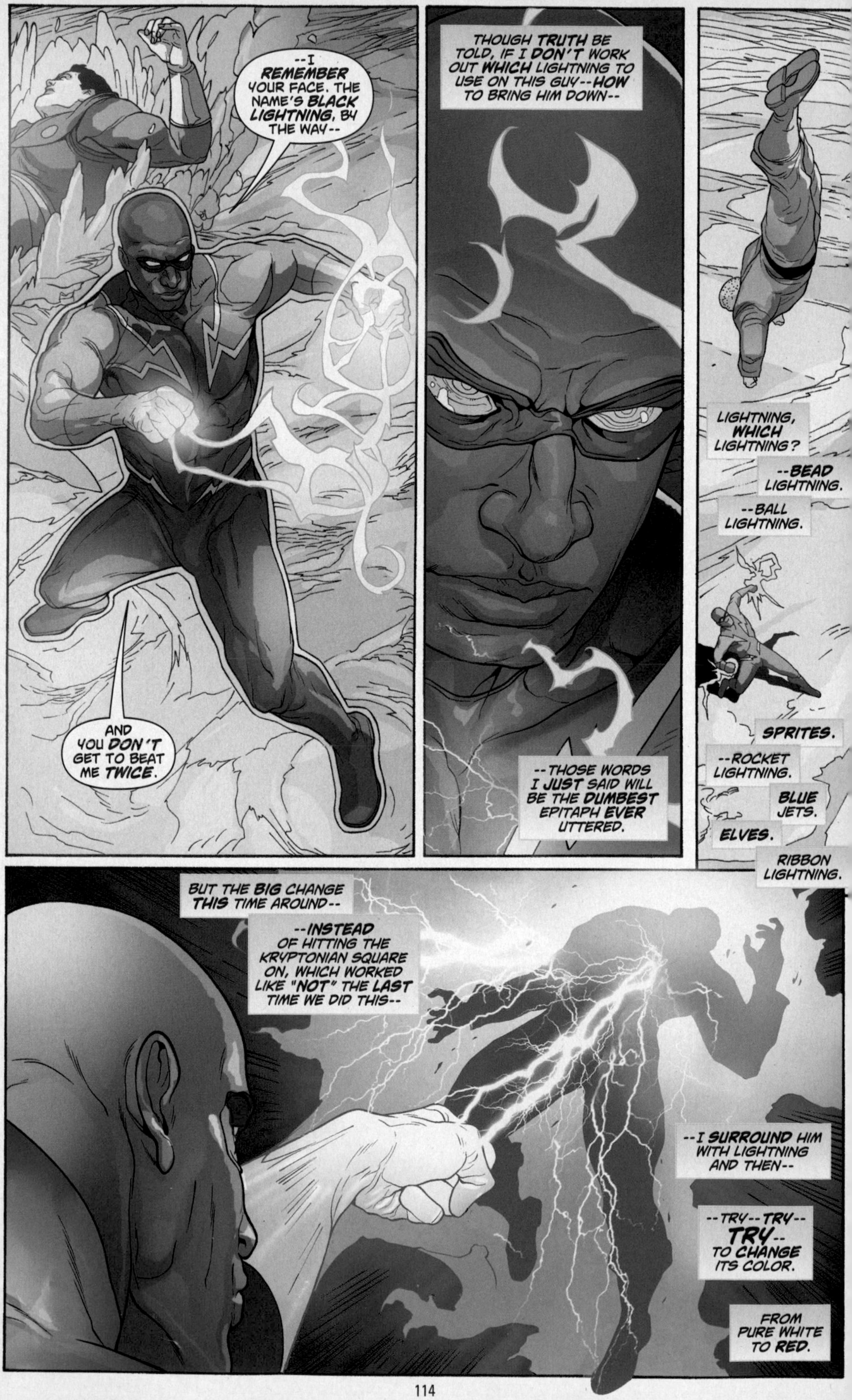
--I REMEMBER YOUR FACE. THE NAME'S BLACK LIGHTNING, BY THE WAY--
AND YOU DON'T GET TO BEAT ME TWICE.
THOUGH TRUTH BE TOLD, IF I DON'T WORK OUT WHICH LIGHTNING TO USE ON THIS GUY--HOW TO BRING HIM DOWN--
--THOSE WORDS I JUST SAID WILL BE THE DUMBEST EPITAPH EVER UTTERED.
LIGHTNING, WHICH LIGHTNING?
--BEAD LIGHTNING.
--BALL LIGHTNING.
SPRITES.
--ROCKET LIGHTNING.
BLUE JETS.
ELVES.
RIBBON LIGHTNING.
BUT THE BIG CHANGE THIS TIME AROUND--
--INSTEAD OF HITTING THE KRYPTONIAN SQUARE ON, WHICH WORKED LIKE "NOT" THE LAST TIME WE DID THIS--
--I SURROUND HIM WITH LIGHTNING AND THEN--
--TRY--TRY--TRY--TO CHANGE ITS COLOR.
FROM PURE WHITE TO RED.

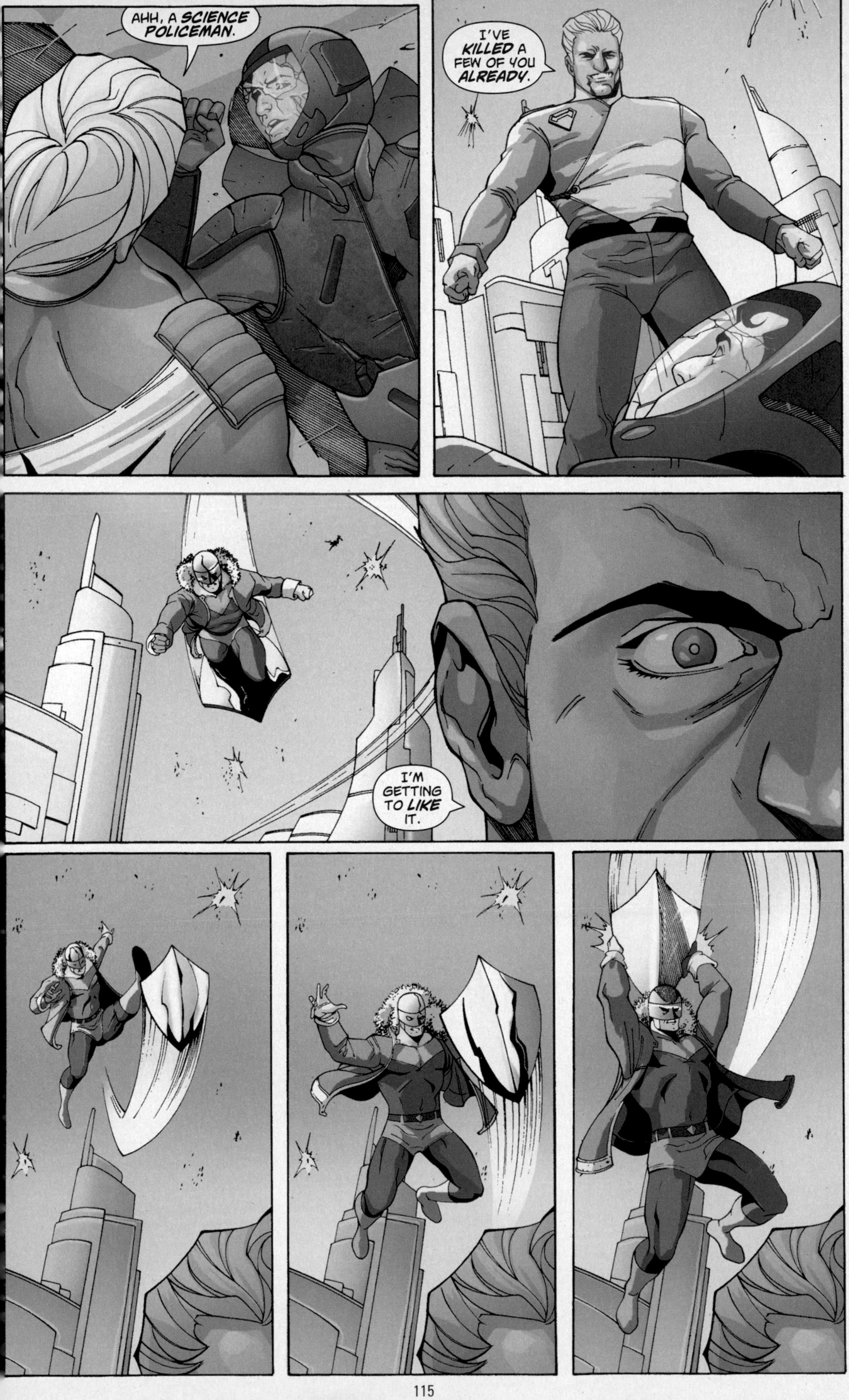
AHH, A SCIENCE POLICEMAN.
I'VE KILLED A FEW OF YOU ALREADY.
I'M GETTING TO LIKE IT.

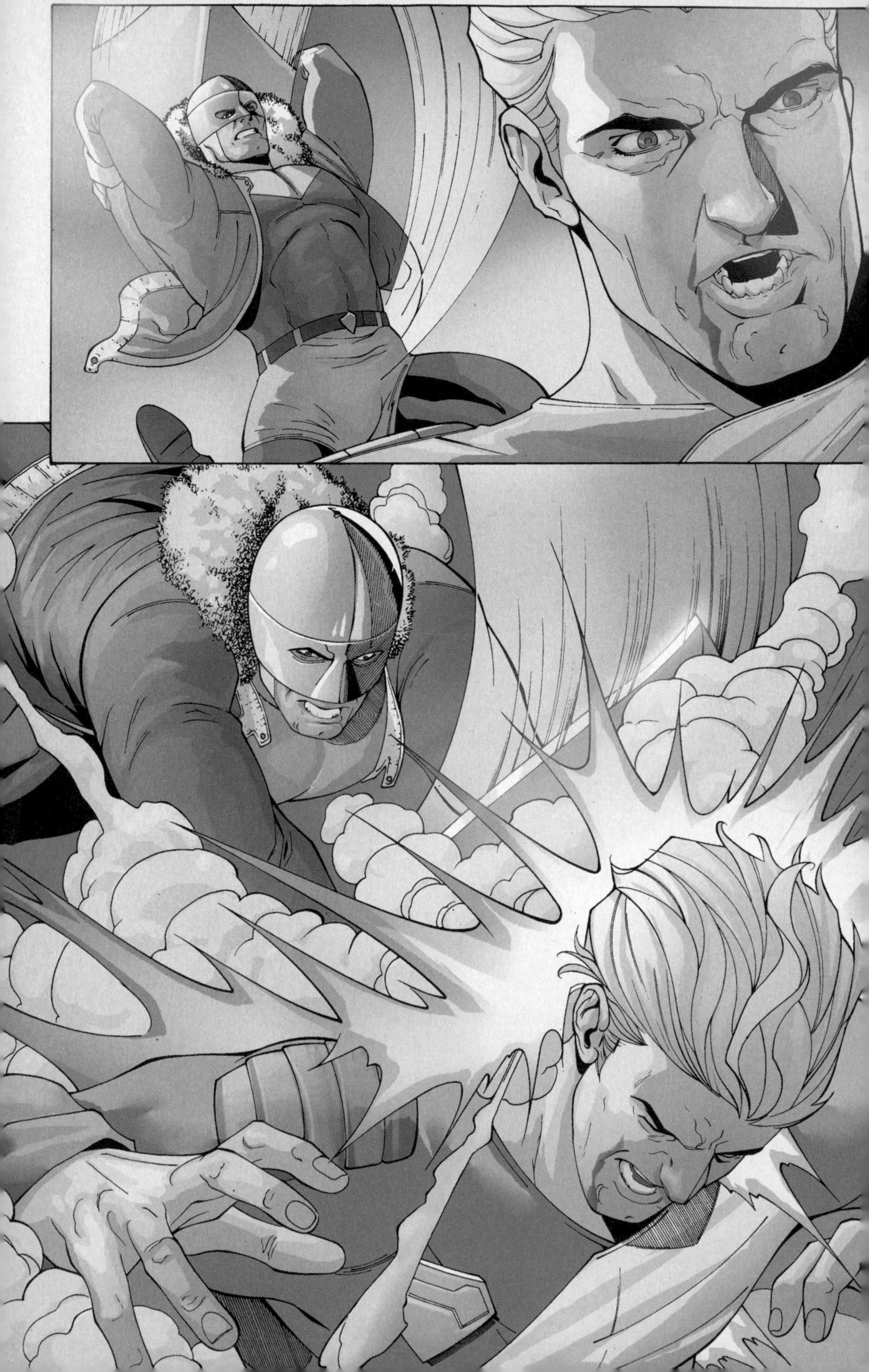

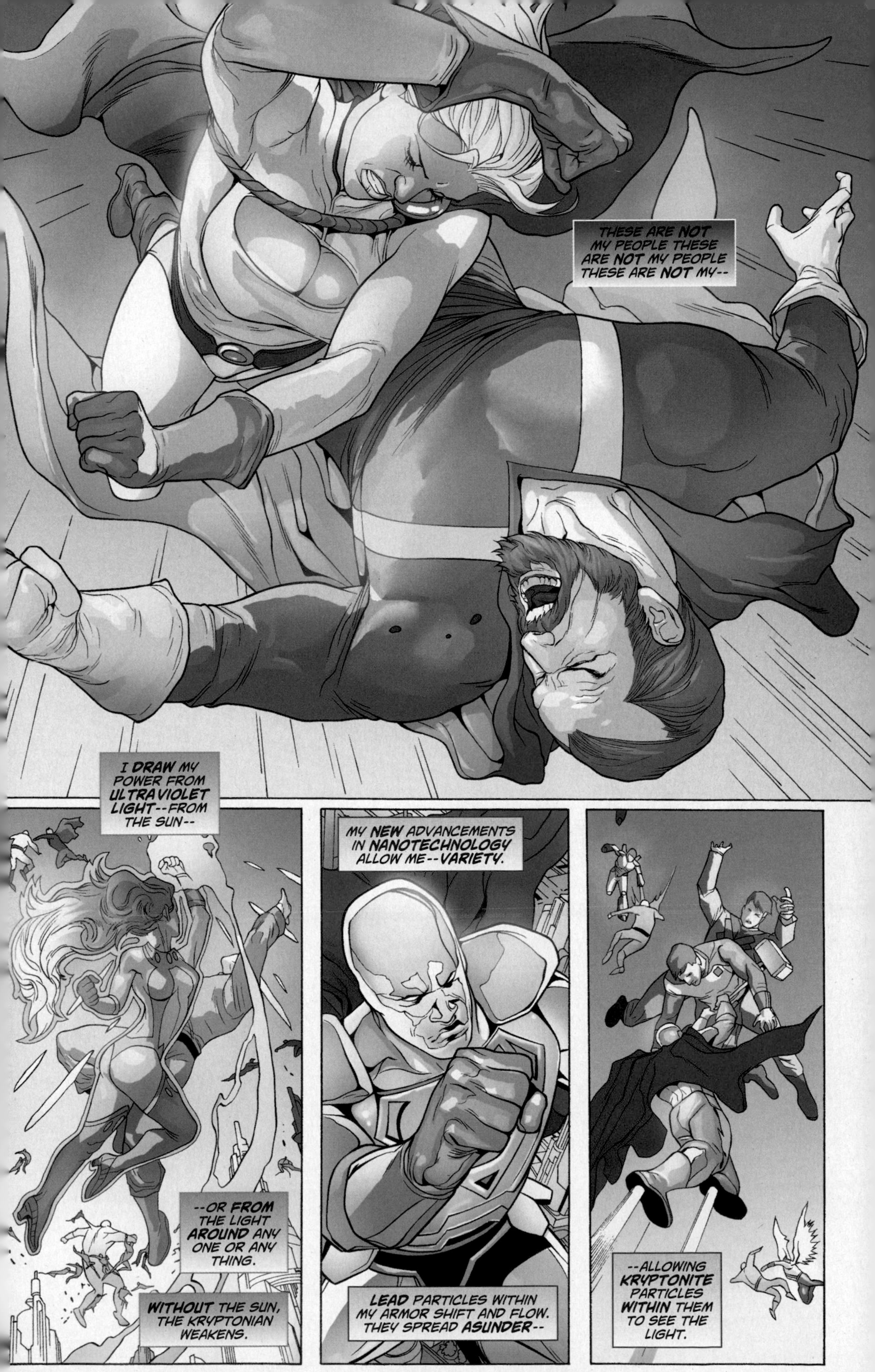
THESE ARE NOT MY PEOPLE THESE ARE NOT MY PEOPLE THESE ARE NOT MY--
I DRAW MY POWER FROM ULTRAVIOLET LIGHT--FROM THE SUN--
--OR FROM THE LIGHT AROUND ANY ONE OR ANY THING.
WITHOUT THE SUN, THE KRYPTONIAN WEAKENS.
MY NEW ADVANCEMENTS IN NANOTECHNOLOGY ALLOW ME--VARIETY.
LEAD PARTICLES WITHIN MY ARMOR SHIFT AND FLOW. THEY SPREAD ASUNDER--
--ALLOWING KRYPTONITE PARTICLES WITHIN THEM TO SEE THE LIGHT.

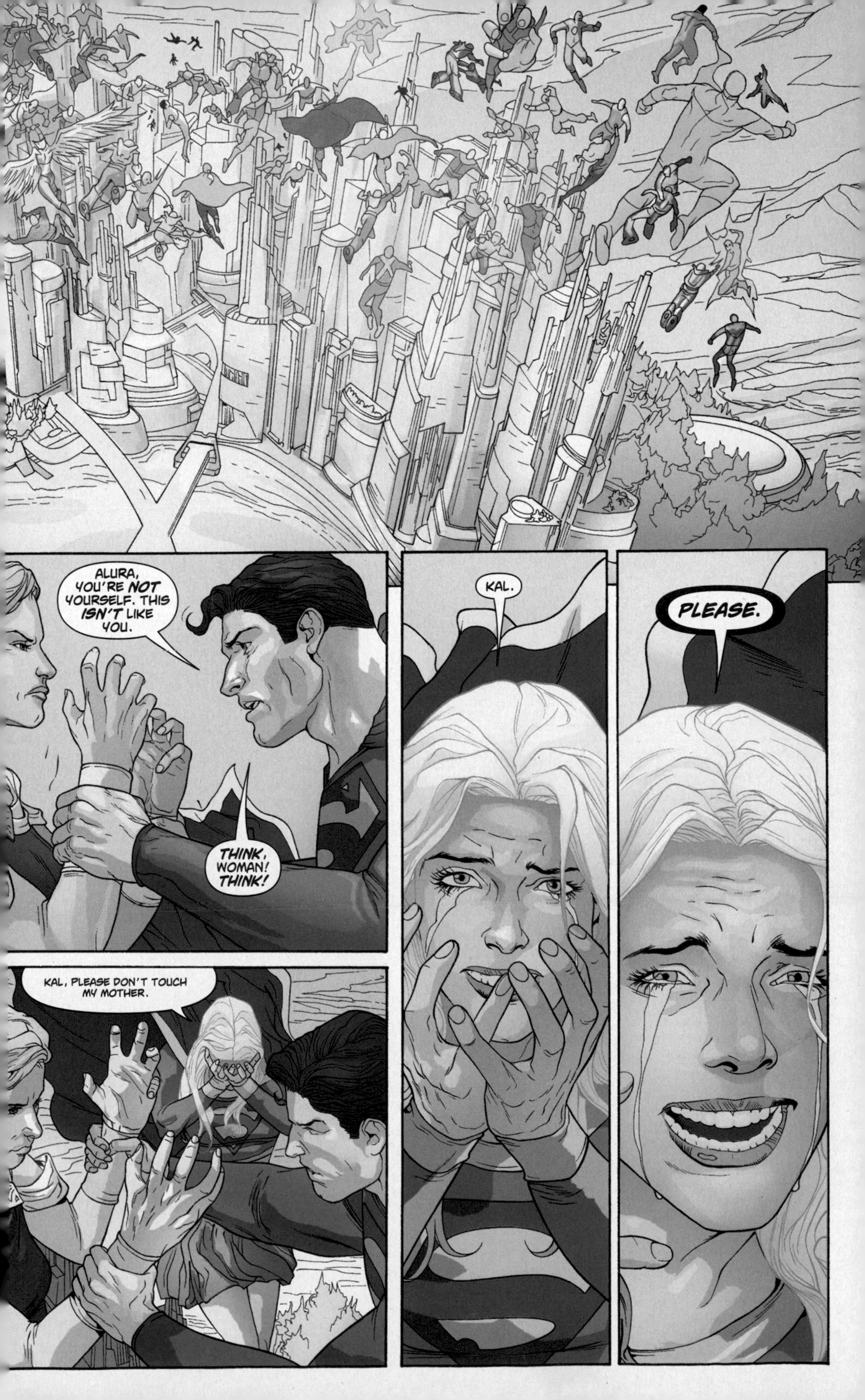
ALURA, YOU'RE NOT YOURSELF. THIS ISN'T LIKE YOU.
THINK, WOMAN! THINK!
KAL, PLEASE DON'T TOUCH MY MOTHER.
KAL.
PLEASE.

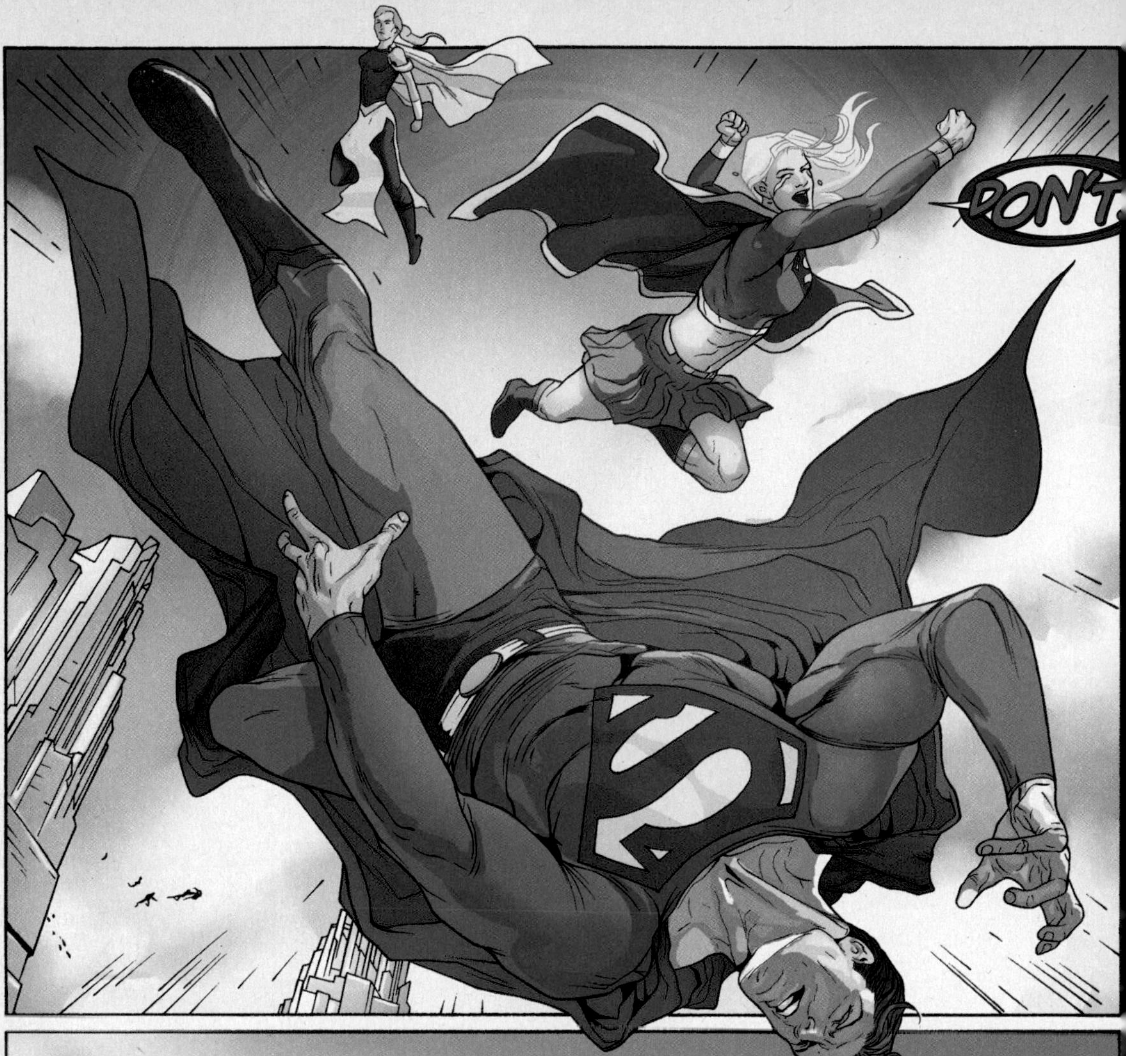
DON'T

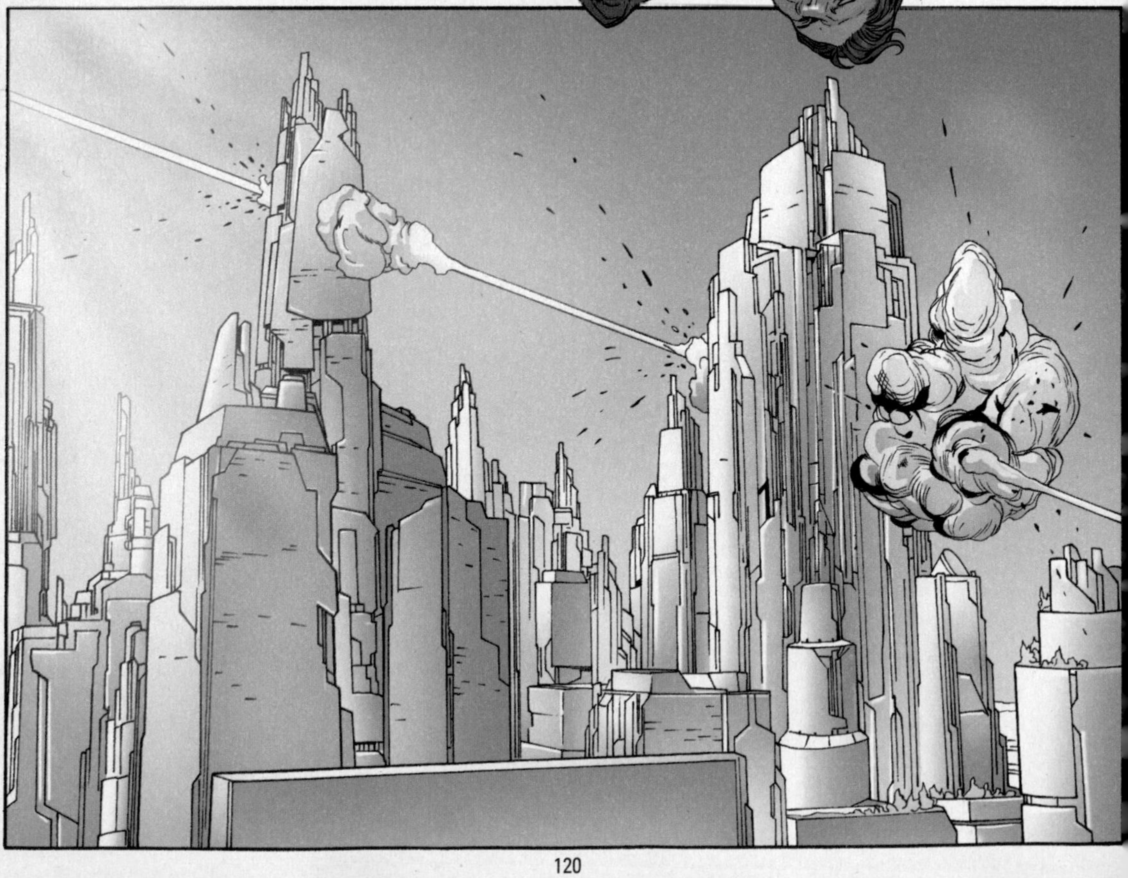

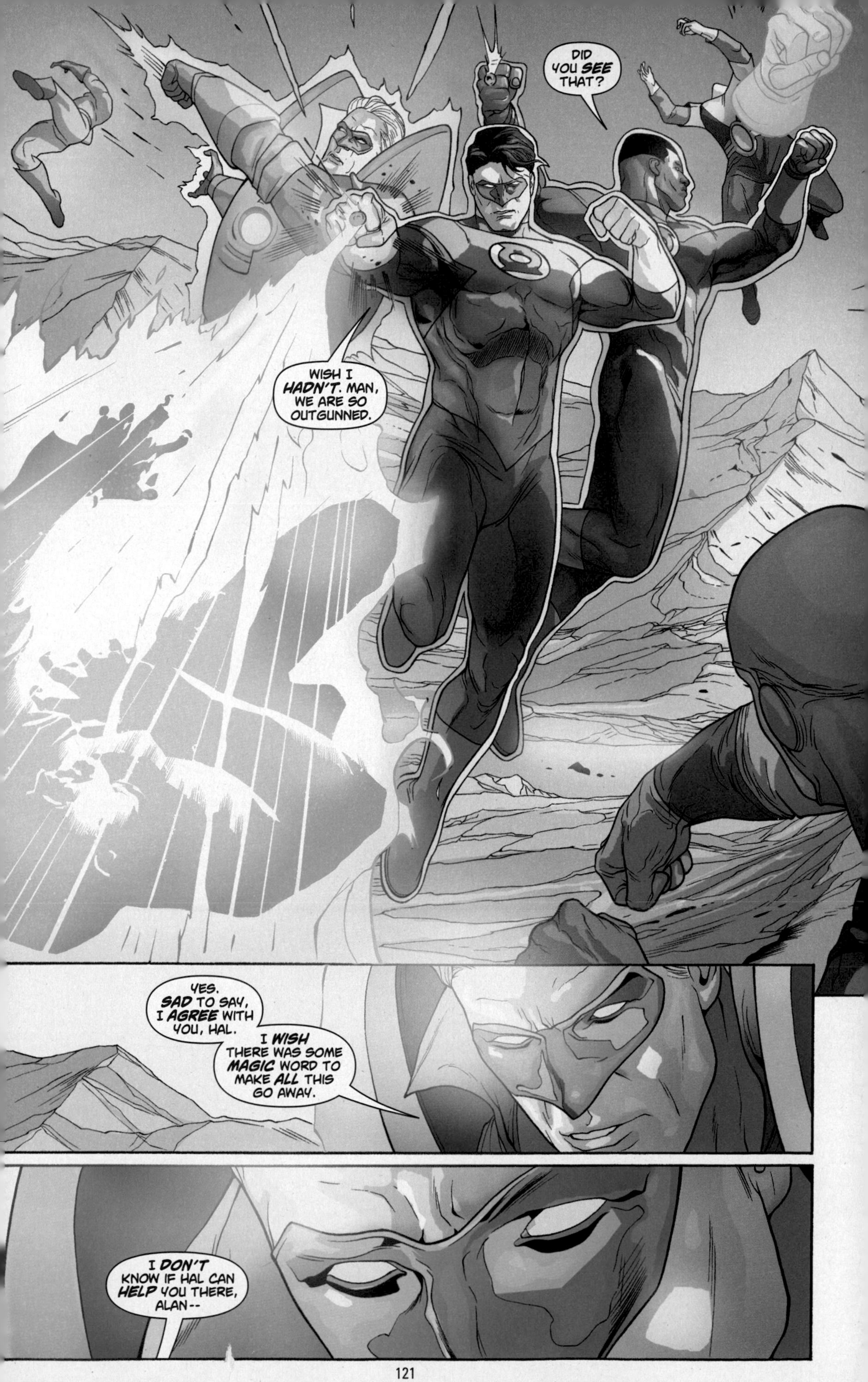
DID YOU SEE THAT?
WISH I HADN'T. MAN, WE ARE SO OUTGUNNED.
YES. SAD TO SAY, I AGREE WITH YOU, HAL.
I WISH THERE WAS SOME MAGIC WORD TO MAKE ALL THIS GO AWAY.
I DON'T KNOW IF HAL CAN HELP YOU THERE, ALAN--

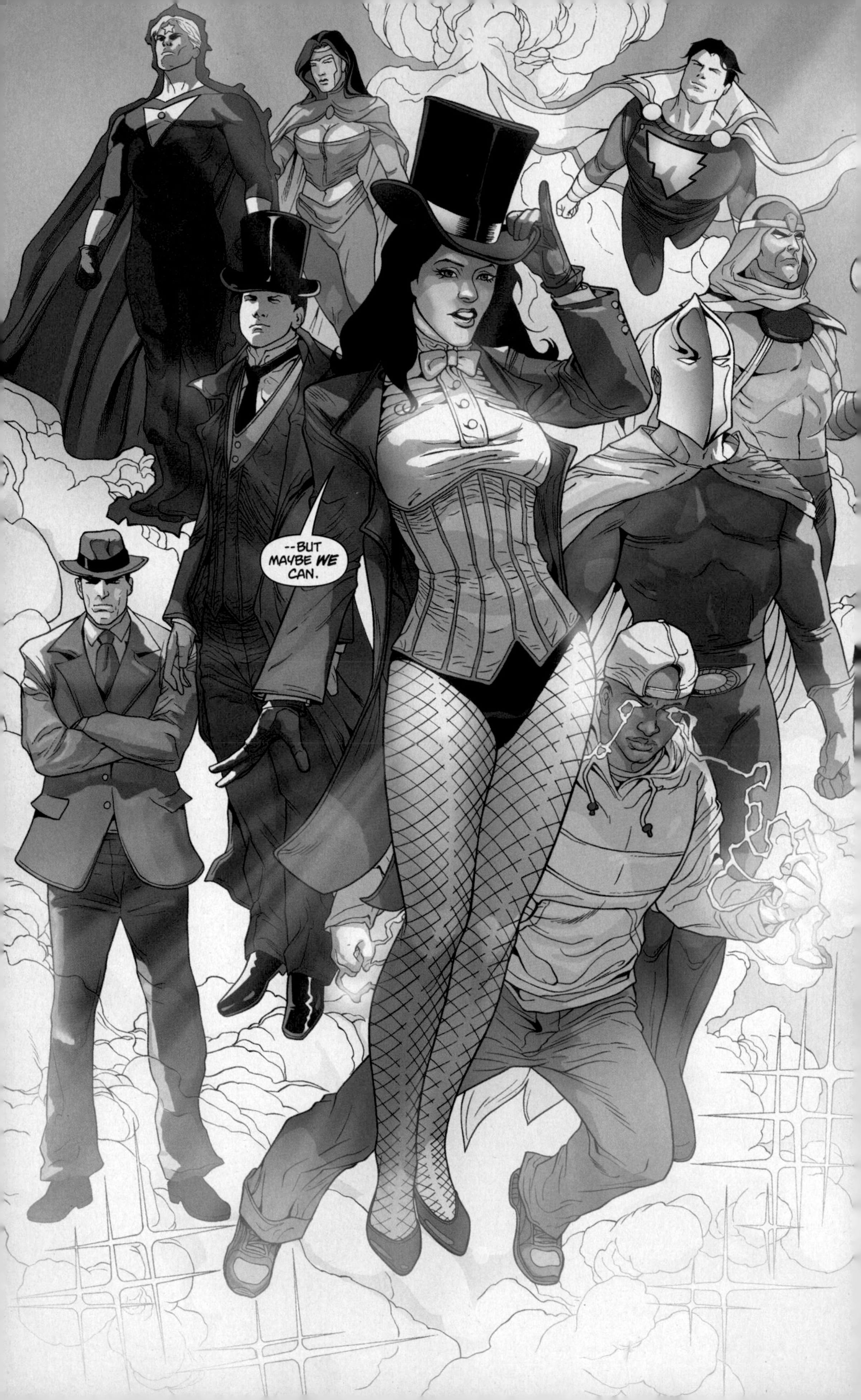
--BUT MAYBE WE CAN.

<BIRTH OF A NATION> ACTION COMICS 873 COVER ART BY **LADRÖNN**

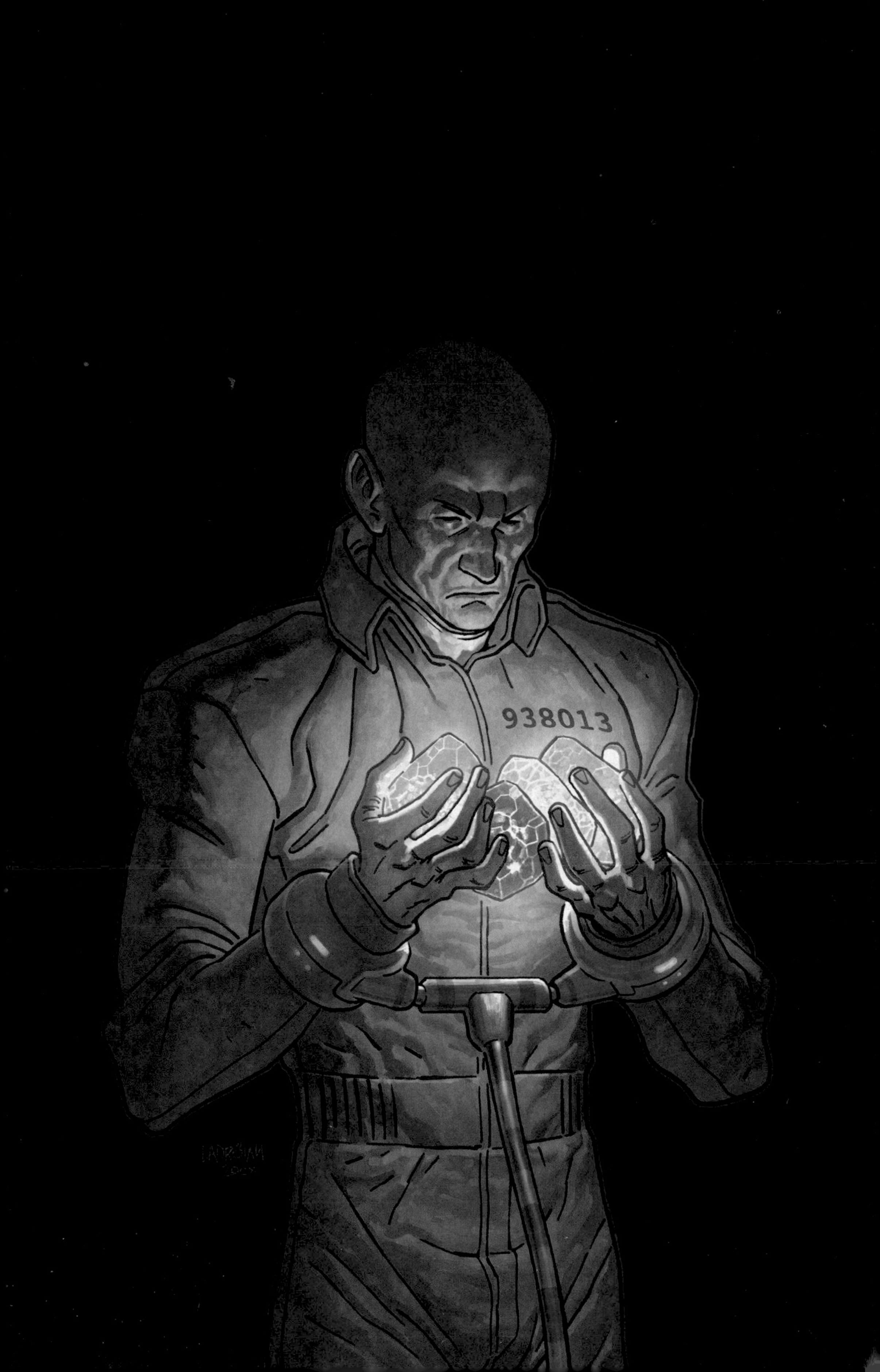
938013

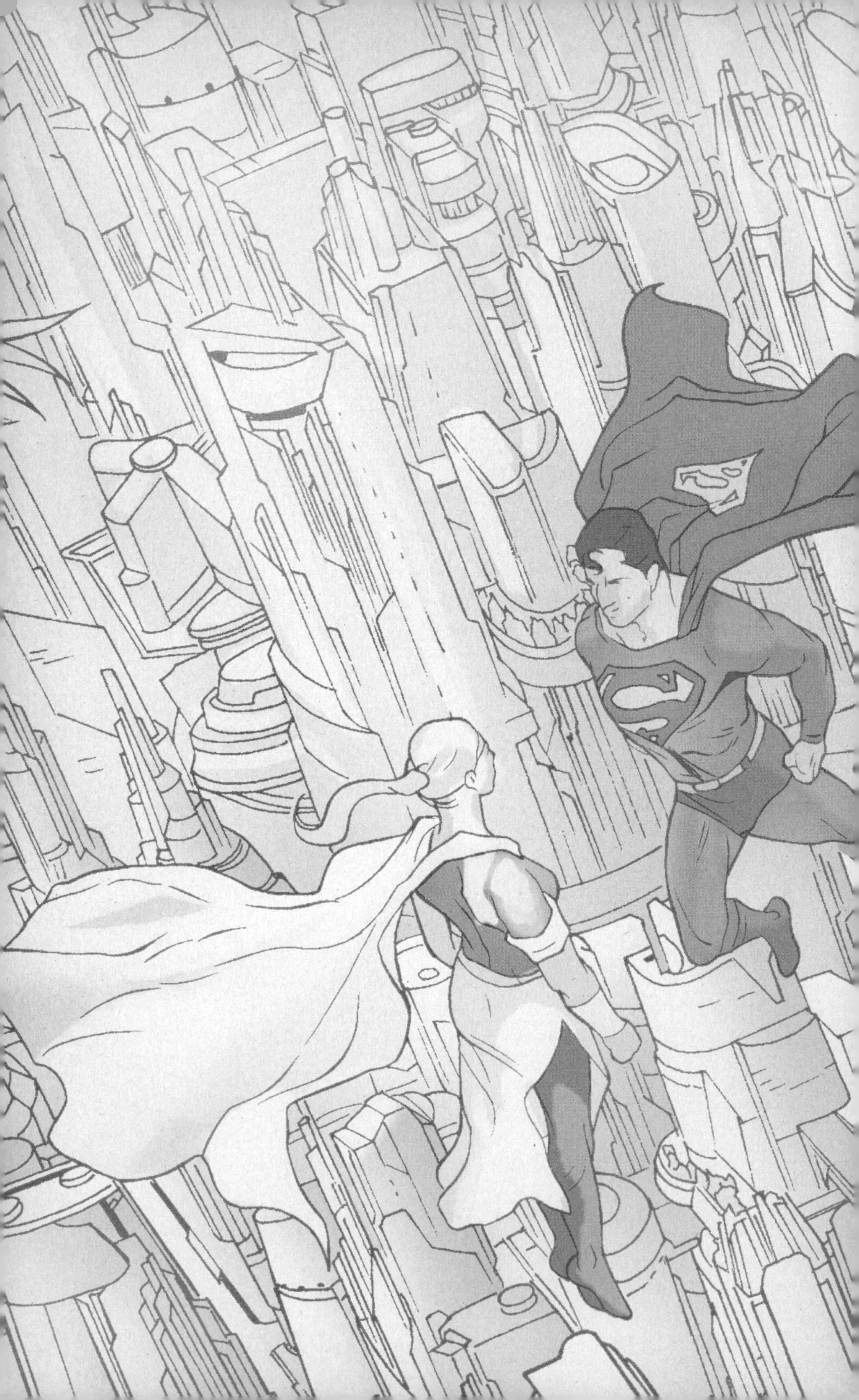

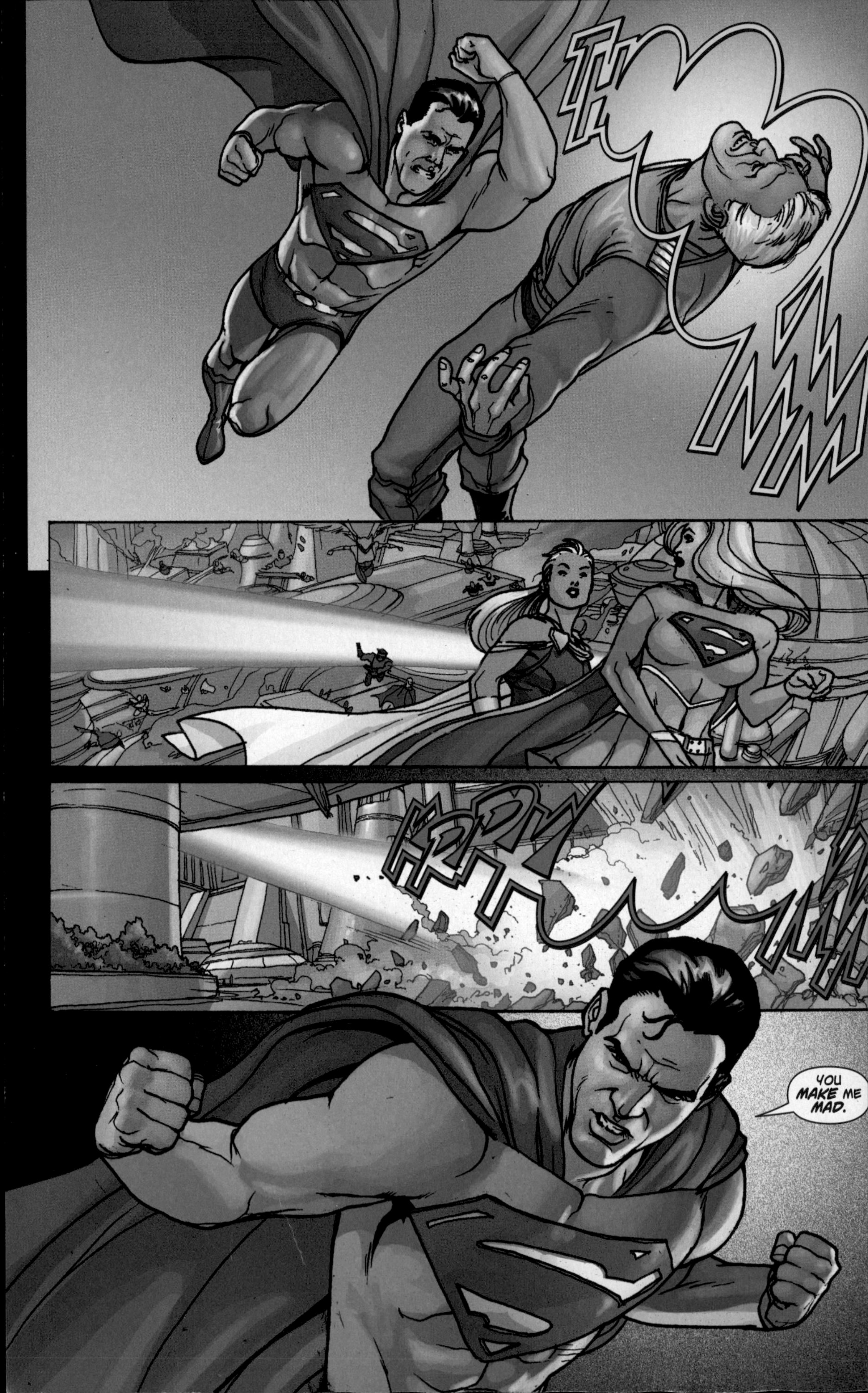
YOU MAKE ME MAD.

KAL? I'M...I'M *SORRY.*

YOUR MOTHER IS *BLINDED* BY GRIEF, KARA.

I *KNOW* IT'S HARD, BUT SHE *CAN'T* LET THE DEATH OF SOMEONE SHE LOVED SO MUCH *CHANGE* HER LIKE THIS.

SHE NEEDS TO DO WHAT ZOR WOULD *WANT.* WHAT ZOR WOULD THINK IS *BEST* FOR EVERYONE. KARA...

"...WHERE *IS* YOUR MOTHER?"

"SHE'S TRYING TO FIX EVERYTHING."

I DO THIS IN YOUR MEMORY, MY DEAR HUSBAND. AND IN YOUR BROTHER'S...

...MAY RAO FORGIVE HIS SON.

WHAT ARE WE *WAITING* FOR, ZEE? NEXT TO *KRYPTONITE* AND THE RAYS OF A *RED SUN,* MAGIC IS THE ONLY THING THAT CAN *KILL* A KRYPTONIAN.

UNLIKE THESE *INVADERS,* THUNDERBOLT, *WE* WON'T BE KILLING *ANYONE.*

THEY ARE NOT *ALL* KILLERS, ZATARA.

WHATEVER *MOJO* YOU'RE GONNA CAST, ZATANNA--

--YOU BETTER DO IT NOW. WE GOT *INCOMING.*

FREDDY? UH, YEAH, ZEE?

THEY HAVEN'T DONE ANYTHING TO TELL THE *PUBLIC* THAT. THEY *REALLY* DON'T KNOW HOW TO WORK A CROWD.

NOW, FREDDY!

GO FOR IT.

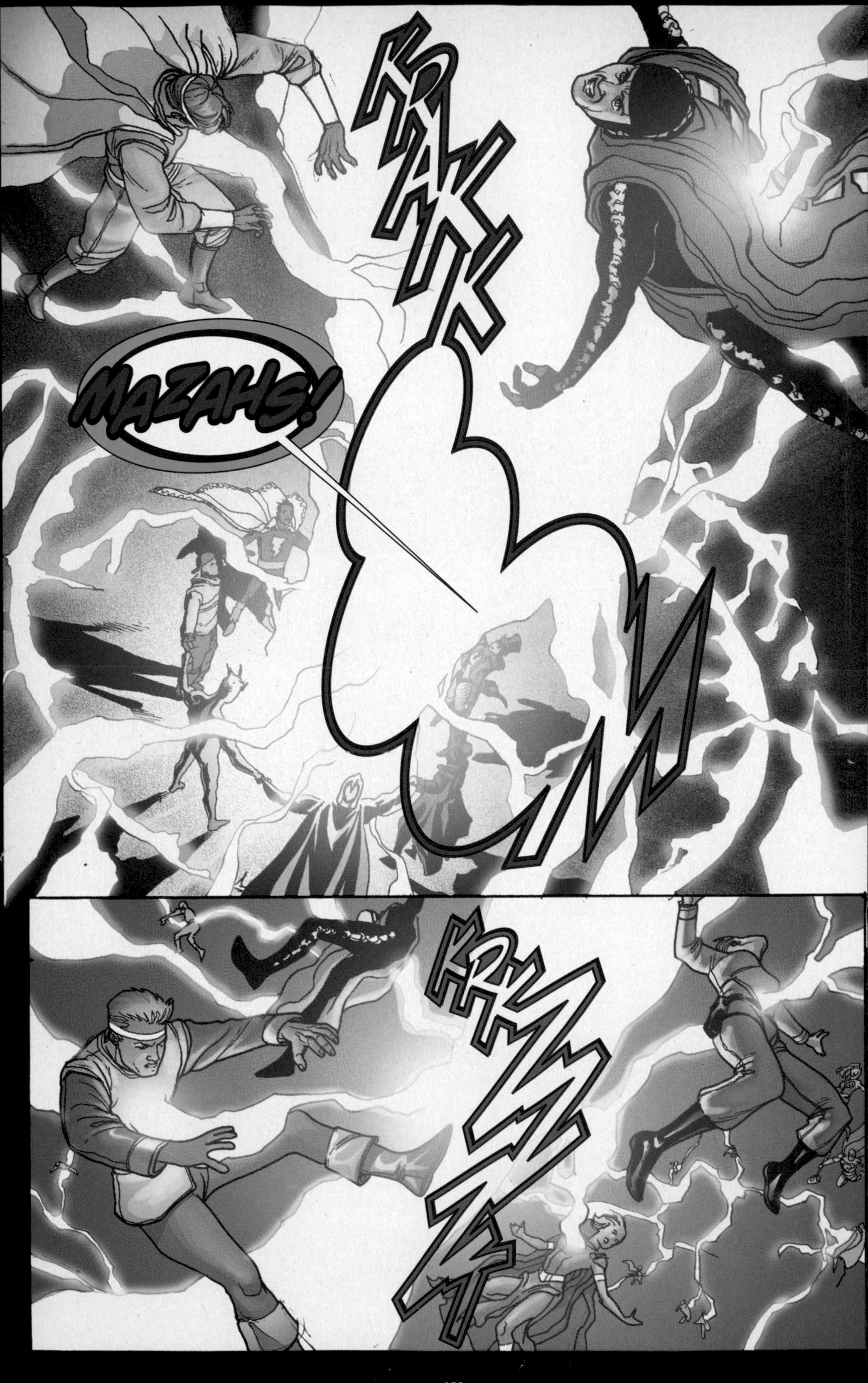
MAZAHS!

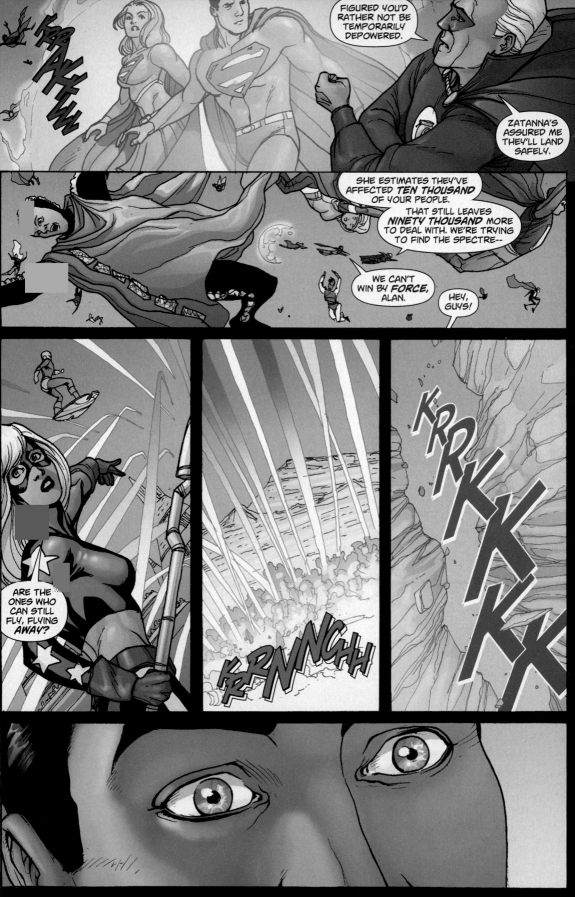

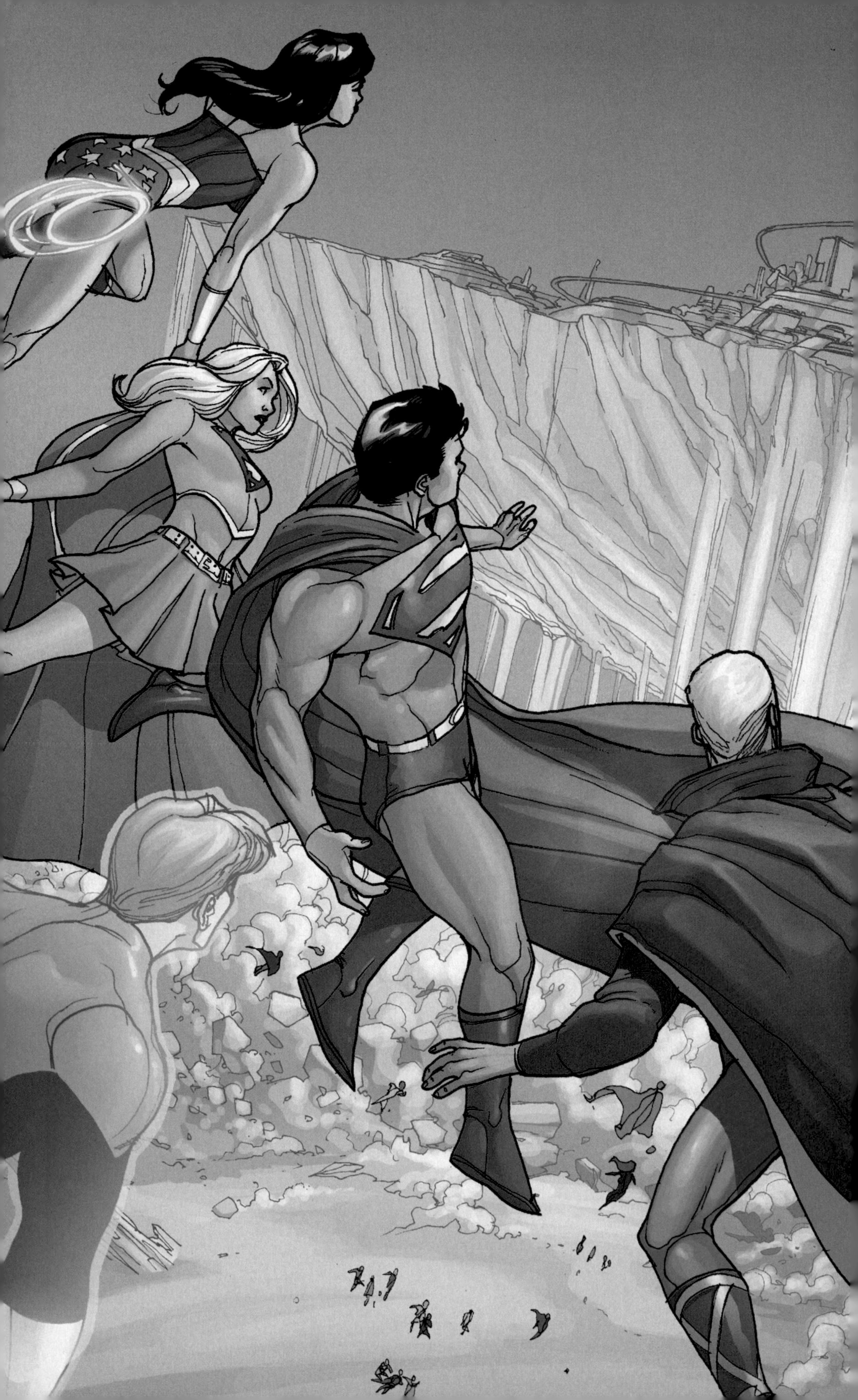

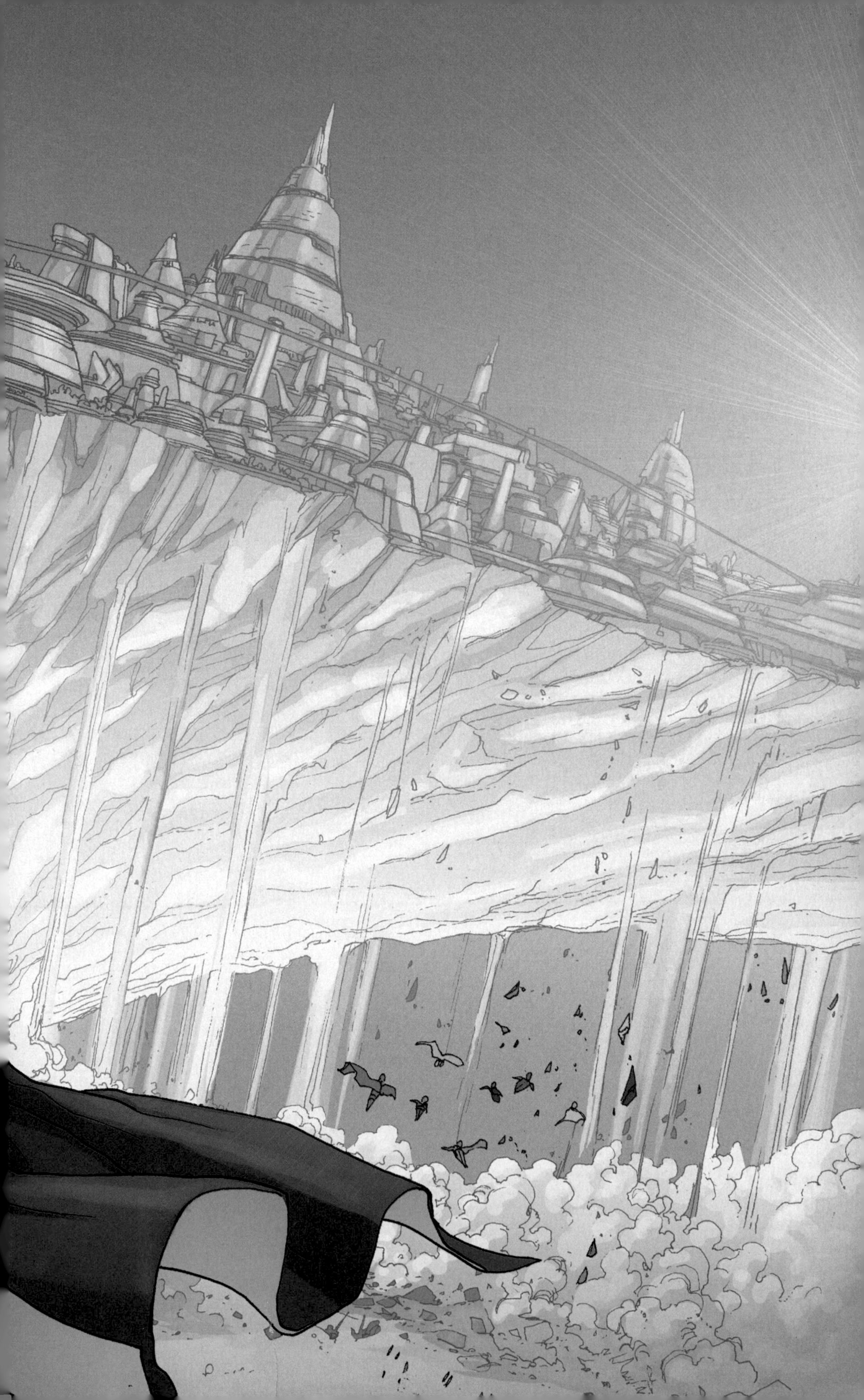

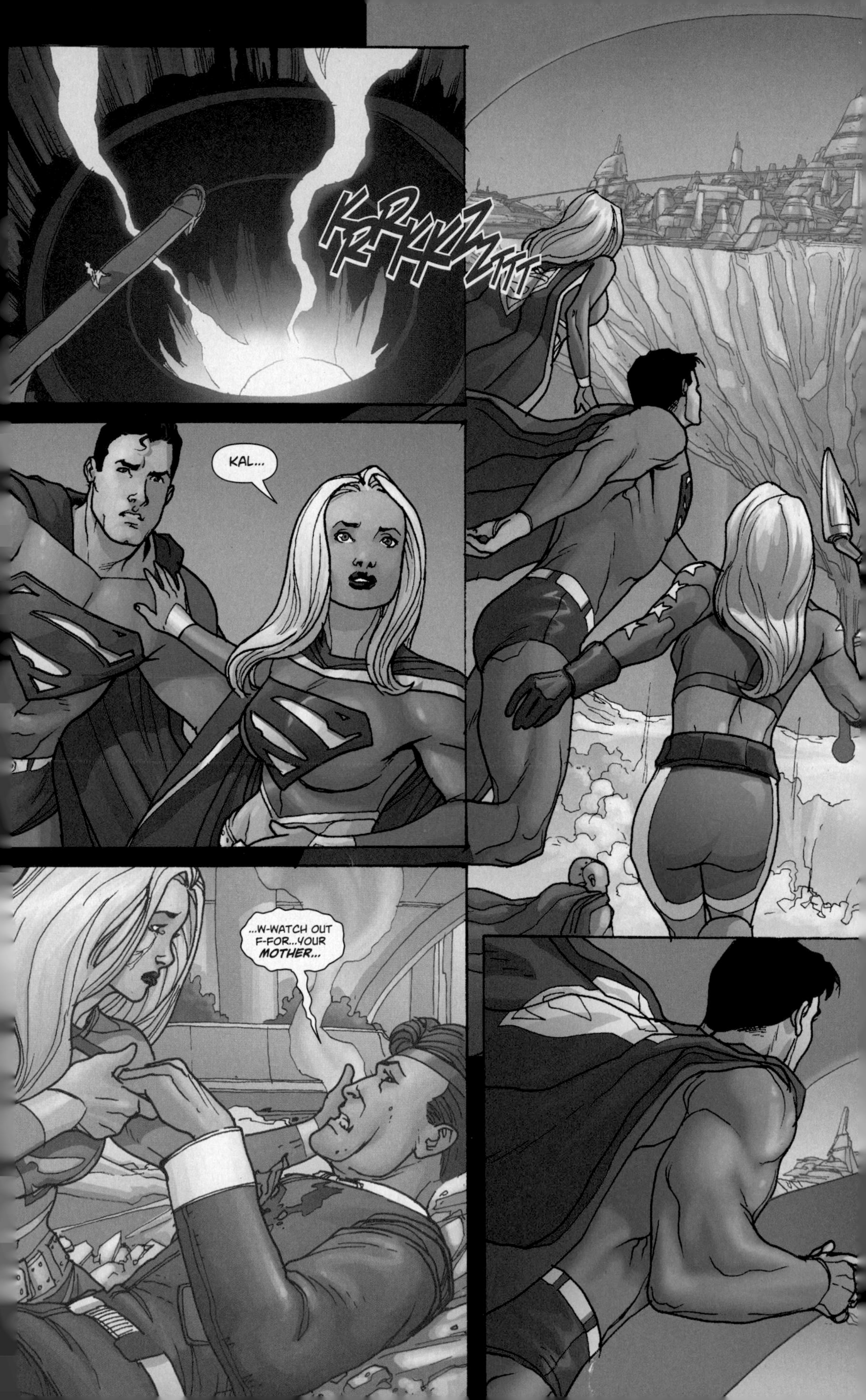
KRRAKZZTTT
KAL...
...W-WATCH OUT
F-FOR...YOUR
MOTHER...

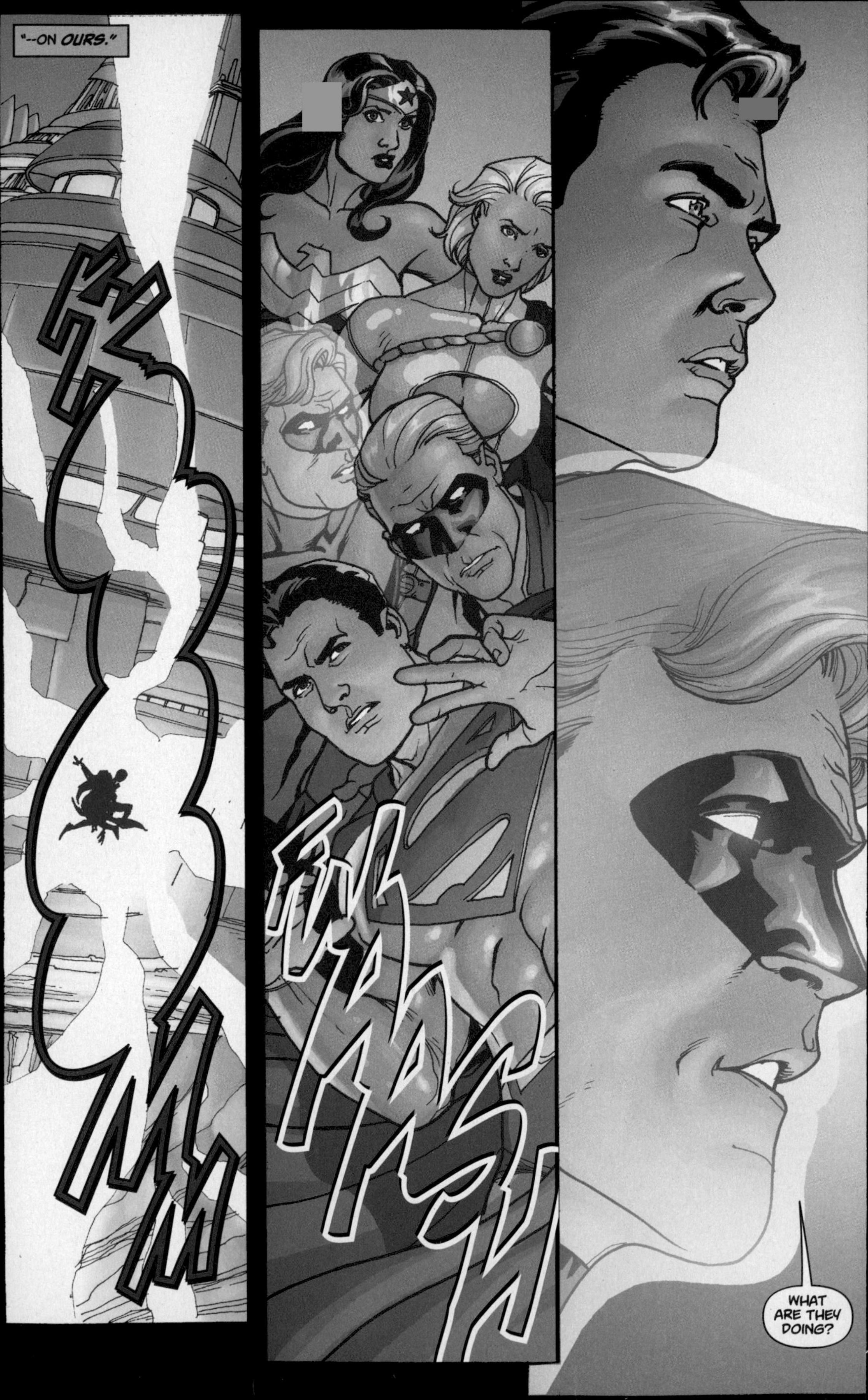
"--ON OURS."
WHAT ARE THEY DOING?

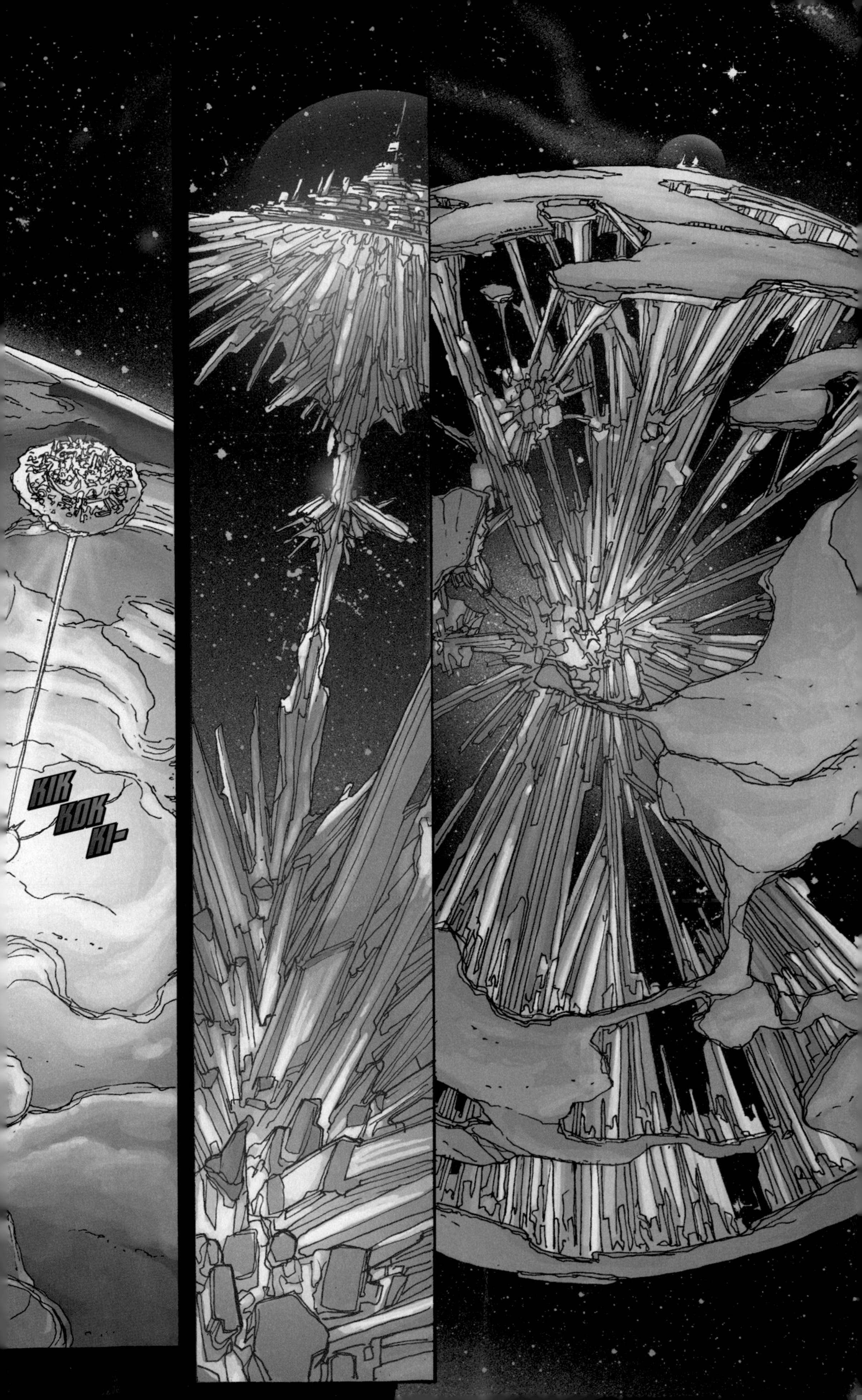
KIK
KOK
KI-

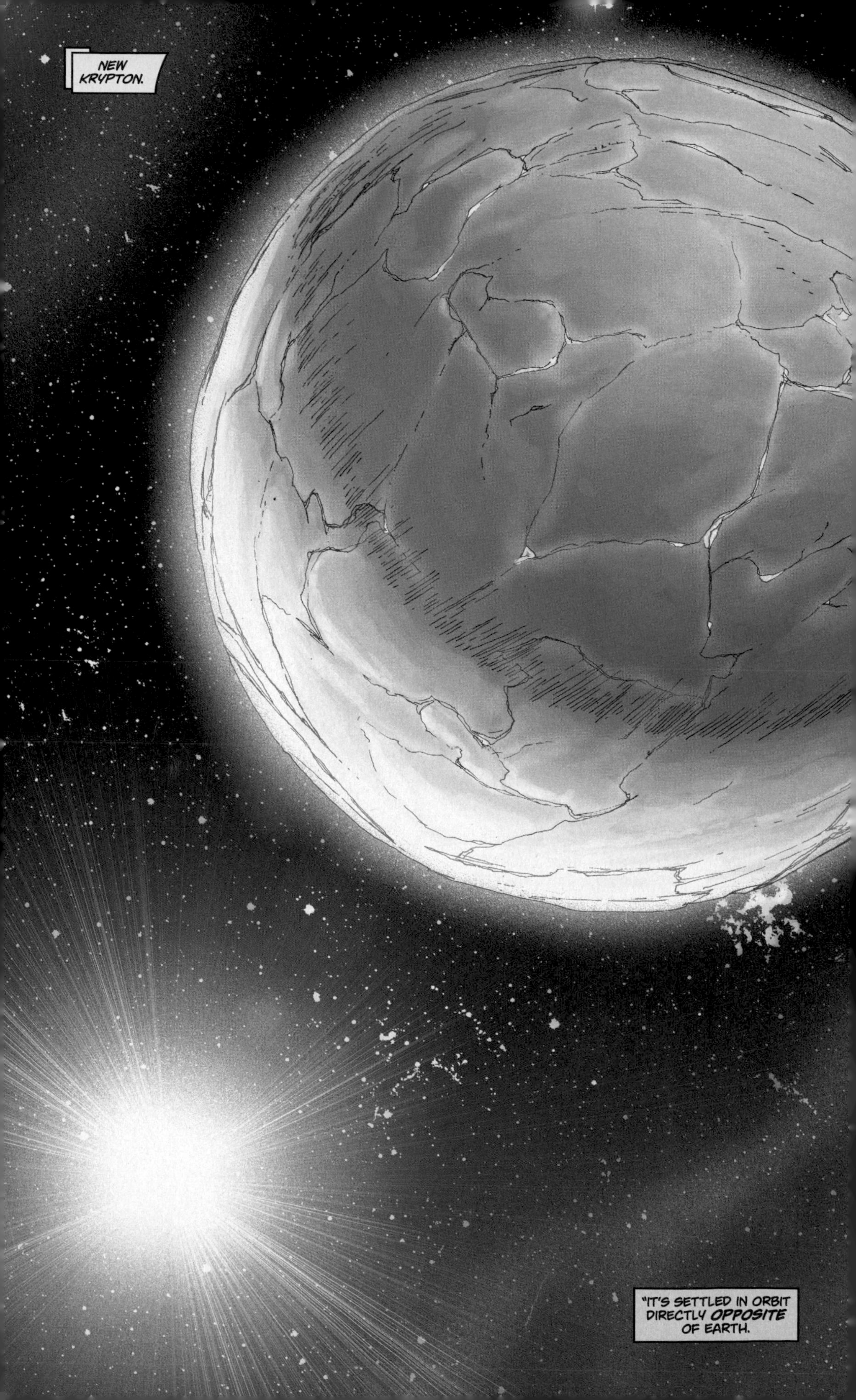
NEW KRYPTON.
"IT'S SETTLED IN ORBIT DIRECTLY OPPOSITE OF EARTH.

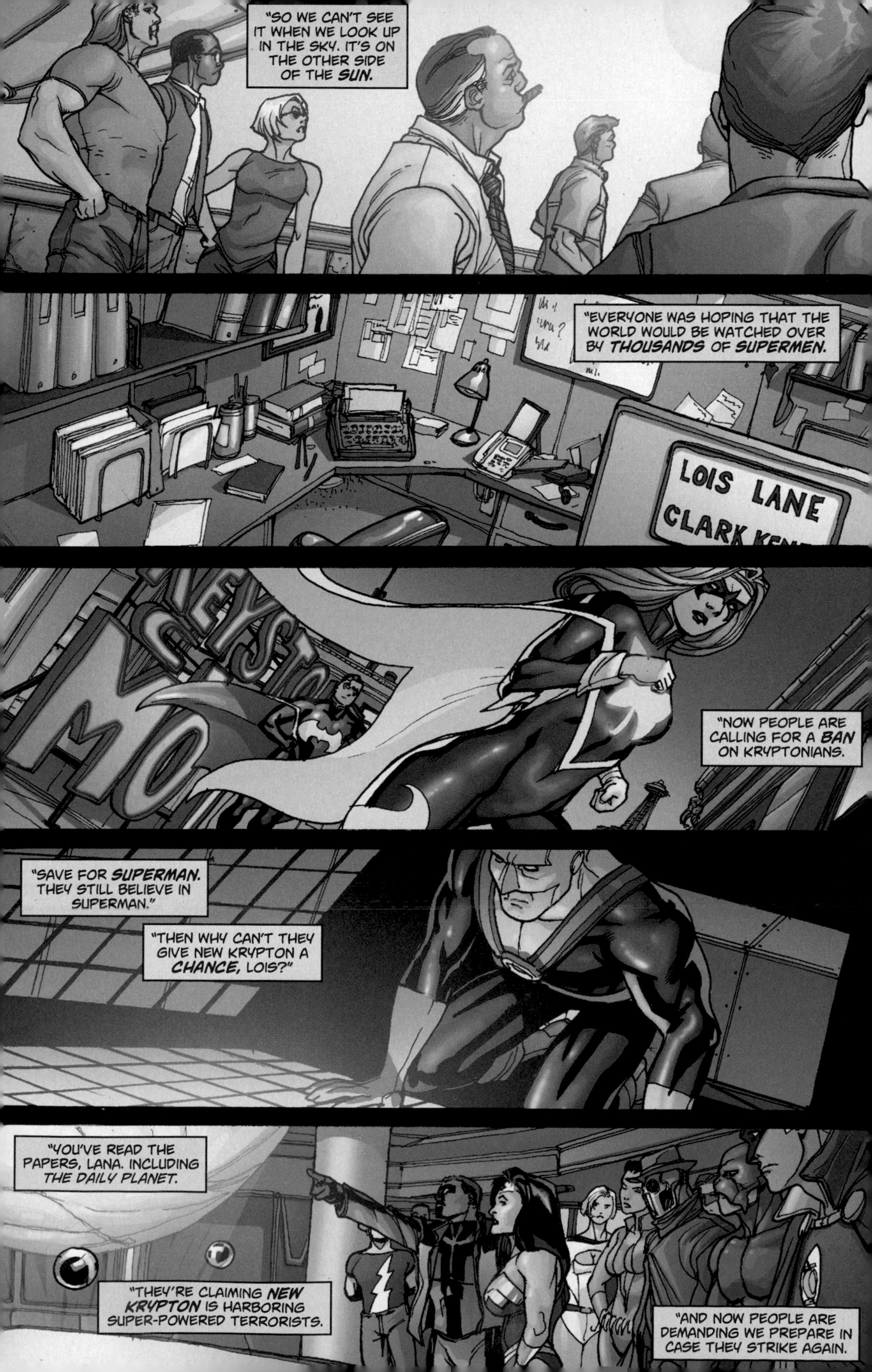
"SO WE CAN'T SEE IT WHEN WE LOOK UP IN THE SKY. IT'S ON THE OTHER SIDE OF THE SUN.
"EVERYONE WAS HOPING THAT THE WORLD WOULD BE WATCHED OVER BY THOUSANDS OF SUPERMEN.
LOIS LANE
"NOW PEOPLE ARE CALLING FOR A BAN ON KRYPTONIANS.
"SAVE FOR SUPERMAN. THEY STILL BELIEVE IN SUPERMAN."
"THEN WHY CAN'T THEY GIVE NEW KRYPTON A CHANCE, LOIS?"
"YOU'VE READ THE PAPERS, LANA. INCLUDING THE DAILY PLANET.
"THEY'RE CLAIMING NEW KRYPTON IS HARBORING SUPER-POWERED TERRORISTS.
"AND NOW PEOPLE ARE DEMANDING WE PREPARE IN CASE THEY STRIKE AGAIN.

"SUPERMAN BROUGHT OUT THE **BEST** IN SO MANY PEOPLE, I KNOW HE CAN BRING THE BEST OUT IN KANDOR TOO.

"HE ONLY NEEDS THE CHANCE TO SHOW THEM THE WAY."

R.R.R.

"HE CAN BRING PEACE BETWEEN WORLDS."

MUST FIND...

...BIZARRO!

"HE THINKS THAT'S WHY SUPERGIRL CHOSE TO GO. TO TRY AND TALK TO HER MOTHER. BUT THE RESPONSIBILITY--"

"IF THAT'S WHY SUPERGIRL WENT, SHE'LL DO IT, LOIS. I JUST WISH SHE'D EXPLAINED HERSELF. IT LOOKS **BAD.** AND CAT GRANT'S **RUNNING** WITH IT."

"BUT IF KARA SUCCEEDS, LANA, SHE'LL HELP ALIENS AND HUMANS COEXIST IN **PEACE.**"

KIK

"HUMANS, LOIS?"

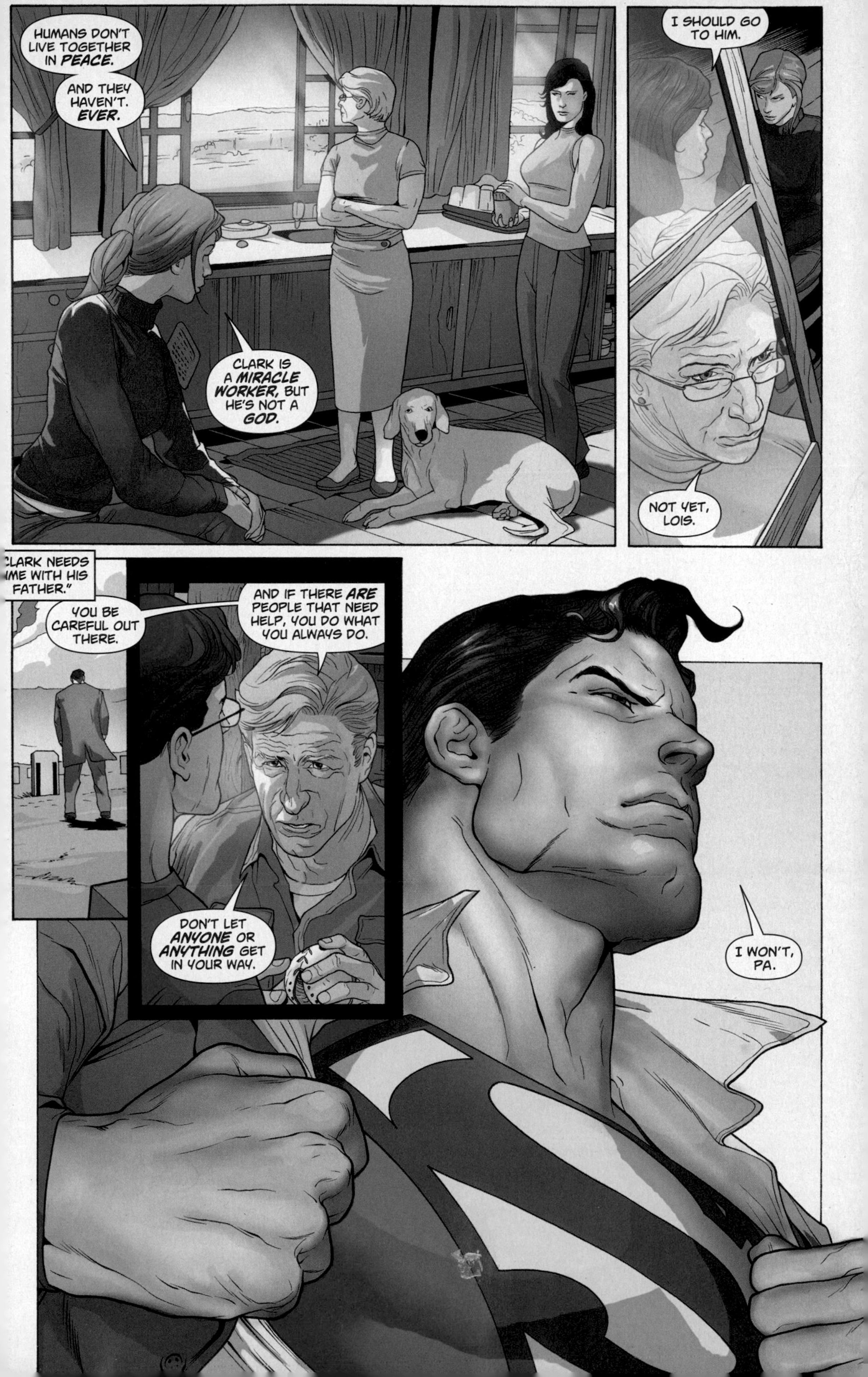
HUMANS DON'T LIVE TOGETHER IN *PEACE.*
AND THEY HAVEN'T. ***EVER.***
CLARK IS A ***MIRACLE WORKER,*** BUT HE'S NOT A ***GOD.***
I SHOULD GO TO HIM.
NOT YET, LOIS.
CLARK NEEDS ME WITH HIS FATHER."
YOU BE CAREFUL OUT THERE.
AND IF THERE ***ARE*** PEOPLE THAT NEED HELP, YOU DO WHAT YOU ALWAYS DO.
DON'T LET ***ANYONE*** OR ***ANYTHING*** GET IN YOUR WAY.
I WON'T, PA.

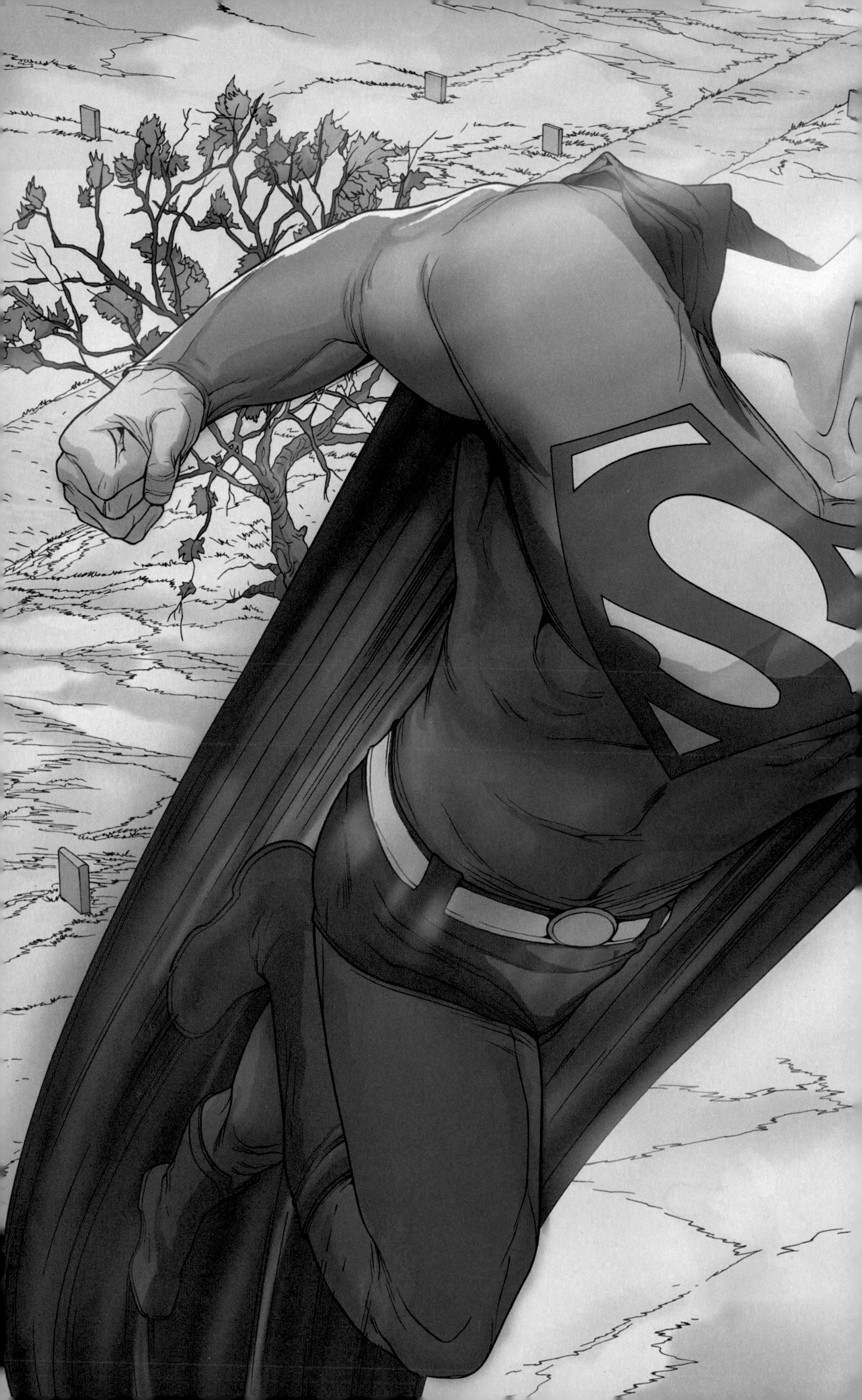

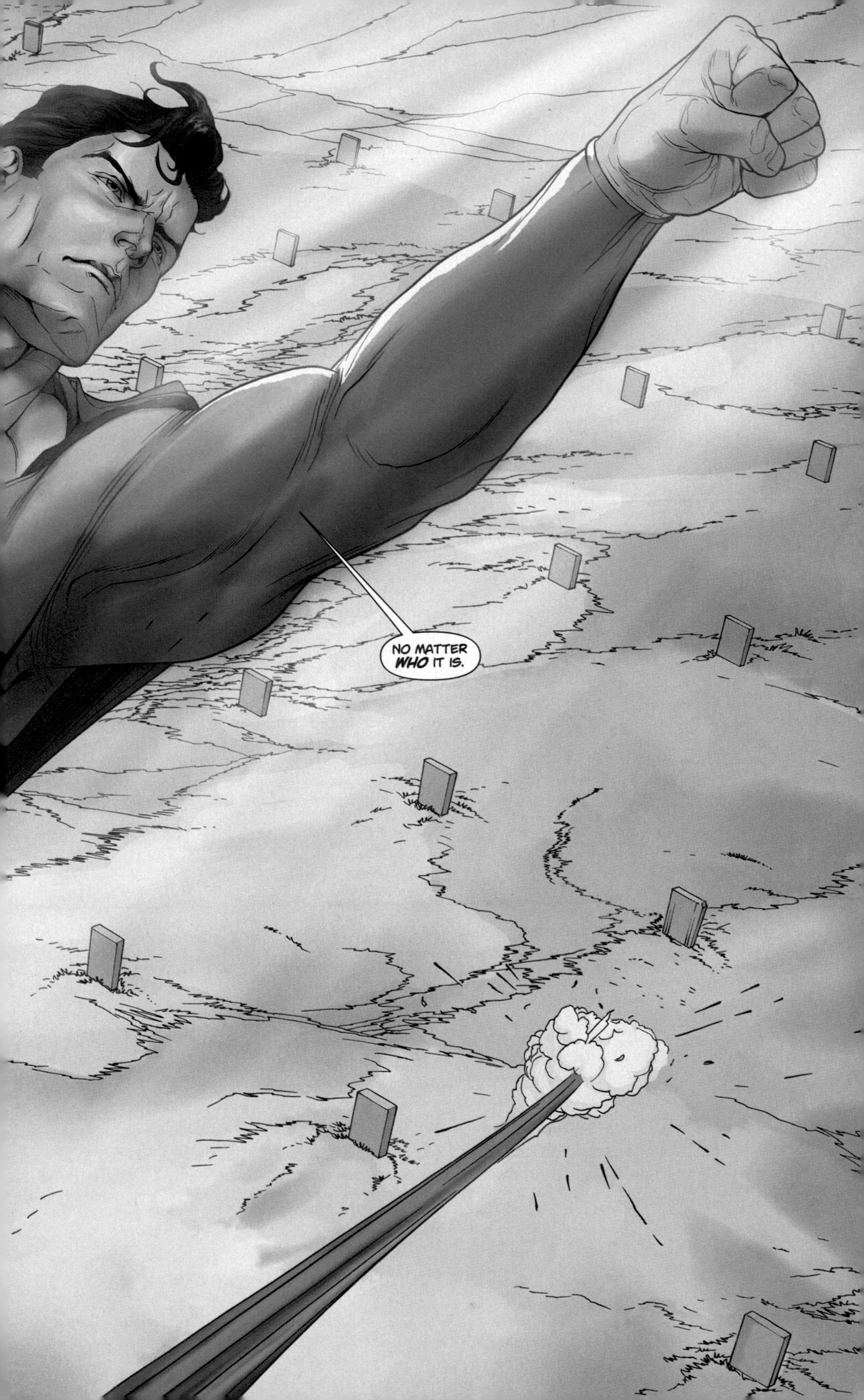
NO MATTER *WHO* IT IS.

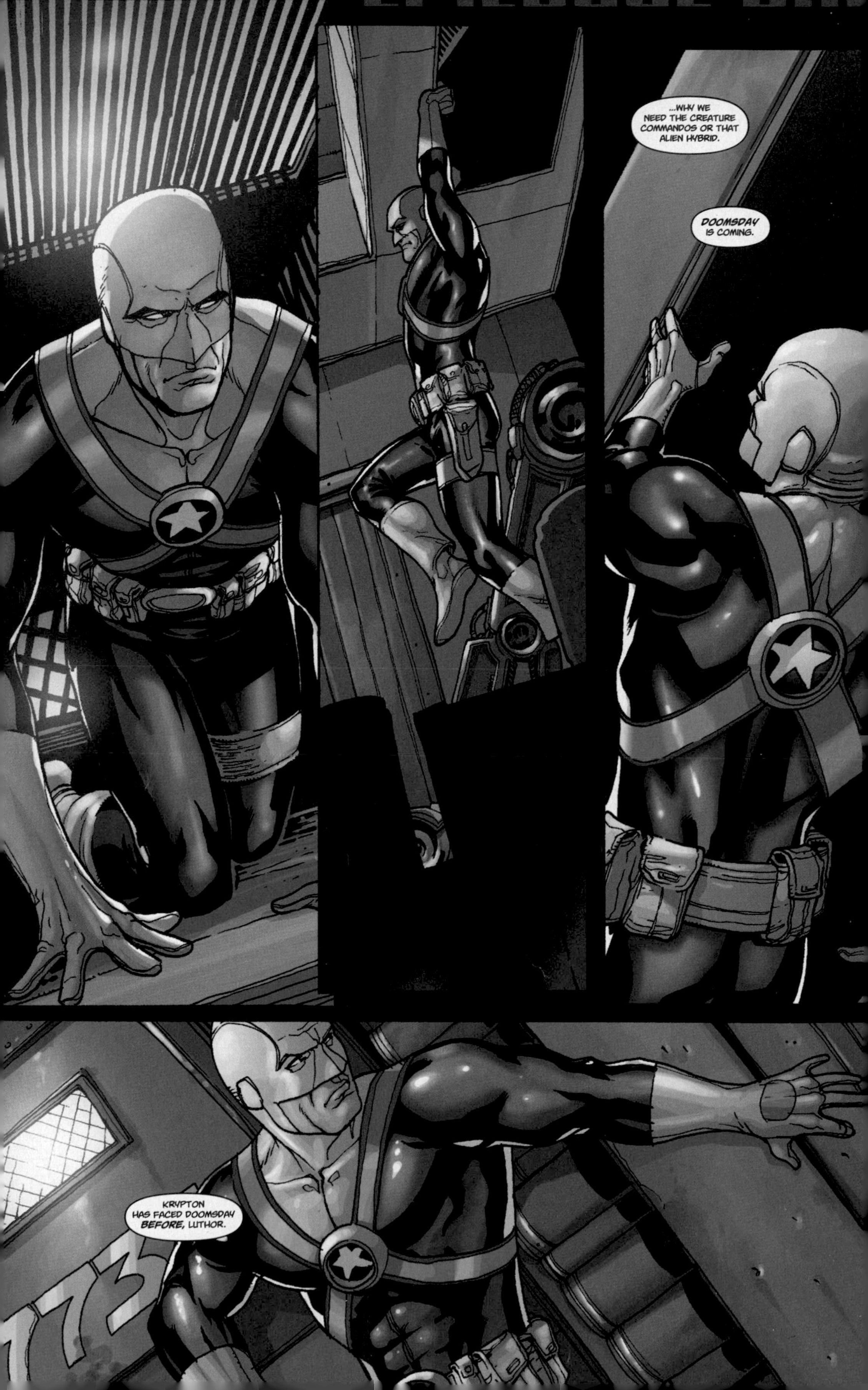
...WHY WE NEED THE CREATURE COMMANDOS OR THAT ALIEN HYBRID.
DOOMSDAY IS COMING.
KRYPTON HAS FACED DOOMSDAY BEFORE, LUTHOR.
773

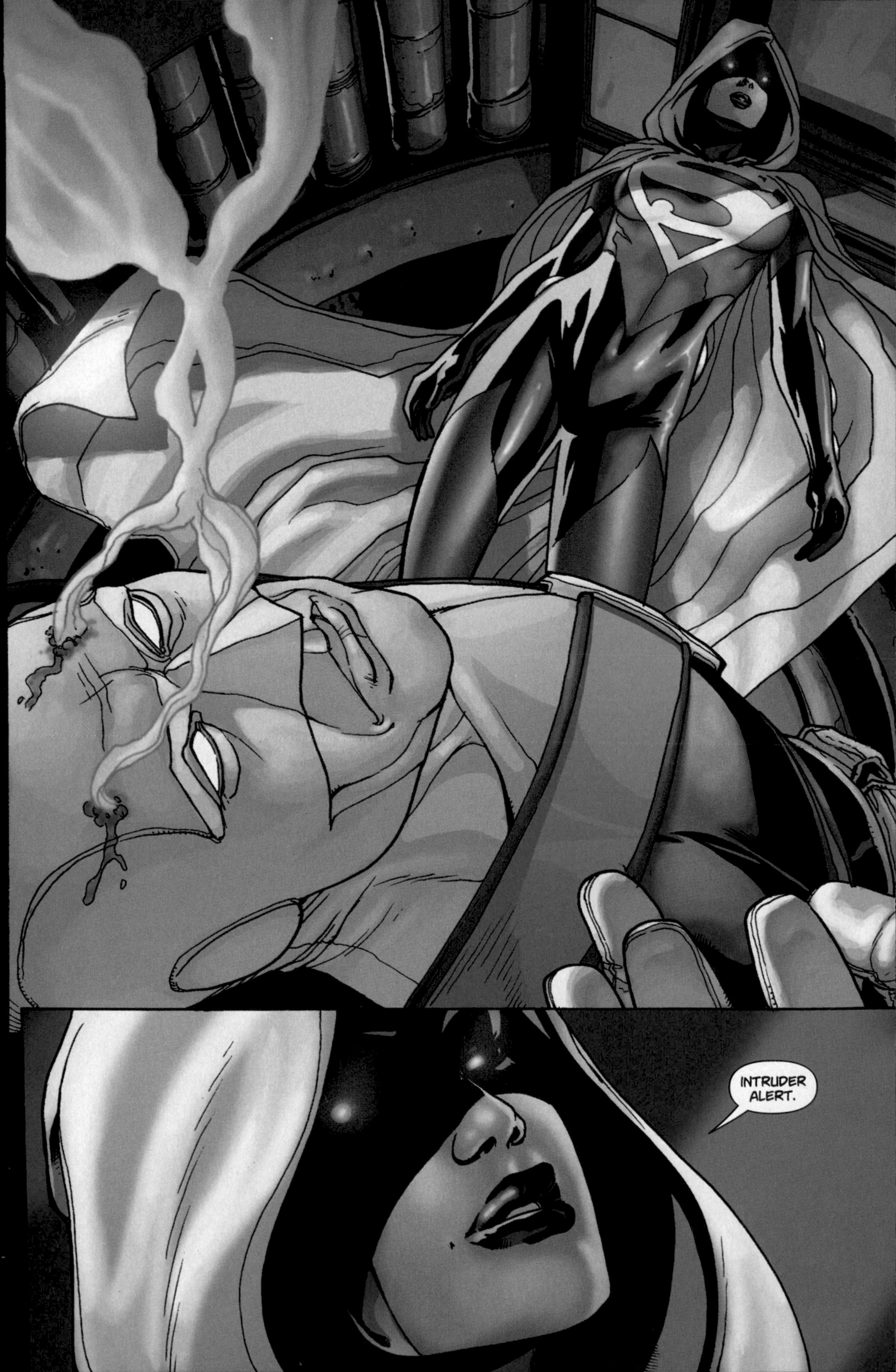
INTRUDER ALERT.

EPILOGUE TWO

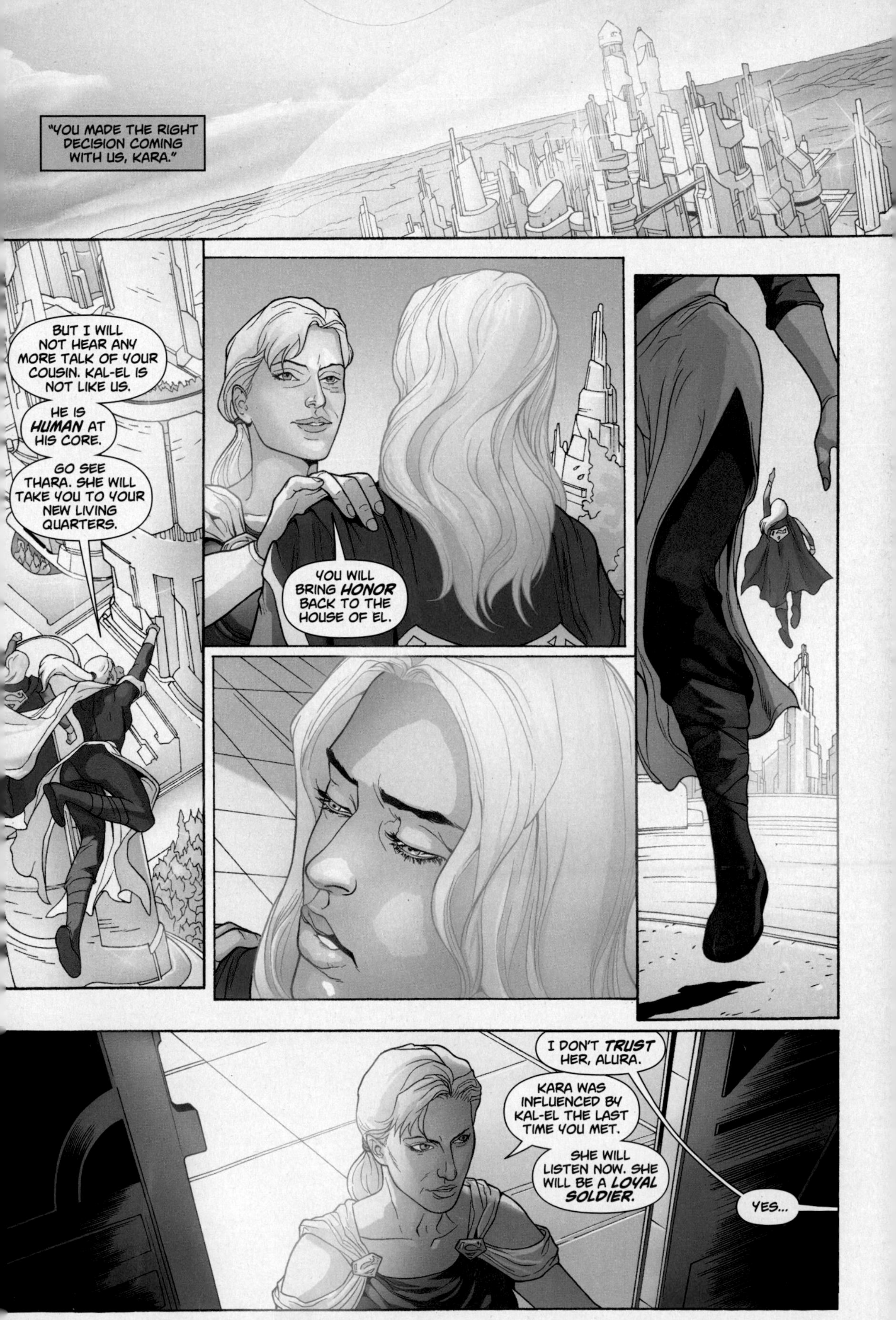

"YOU MADE THE RIGHT DECISION COMING WITH US, KARA."
BUT I WILL NOT HEAR ANY MORE TALK OF YOUR COUSIN. KAL-EL IS NOT LIKE US.
HE IS HUMAN AT HIS CORE.
GO SEE THARA. SHE WILL TAKE YOU TO YOUR NEW LIVING QUARTERS.
YOU WILL BRING HONOR BACK TO THE HOUSE OF EL.
I DON'T TRUST HER, ALURA.
KARA WAS INFLUENCED BY KAL-EL THE LAST TIME YOU MET.
SHE WILL LISTEN NOW. SHE WILL BE A LOYAL SOLDIER.
YES...

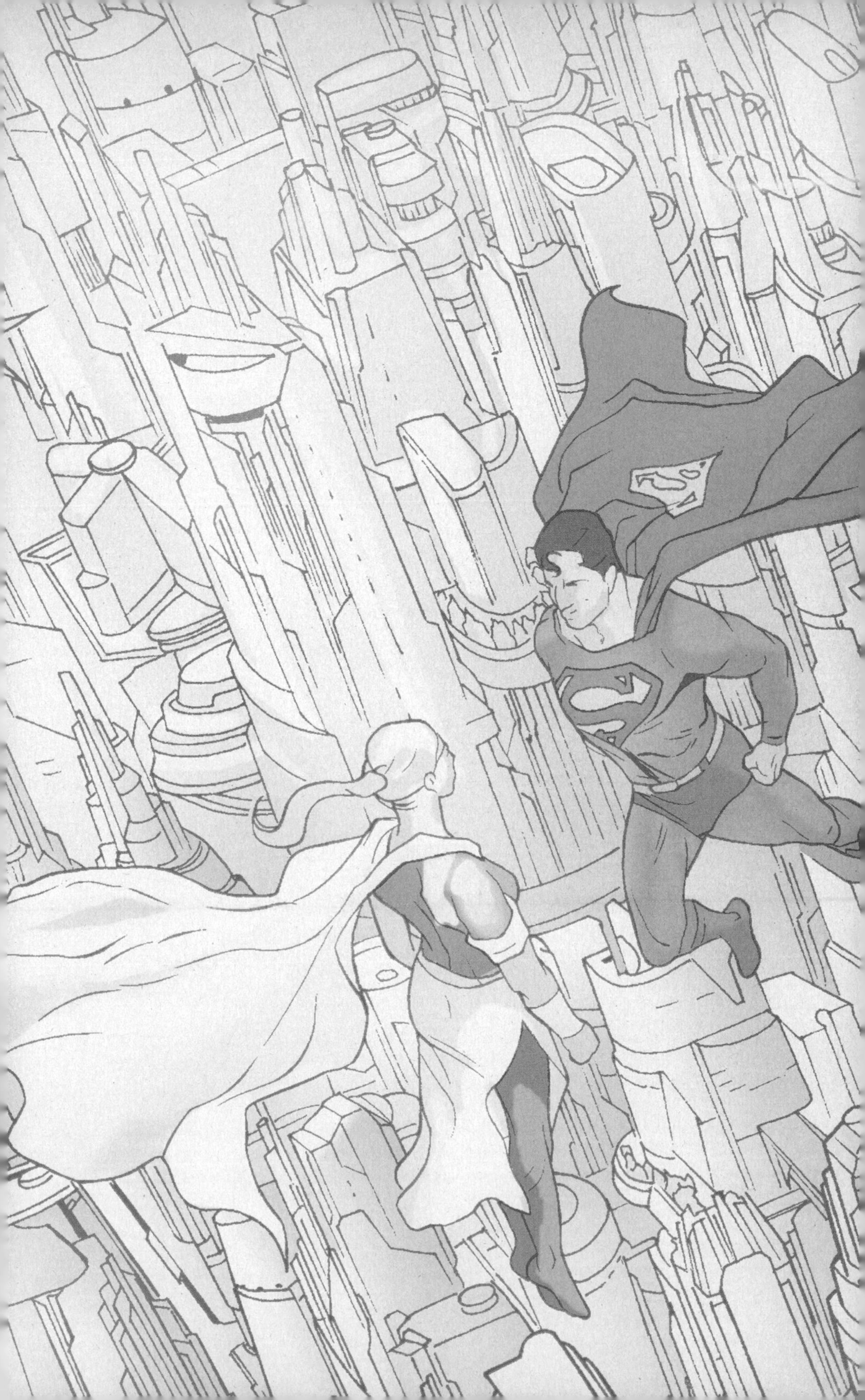

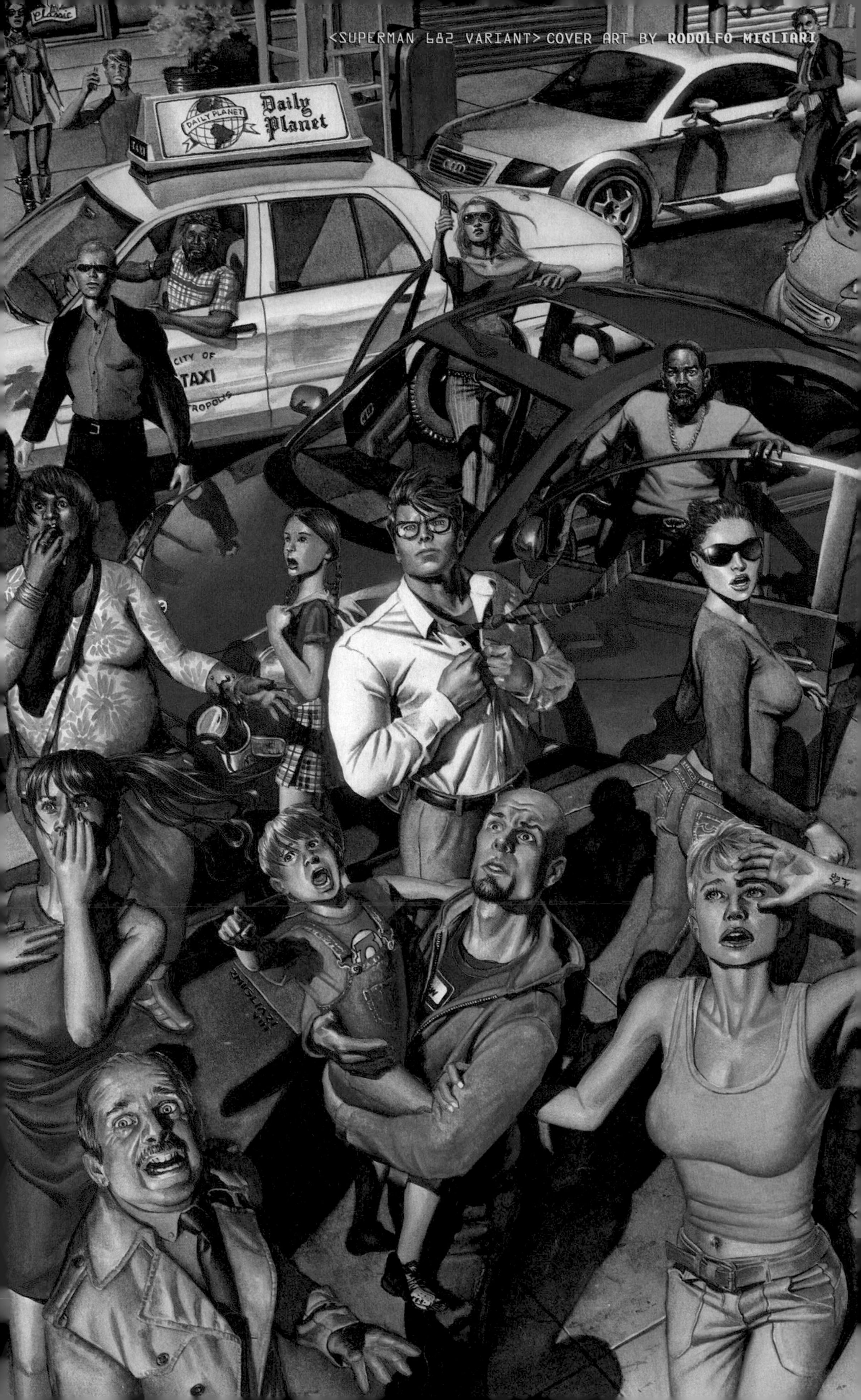
Classic
Daily Planet
DAILY PLANET
CITY OF
TAXI
TROPOLIS
<SUPERMAN 682 VARIANT> COVER ART BY **RODOLFO MIGLIARI**

<ACTION COMICS 872 VARIANT> COVER ART BY **CHRIS SPROUSE** AND **KARL STORY** WITH **GUY MAJOR**

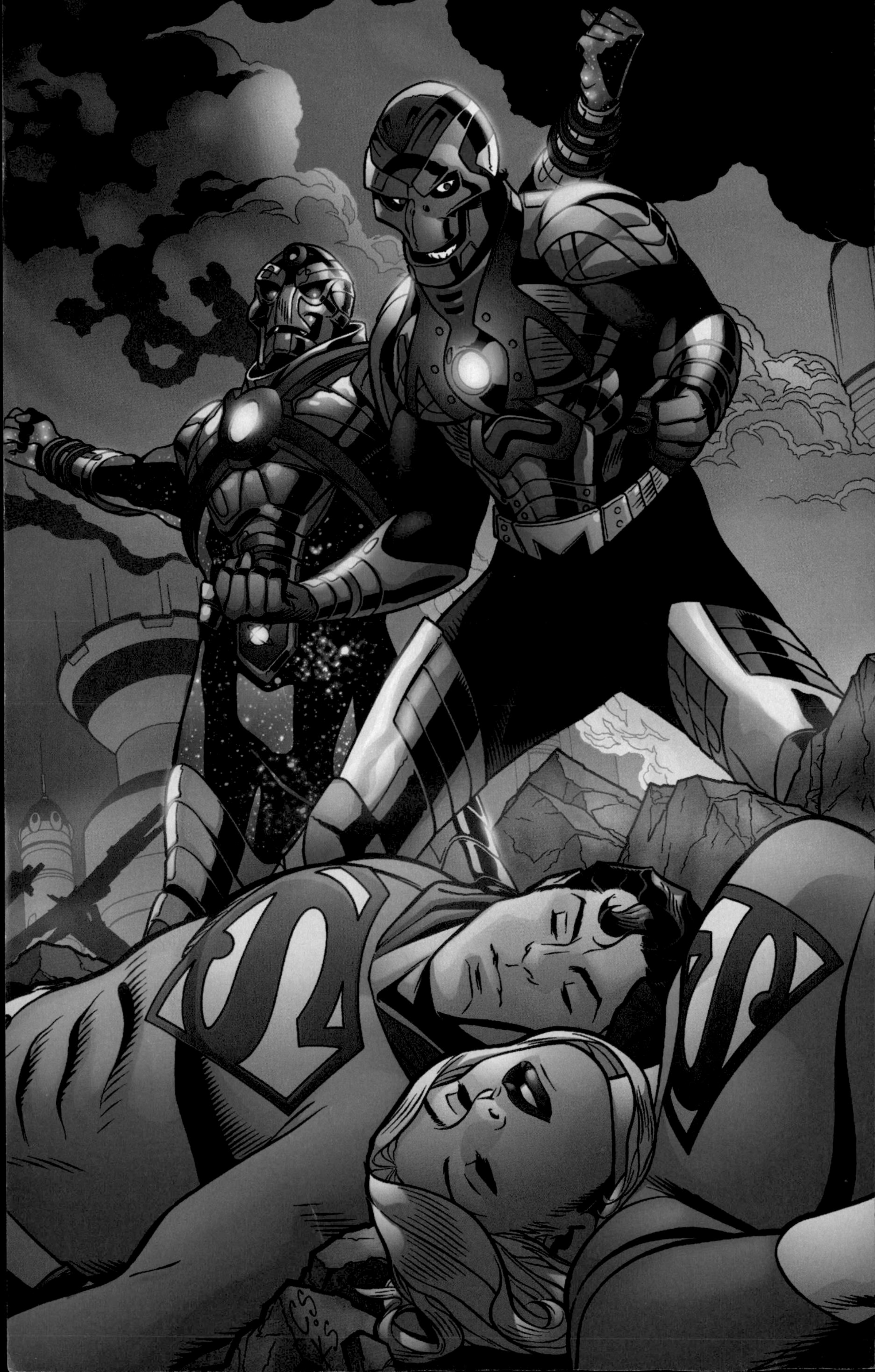

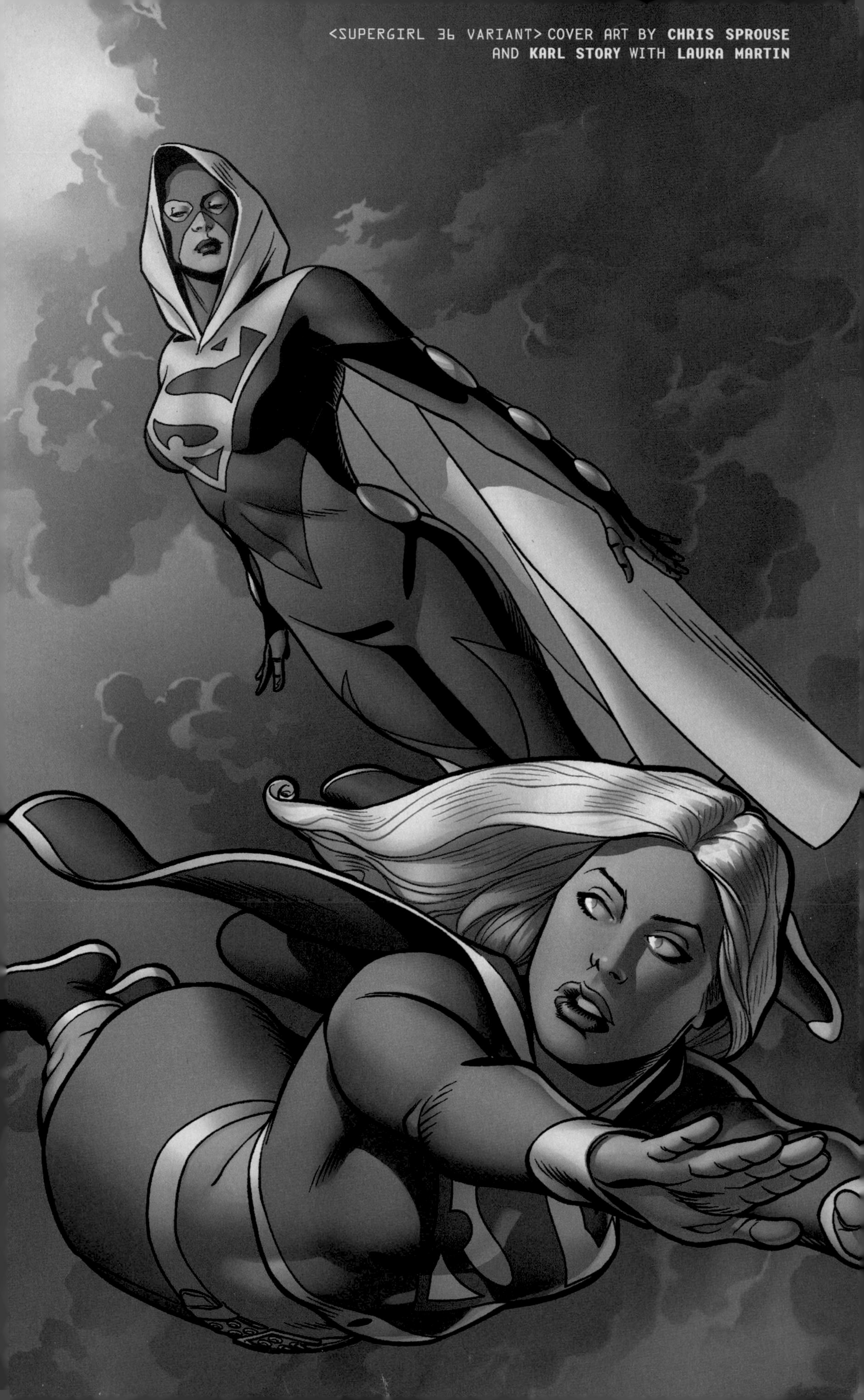

<SUPERGIRL 36 VARIANT> COVER ART BY **CHRIS SPROUSE**
AND **KARL STORY** WITH **LAURA MARTIN**

UNUSED PAGE FROM <SUPERMAN NEW KRYPTON SPECIAL #1>
DEPICTING KRYPTONIAN CRIMINALS GENERAL ZOD, URSA AND NON DISCOVERING KANDOR'S SURVIVAL
WRITTEN BY **GEOFF JOHNS**
ART BY **JAMAL IGLE** AND **KEITH CHAMPAGNE** WITH COLOR BY **HI-FI**

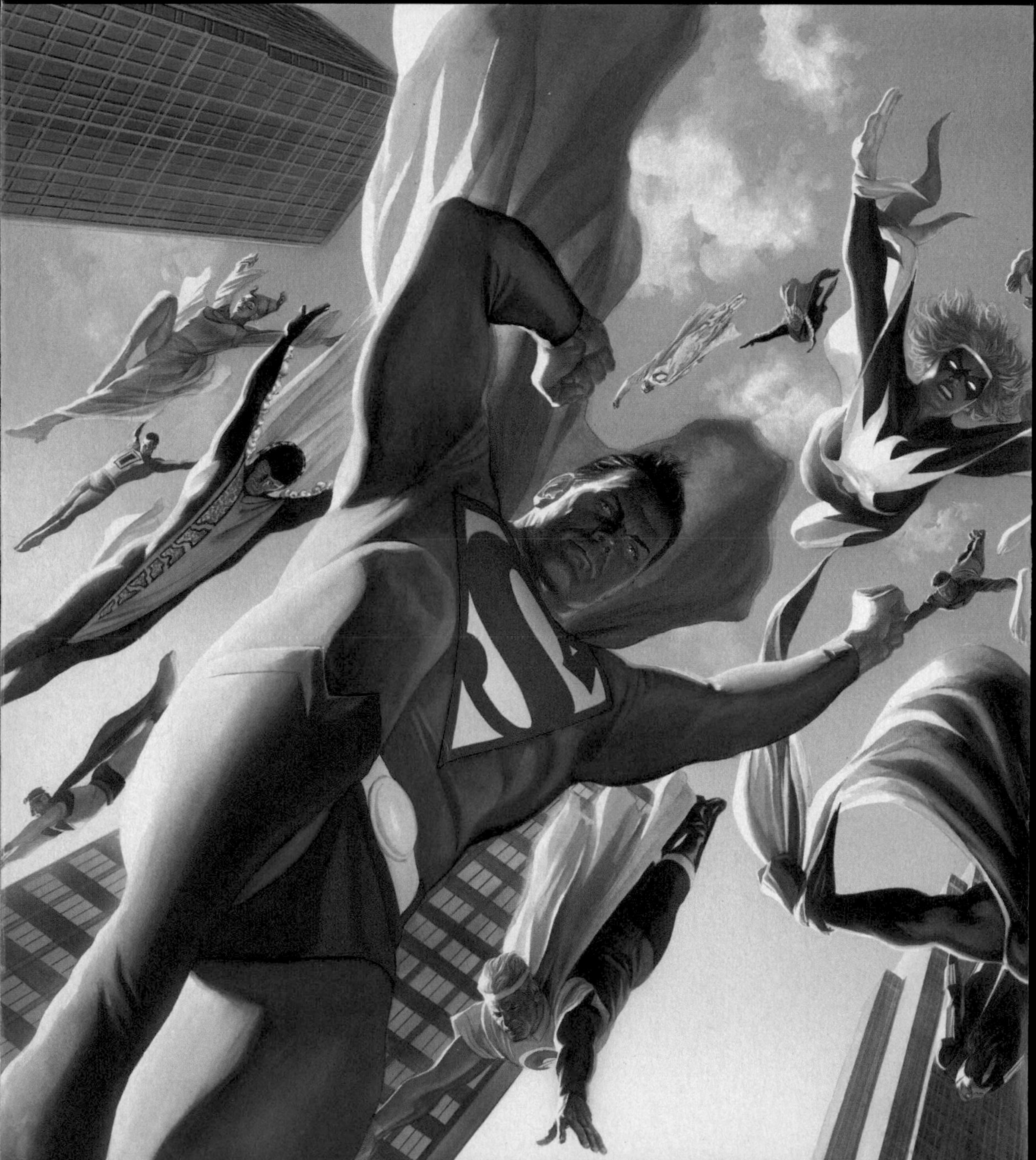

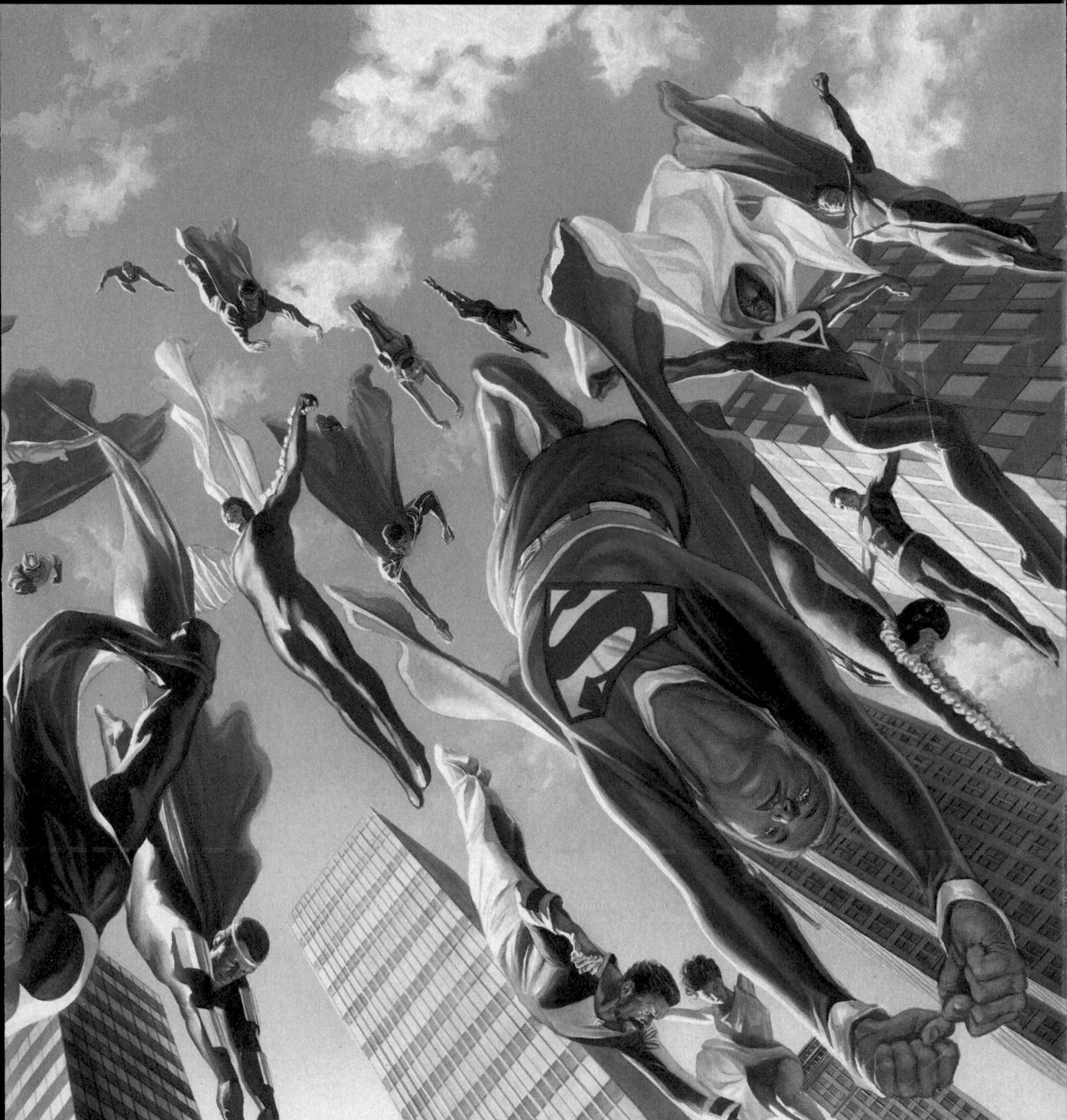

ORIGINAL COVERS TO <SUPERMAN 681, ACTION COMICS 871, AND SUPERGIRL 35>
BY **ALEX ROSS**

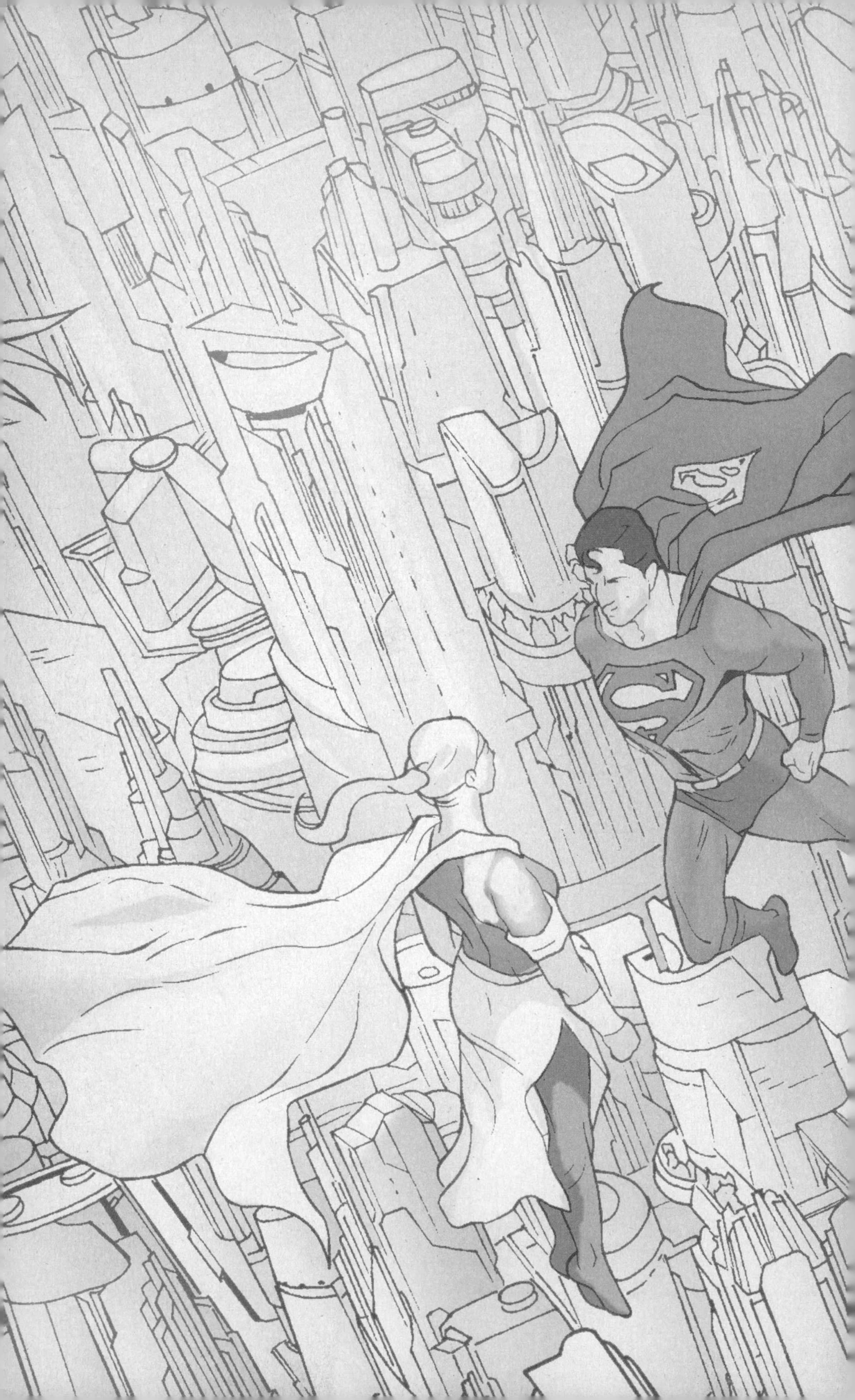

FROM THE WRITER OF
BATMAN: THE LONG HALLOWEEN

JEPH LOEB

with TIM SALE

This coming-of-age tale is an emotional and insightful examination of Clark Kent's transformation from a powerful boy into a heroic man. Told through the course of four seasons in the Man of Steel's adolescent life, it illustrates that it is the person, not the powers, that makes the Man of Steel a hero.

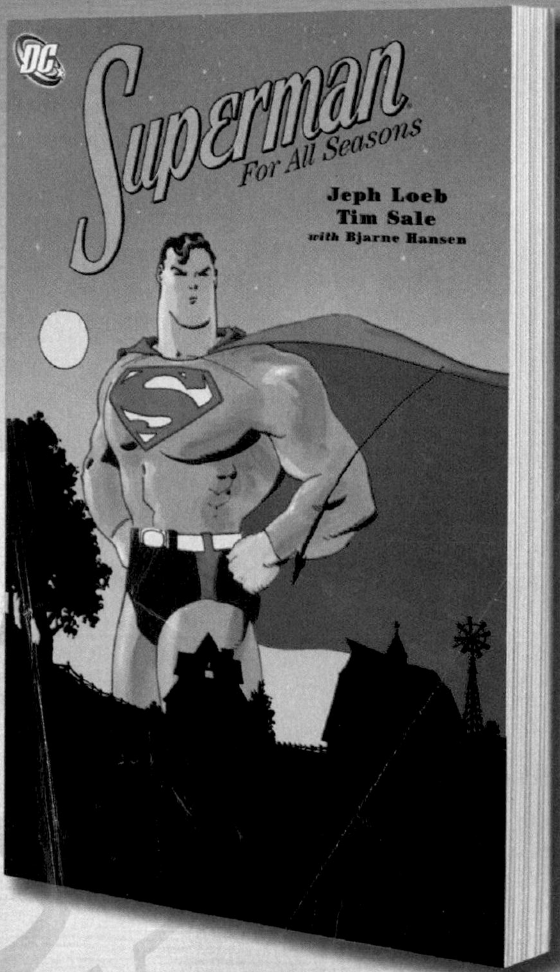
Superman
For All Seasons
Jeph Loeb
Tim Sale
with Bjarne Hansen

MORE CRITICALLY ACCLAIMED TALES OF THE MAN OF STEEL

SUPERMAN:
FOR TOMORROW VOL. 1

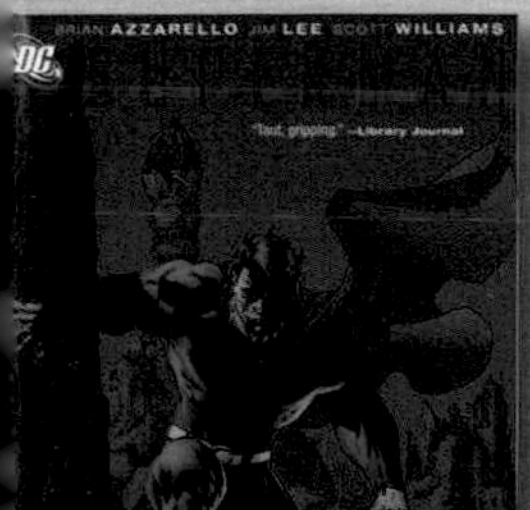
FOR TOMORROW

BRIAN AZZARELLO
JIM LEE

SUPERMAN:
FOR TOMORROW VOL. 2

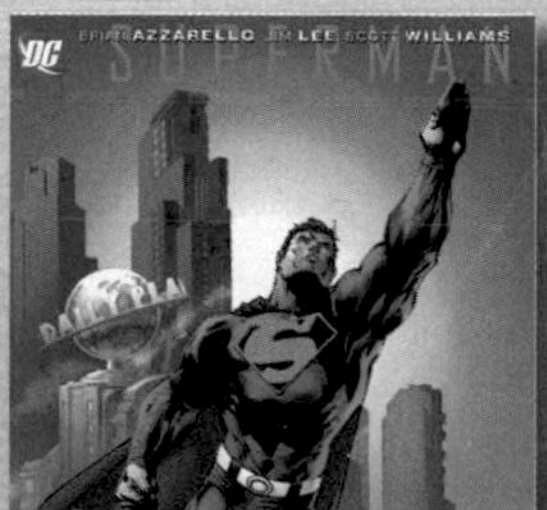
AZZARELLO JIM LEE SCOTT WILLIAMS
SUPERMAN
FOR TOMORROW
INCLUDES AN AFTERWORD AND SKETCH SECTION BY JIM LEE

BRIAN AZZARELLO
JIM LEE

THE DEATH
OF SUPERMAN

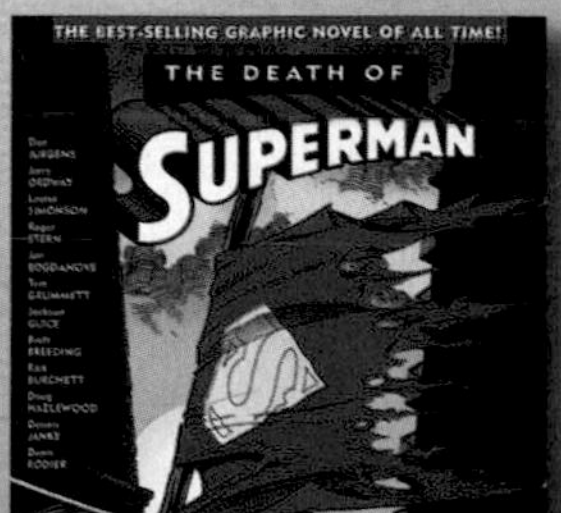
THE BEST-SELLING GRAPHIC NOVEL OF ALL TIME!
THE DEATH OF
SUPERMAN

VARIOUS
WRITERS & ARTISTS

SEARCH THE GRAPHIC NOVELS SECTION OF
DCCOMICS.COM
FOR ART AND INFORMATION ON ALL OF OUR BOOKS!

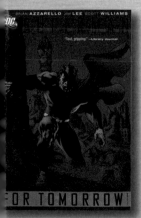

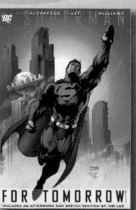

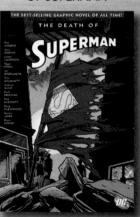

MORE CLASSIC TALES OF THE MAN OF STEEL

SUPERMAN:
THE MAN OF STEEL
VOLS. 1 - 6

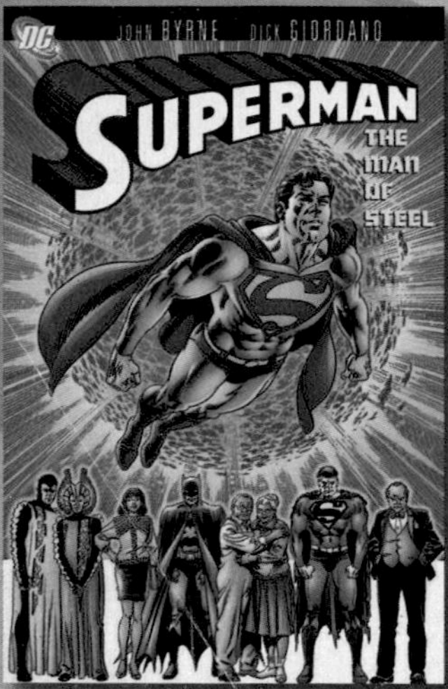
JOHN BYRNE
DICK GIORDANO
SUPERMAN
THE MAN OF STEEL

JOHN BYRNE

SUPERMAN:
BIRTHRIGHT

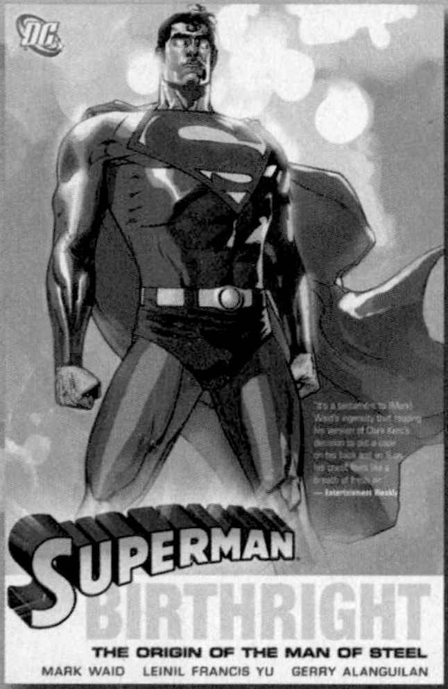
SUPERMAN
BIRTHRIGHT
THE ORIGIN OF THE MAN OF STEEL
MARK WAID LEINIL FRANCIS YU GERRY ALANGUILAN

MARK WAID
LEINIL YU

SUPERMAN:
CAMELOT FALLS
VOLS. 1 - 2

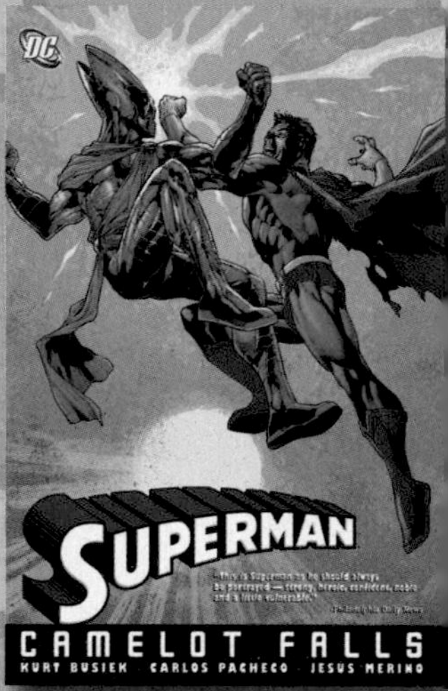
SUPERMAN
CAMELOT FALLS
KURT BUSIEK CARLOS PACHECO JESUS MERINO

KURT BUSIEK
CARLOS PACHECO

SUPERMAN:
OUR WORLDS AT WAR

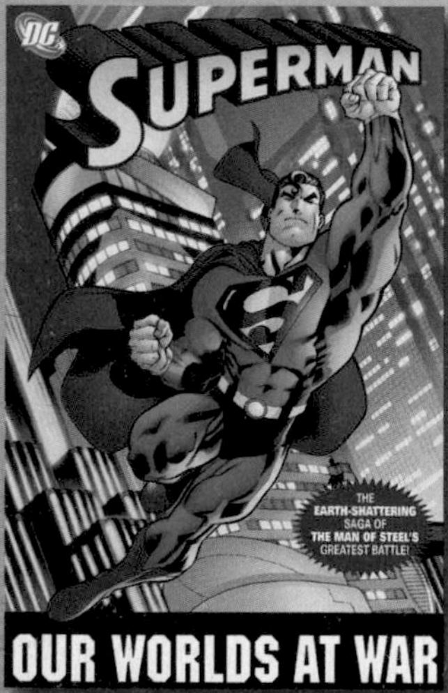
SUPERMAN
THE EARTH-SHATTERING SAGA OF THE MAN OF STEEL'S GREATEST BATTLE!
OUR WORLDS AT WAR

VARIOUS
WRITERS & ARTISTS

SUPERMAN:
RED SON

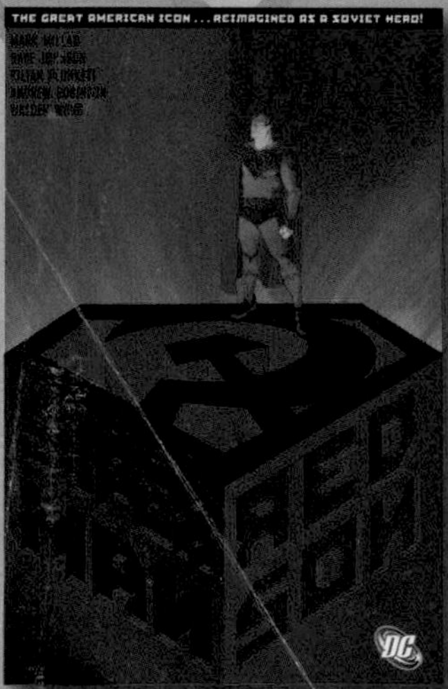
THE GREAT AMERICAN ICON... REIMAGINED AS A SOVIET HERO!
RED SON

MARK MILLAR
DAVE JOHNSON
KILLIAN PLUNKETT

SUPERMAN:
SECRET IDENTITY

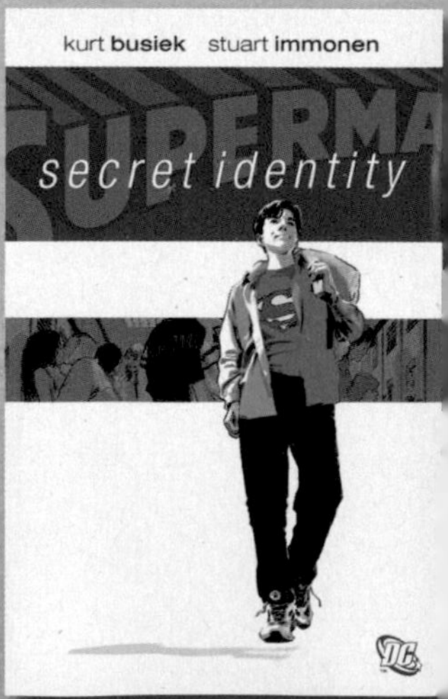
kurt busiek stuart immonen
secret identity

KURT BUSIEK
STUART IMMONEN

SEARCH THE GRAPHIC NOVELS SECTION OF
DCCOMICS.COM
FOR ART AND INFORMATION ON ALL OF OUR BOOKS!